Victoria and Albert

Also by David Duff

VICTORIA IN THE HIGHLANDS

VICTORIA TRAVELS

Victoria and Albert

DAVID DUFF

TAPLINGER PUBLISHING COMPANY
NEW YORK

First published in the United States in 1972 by
TAPLINGER PUBLISHING CO., INC.
New York, New York

Library of Congress Catalog Card Number: 72-2203

ISBN 0-8008-7967-8

Contents

Illustrations

Introduction

*Q*UEEN VICTORIA said of Coburg: "If I were not who I am—this would have been my real home, but I shall always consider it my *second* one."

In this walled and historic German town, as throughout the Duchy of Saxe-Coburg and Gotha, she was known simply as *Die Queen*. She liked to think of her family as the House of Coburg, her mother being a Princess of Coburg and her husband the younger son of the reigning Duke. Prince Albert was born at the ducal country seat of Rosenau, spent his childhood in Coburg and there left his heart when he travelled to London to marry the British Queen. A son and a grandson of Victoria and Albert were the last two reigning Dukes, the ducal structure being wiped away in 1918.

Accordingly, for a century, the links between Britain and the Duchy were many and, although to the major part of the British people Albert's birthplace remained a remote German territory, there developed in Coburg an affinity with Britain which, surviving wars and revolutions, can be sensed today. Visually the influence can be noted in the exotic English Gothic architecture of buildings erected in the nineteenth century.

Despite the tides of hate and change which have flowed over Germany, the memory of Victoria and Albert here remains. A street bears the Queen's name. The picturesque market place is dominated by a bronze statue, ten feet high, of the Prince Consort. On 26th August—the Prince's birthday—1865, the Queen and her nine children gathered there for the unveiling. It was, the Queen wrote, "the most beautiful, touching and solemn ceremony I *ever* saw".

In the Ehrenburg Palace portraits of the British Royal Family hang side by side with those of their German cousins. Here the treat for the tourists comes when a curtain is drawn back to reveal the imposing mahogany water-closet which was installed, on the Queen's order, for her own use. She instructed the Superintendent of Works that he must test it and sit on it to ensure that it was the right height.

Queen Victoria paid six visits to Coburg, spanning a period of fifty years. That she did not travel there more often during her widowhood was due to the scandalous behaviour of her brother-in-law, Duke Ernest II, whose attitude to women was in marked contrast with that of Albert the Good. Although Duke Ernest had failed to produce an heir, in his advanced years he became a most accomplished seducer, fathering a tribe of illegitimates. When the Duke of Connaught was asked why it was that so many people greeted him in a familiar way, he explained that they were the offspring of Duke Ernest. Even today, if anyone of the name of Ernest is introduced to senior citizens, they ask, with a smile, "Ernest II?"

From the ramparts of the magnificent medieval castle of Veste Coburg, or the Festung, which stands five hundred feet above the valley, I could see, on a clear day, the woods of the Thüringerwald, stretching out to Gotha, forty miles away. Those woods were the playground of Prince Albert as a boy. Now they are cut off by the frontier which divides Germany, slicing through the territory of the one-time Duchy. Beyond that frontier there is no trace left, or mention made, of the Princes and Princesses of Coburg who ventured forth to populate all the palaces of Europe. No one reads the *Almanach de Gotha* any more.

A knowledge of Coburg—its buildings, its history and its countryside—provides a part of the answer to the riddle of the character of Prince Albert. It is simple to realise how, privileged as he was, the magic of the old time Duchy impregnated his soul. To look out from the battlements of a castle which was besieged in the Thirty Years' War, to stand in the Church of St. Moriz where Martin Luther preached, to imbibe the treasures and the splendour of the Ehrenburg Palace, to wander at night through the town streets which are so little changed, to sit under the trees in the parkland of the Rosenau, to listen to the bird song of the woods, is to understand why there was always a loneliness in the heart of the Queen's husband. She knew it well.

I am indebted to many people in Coburg—in particular Herr Bruno Bartl and Herr Herbert Appeltshauser —for help with information, translation and illustrations. Once again my thanks go to my wife and Mrs. Fenella Baines for advice and assistance with the manuscript, and to Mrs. J. M. Rochester for typing and for help with proof-reading and indexing.

DAVID DUFF

Weybread, May 1970–March 1972

PROLOGUE

One Night of Love

*B*ARELY FIVE FEET TALL, she lay in the large wooden bed at Windsor Castle. The dressers bobbed and retired. Lehzen, the governess who had watched over her every night since she was five, kissed her and moved away through the dressing-room to her own room which lay beyond. There was only the door between them.

The boy was playing the piano in these private apartments—at moments of stress he always turned to music. He came to her bedside in his dressing-gown. He was tall, handsome in an operatic way, still pale from the beating meted out to him by a hostile English Channel. Twelve hours earlier, "a good deal perplexed and agitated",[1] he had married the British Queen in the Chapel Royal, St. James's Palace. He was still smarting from the ordeal of facing the shafts of cynical, appraising eyes looking out from the coroneted heads of those who had ruled England for a thousand years. He was three months younger than the girl with the pale blue eyes who looked up at him from the bed. She was most conscious of this—three months seems a long time when one is only twenty.

Love and hate—peace and war. Behind the dressing-room door Baroness Lehzen, lying sleepless, increased her determination that this stripling of a youth should not rob her of one tittle of the power that she had held over the Queen through fifteen years of love and patience.

On that night of the 10th of February 1840, when Victoria Regina took a German princeling to her bed, something of England died. The Victorian era began and a measure of glory lay ahead for the British Empire.

Early next morning Albert and Victoria were out walking in the park—she breathless as she hurried to keep pace with his long strides. "Strange that a bridal night should be so short," commented diarist Charles Greville. The Duchess of

Bedford watched the pair: she thought that Victoria was "excessively in love with him, but he not a bit with her".[2]

Yet in nine more months and ten more days a child was born to them—a daughter.

Part One

CHAPTER ONE

Albert

A LBERT, PRINCE CONSORT, Prince of Saxe-Coburg and Gotha, was God's peculiar gift to the Church in the second half of the nineteenth century. The legend of his goodness was initiated in his lifetime. As year succeeded year after his death, greater became the goodness and wider spread the word. Only when his widow died and the son who bore his name, but would not use it, became Edward VII, did the tide of propaganda turn to the ebb.

The life story of Albert, dealt with singly or merged with those of his wife and family, was compiled many times. Each was a pulpit from which poured a sermon perpetuating his goodness and his noble ways. *Albert the Good* was written by W. J. Wintle for the Sunday School Union, and *The Home Life of the Prince Consort* by the Rev. Charles Bullock, editor of "Home Words". Certain of these royal eulogies sold over 300,000 copies, supplies being available direct to the clergy at the rate of 6*s*. 3*d*. per hundred.

Solid behind the campaign was Queen Victoria, single-minded in her intent to enshrine her husband's memory, by written word and painted likeness, by monument and statue, by medal and benevolence, beyond her vision of the years.

Thus in the drear classrooms and church halls of the industrial slums, in the Sunday Schools of the isolated villages, in the mission houses of the expanding Empire, the example of the dead Prince was held up before, and firmly knocked into, the minds of the young as the bright and kindly light which they must follow through six days of unremitting toil and one of prayer and meditation, through marriage and parenthood, through illness and sorrow, until, like he, they were called to rest.

Albert's goodness was based on four main platforms. He was most abstemious with alcohol; his sexual activities were confined exclusively to his wife; he worked hard and well for very long hours; he died full of faith and prepared to meet his Maker at the end of a race well run.

At the time a paragon fulfilling these requirements was much needed in the British shop window. Drink was cheap, strong and a national menace to health and domestic happiness. The fearful extravagances indulged in by Queen Victoria's "wicked uncles", and as a result Society, in the sphere of sex, had corroded moral standards throughout the class structure. Hard work was necessary for the expansion of Britain's industry—and the private requirements of the industrialists. Faith and the courage to bear suffering were essential when death came early to the mean streets and medicine was entirely incapable of dealing with the tragedy of occupational diseases.

But how much credit can be accorded to Albert for this so-termed "goodness"? He did not drink because he did not like alcohol—it upset his nervous stomach. He did not sleep with women because the mere thought of extra-marital relations made him feel physically sick. He worked hard because he loved to reason and to exercise his brilliant brain, and also because it gave him power. It was strange, but not good, that a man of just turned forty, with four fine homes, a loving wife and nine children, with ample opportunities for sport and travel, with ample scope to indulge in the arts and music which he relished, and with half a million pounds in the bank, should admit that he did not cling to life. To confess that he found the days like unto a treadmill[3] and would not fight if the fever came upon him, was a poor reflection on his family and his adopted country. It was an odd example to set to working families waging the fight in crowded slum dwellings and with but a few shillings a week on which to live.

Yet Albert had the lone label of "the Good" to carry with him into the centuries ahead. There were other labels which would have been more appropriate, such as "Albert the Able" or "Albert the Efficient". His grandson, King George V, classified him as an intellectual.[4] Albert's own ambition was to be remembered as "the 'noble' in the true sense of the word".[5]

It was the hearse that bore him from the treadmill to the bright clouds of goodness upon which he was to rest. If he had lived to man's allotted span, the clerical propagandists might have had to look elsewhere for their paragon. It has been said that, although Albert may have been the right man for Victoria when he married her, he was a danger to Britain when he died.[6]

Two women who were in a unique position to know the secrets of Court life and who both had the confidence of the Queen gave their considered opinion of the Prince Consort. They were Ladies of the Bedchamber—Jane, Marchioness of Ely, and Jane, Lady Churchill. On Lady Ely's death in 1890 Queen Victoria wrote: "No one can ever replace this dearest kindest friend. She understood all my feelings and likings perhaps more than anyone else . . ."[7] Lady Churchill died on Christmas Day 1900, after forty-six years of royal service.

Both Lady Ely and Lady Churchill believed that there would have been direct conflict between the Throne and the People if the Prince Consort had lived.[8]

Albert's outlook towards his position was covered by words of Lord Bowen: "Royalty in its own estimation is an exclusive caste, totally apart and essentially above the rest of mankind. Such is their own elevation to Royalties that they are incapable of seeing the gradations of society as we see them."[9]

He was, in all ways but one, a modern-thinking man and part of his handicap was that he was born too soon—he was dreaming of powered-flight fifty years before aeroplanes flew.[10] The exception was his view on the Monarchy. He resisted with every method at his command and every reason in his argument any encroachment on the powers of the Crown. His life in Britain has been described as "a long attempt to put back the hands of the clock and reinstate authority which had already been delegated to Parliament".[11] In his last years backward, reactionary steps were taken, and the steps would have been longer still but for the resistance and wiles of Lord Palmerston. If his physical strength had matched his determination, either Parliament would have had to give ground to "King Albert", or the chorus of the people would have brought about the abolition of the Monarchy. Bearing in mind the upsurge of Republicanism in 1870, the latter appears the more likely. An autocratic Prince from Germany would have made a far better target for the revolutionary leaders than the meanness of the Queen and her favours to John Brown. It would have taken more than the illness of the Prince of Wales to turn the tide.

In the opinion of Gladstone, the Prince Consort failed to grasp the essential differences between the Crown of Great Britain and other regal systems, his mind being overfilled with the idea of being a coadjutor.[12] He attempted, by developing the Queen's innate sense of duty, by unswerving worship of duty himself and by wearing "the lily of a blameless life", to offset the flow of power from the Crown to Parliament. In part he succeeded and in part he failed. Reason for the failure was, to an extent, that he rated facts above imponderabilia,[13] and because he lacked the common touch.

Albert was an un-clubbable man: "He was unlike a man in many things and like the schoolmaster abroad in others."[14] He never walked out unless accompanied by an equerry—in contrast with his wife's uncles who, unpopular as they were at times, were accustomed to move alone among the people. He seldom unbent, confiding only in those in his intimate entourage. He hedged himself about with privacy, forbidding those who served him to keep diaries and waging constant war on journalists who pried into royal affairs. He was unbending on matters of royal etiquette. Dr. Lyon Playfair,* who had a long business association with the Prince, revealed that he was never once asked to sit down.[15] The same rule applied to the ladies. Lady Russell was a guest at Windsor soon after the birth of a child, and was showing obvious signs of fatigue. The Queen whispered to her that she might sit down but arranged that Lady Douro should stand in front of her so that the Prince should not notice the breach of etiquette.[16] How the Duchess of Sutherland, with her £365,000 a year, could bring herself to stand the whole evening at the opera behind the chair of an insignificant German princeling was a question asked in many British homes.[17]

Albert was a sarcastic man, a jealous man and an egocentric. He had a contempt of mankind in the abstract and seldom knew pleasure.[18] His wife admitted that at times he was harsh and a great tyrant, and that he "laughed and sneered constantly" at the sufferings of women and their "unavoidable inconveniences".[19] But she did not always recognise his sarcasm. When Albert told her that Feodora, her half-sister, was worthy of a crown, she really believed it.[20] "Bertie",

* 1st Lord Playfair.

Prince of Wales, was referred to as "our hero" after his highly successful tour of Canada and America in 1860, and one of the Prince's tutors had to implore that "irony and mockery" should not be used when the occasion arose for correction.[21]

Albert was exceedingly jealous on the point of his power over his wife. Relentlessly he sawed away at the link of friendship, love and understanding which had bound Queen Victoria to Lord Melbourne through three vital years. He was not content until she denounced her love as foolish, while the old statesman's life ebbed out in loneliness at Brocket. Looking back at the diaries written before her marriage, Victoria admitted that they did not now awake very pleasant feelings. "The life I led then was so artificial & superficial, & yet I thought I was happy. Thank God! I know now what *real* happiness means!"[22]

As for Baroness Lehzen, Albert used stronger methods. "Crazy, common, stupid intriguer,"[23] he called her, and in the end the governess, who had given every day of seventeen years to the care of Victoria, surrendered and slipped away without even saying goodbye. Yet the woman with whom the Queen was at loggerheads, the Duchess of Kent, her mother, Albert made his close ally. In this direction, at least, he proved wise and kind.

He was anything but wise and kind in his attitude to his eldest son. Here the egocentricity showed. He was determined to reproduce his own image in the next generation—alike in body and soul. When he failed, he showed unpleasant streaks of bitterness which converted the son into the antithesis of the original intention.

Albert had little sense of humour, but realised the importance of laughter in the English way of life. He was a parallel with the German philosopher who admitted that he started making "zee leetle jokes" as soon as he saw the white cliffs of Dover and did not cease so doing until, with infinite relief, he disembarked at Flushing. General Sir Henry Ponsonby, Private Secretary to Queen Victoria for twenty-five years, was in 1856 appointed Equerry to the Prince He said of Albert that he had "unmistakable marks of the Snark".[24]

> *The third is its slowness in taking a jest.*
> *Should you happen to venture on one*

It will sigh like a thing that is deeply distressed
And it always looks grave at a pun.

So Albert kept his little collection of jokes, trotted them out
at regular intervals and always laughed heartily himself.
One of his favourites concerned the evening when the Queen
asked Lady Bloomfield to sing. In trepidation, Lady Bloomfield attempted one of Grisi's airs. She left out the shake at the
end. The Queen turned to Lady Normanby and asked:
"Does not your sister shake?" "Ma'am," came the reply,
"she is shaking all over."

Genuine and uncontrolled laughter only came from the
Prince when he witnessed personal and accidental discomfi-
ture, such as a tall person hitting his head on a low door, or a
guest slipping on a floor mat or sitting on his hat.[25]

Although as a boy he had thrown glass phials containing
sulphuretted hydrogen about the auditorium of the Coburg
theatre and roared with laughter at the confusion caused,[26]
in adult life Albert developed a horror of the practical joke.
Lord Clarendon wrote: ". . . scrambles and larks . . . curdle
the blood in the Consort's veins."[27] The change may have
been caused by the antics of the Prince of Wales, who indulged
in the nastiest of tricks. He once smeared with red ink the
wedding dress of a Palace housemaid as it lay ready for use on
her bed. He was flogged for this. When "Bertie" was allowed
to set up his own establishment at White Lodge, one of the
written instructions from his father was that "*A practical joke*
should never be permitted."[28] "Junketing" was also looked
upon with grave disfavour by the Consort, and the Princesses
were given strict orders not to junket with members of the
Household.[29]

Albert was pure German. Before leaving Coburg in 1839
he wrote to his grandmother: "I shall never cease to be a true
German, a true *Coburg* and *Gotha* man (*ein treuer Deutscher,
Coburger, Gothaner zu sein*)."[30] Many years later he repeated
to a friend: "I shall never cease to be a true German."[31]
Lord Aberdeen, who admired the Prince, said that his only
fault was "excessive Germanism".[32] The problem of serving
two masters therefore arose. By 1860 Albert was convinced
that Napoleon's dreams were full of Belgium and the Rhine.
He was therefore anxious to keep Britain up to "the proper
point of hostility" so that any French move could be treated

as a British quarrel. Lord Clarendon commented: "In this he may not be wrong but he can't quite declare at the same time that in advising the Q. & controlling the foreign policy of her Govt. he is guided by *British* interests."[33]

Albert did not care for the English people and "he resisted Anglicisation as if it were in some way degrading".[34] In the way that he dressed and talked, rode and shot, even in the way that he shook hands, he remained foreign—even arrogantly so. Hard and undemonstrative as he was, he missed the sentimentality of Coburg. He wrote to his brother in 1857: "Sentimentality is a plant which cannot grow in England, and an Englishman, when he finds that he is being sentimental, becomes frightened at the idea, as of having a dangerous illness, and he shoots himself . . ."[35]

The main clash came with the aristocracy. Here he had everything to gain by becoming popular with its members and winning their confidence, and yet he went out of his way to antagonise and upset them. Duke Ernest touched on this point in his Memoirs: ". . . many peculiarities of Society were from the first more congenial to me than they ever became to my brother. The love of the Nobility for every kind of sport found much more response and understanding from me than from him, and in this way it was possible for me to obtain access to the otherwise reserved English character . . . It is a subject on which I often squabbled with him in all affection."

The problem here was not only nationalistic, for Albert would not have been popular with the aristocracy if he had been British born. This was a conflict between the squire and the professor, between ritual and reason, between the old order and the new. The English way of country life had altered little since the gay days of Charles II. Albert had had mathematics, modern thinking and art crammed into him in Brussels, Bonn and Rome. The pastimes and beliefs which England had held sacred for centuries past meant little or nothing to him. This was not entirely coincidental, as his training had been angled that way. M. Perthès, under whom Albert studied at Bonn University, gave his opinion that his former pupil would be sure "silently to influence the English aristocracy".[36] So a self-satisfied young man of just twenty set out from a tiny principality intent on teaching a powerful foreign nation, steeped in history, how to live life his way.

Directly, the Prince had little effect on the members of the British upper classes, and they forgot all about him once he was dead. Lord Orford remarked: "That at least was one foreigner safely out of the way."[37] Indirectly, he was to affect them very deeply.

It was easy to understand why Albert was unpopular. He rode, not for the pleasure, but for a period judged sufficient to give him adequate exercise. His objective when shooting was to bag the maximum amount of game in the minimum of time. He considered eating and light conversation a waste of valuable minutes which might otherwise have been spent absorbing knowledge or reading a good book. He refused to dally with the gentlemen after the ladies had left the dinner table. He would pass the loveliest ladies in the land, who had taken considerable trouble to be so, without even a glance in their direction. His handshake was as inspiring as the touch of a cold fish. And he cried when relations and German members of his entourage died, which was considered quite extraordinary.

Albert was an astute businessman and loved money, as all the Coburgs did—if he had liked money less, the British would have liked him more—but he differed from other members of his family in that he was prepared to work for it. The people, remembering well the £50,000 handed out to poor Charlotte's husband, Leopold of Coburg, by this time King of the Belgians, knew that they would have to pay a high price for obtaining an Heir to the Throne. They also knew that each subsequent child would, in turn, have to be provided for and therefore hoped that the royal tribe would be small. But Britain in the "Hungry Forties", when a farm labourer's wage was seven shillings for a seventy-two-hour week, was in no mood to squander money on a foreign Prince. Many families never tasted meat and so severe became the famine that the rumour gripped Luton that the Queen was planning to have all children under five put to death.

Albert saw human problems in the abstract. He was prepared to spend long hours in committee discussing relief and welfare, but dissociated himself from personal sacrifice. He never recovered from the shock of having his planned income of £50,000 a year cut by Parliament to £30,000, although his wife swelled this by handing him valuable sinecures. "The Tories cut off my apanage," he complained to his brother in

1857.[38] He was forever comparing his lot with fortunate, fuddly Prince George of Denmark upon whom Queen Anne bestowed £100,000, although he did no work and only one of the children whom he sired reached the age of ten.

Albert was quick to pick up the money trail. He slashed outgoings by completely reorganising the household arrangements at Buckingham Palace and Windsor—one economy was to cut the wages of the housemaids from £45 per annum to £12. Under his able administration the income from the Duchy of Cornwall rose from £16,000 to £66,000 and that of the Duchy of Lancaster from £27,000 to £60,000.[39] The Windsor farms were made to pay. There were rumours that he was dabbling in railway shares.[40] The purchase of pictures, some falling to royal bids at auction sales, showed the skill and knowledge of the buyer.[41] By 1846 it was possible to buy the Osborne estate in the Isle of Wight and set about the building of the new House, at a total cost of some £200,000.[42] Birkhall, on Deeside, was next to fall into the royal net, this being followed by the purchase of a forty years' lease on Abergeldie Castle from the Gordons. The Prince's plum came in 1852 when he bought, in his own name, the 17,400 acre Balmoral estate from the Fife Trustees for 30,000 guineas. He then built the new Castle.[43] By the time the Prince of Wales came of age a sum of £600,000 had been put aside by his father and out of this Sandringham was purchased for £220,000.[44] Any big commercial undertaking would have gladly given him a seat on the board.

Yet Albert was a mean man, and it showed. When he won prizes at agricultural shows for the animals and produce of the Windsor farms, he would quietly slip the silver coins into his pocket, to the horror of the assembled gentry and the disgust of other competitors less fortunately placed than himself.

In farming he believed that, if one looked after the pence, the pounds would look after themselves. He grubbed up hedgerows to gain more land and rid himself of the birds which ate the grain—Napoleon III, on his visit to Windsor in 1855, declared himself to be all on the side of the birds.[45] But the Berkshire farmers took exception to the royal competition. Claiming his privilege as husband of the Queen, the Prince did not pay rates. As he was a competitive farmer, in 1846 a demand was made that he should do so. After a legal argument, Albert agreed, but with bad grace. It rankled.

Seventy-four-year-old Richard Webley, a labourer on the Flemish farm, had retired two years previously on a pension of five shillings per week. When next he went to draw his money, he was told that he need not come again as, now H.R.H. had to pay poor rates, the parish must support him.[46]

Apart from his foreign birth, Albert suffered from two major handicaps. The first was that he was a puppet, thinking thoughts and speaking words implanted in him by another man, Baron Christian Stockmar. Stockmar, then a young doctor, had accompanied Prince Leopold to England at the time of his marriage to Princess Charlotte of Wales. After the death of the Princess the following year, he became Leopold's political agent. He became more than that—Coburg company secretary, charged with the task of spreading the Coburg creed and seed about Europe. Able and clear-minded Stockmar was beside Victoria when she became Queen. Thereafter he accompanied Prince Albert on a long tour of Italy, changing a studious boy, who was not interested in politics and never read the newspapers, into Leopold's ideal of a husband for the British Queen—"a walking dictionary for reference on any point which her own knowledge or education have not enabled her to answer".[47] Stockmar spent much of the year at Windsor after the marriage and at the end of the day Albert would rush to his room, with his papers, his queries, his reports. When, in his old age, Stockmar retired to Coburg, Albert found the lack of support and advice overpowering. In 1863 the Queen gave her opinion that, if Stockmar had been at Windsor in December 1861, her husband would not have died.[48]

The second handicap under which Albert laboured was that of health. He was born in an age when the survival of the fittest still applied. If a man retired to his bed, it was assumed that he had gone there to die. Great medical advances were only around the corner of time but still out of reach of even the husband of the Queen.

Victoria was no nurse. Of great physical strength and endurance herself, she was apt to be impatient with illness. In February 1861, when the Prince was unwell, she wrote to her eldest daughter in Germany: ". . . dear Papa never allows he is any better or will try to get over it, but makes such a miserable face that people always think he's very ill. It is quite the contrary with me always; I can do anything before others and never show it, so people never believe I am ill or even suffer."[49]

In 1862, when she began her campaign for the deification of Albert, she penned the following somewhat contradictory statement: ". . . the Prince had very good health. At any rate he had begun with a fine constitution. Every one of the chief organs of life was well developed in him, with the exception of a heart that was not quite equal to the work put upon it; so that he mostly had but a feeble pulse."[50]

"He had begun with a fine constitution . . ." Yet as a child his nose bled, his chest was weak and he constantly suffered "alarming attacks" of croup.* He tired quickly and was known to fall asleep during meals and tumble from his chair to the floor.[51] By his mid-twenties he had suffered "frightful torture from rheumatism".[52] He himself admitted that he had a weak stomach "with which I came into this world, and which I shall take with me to the grave".[53] He was middle-aged before he was thirty. He was always pallid when at sea and prostrated by rough weather. He suffered from sickness before making important speeches, and migraines after they were over. He constantly purged himself with hot water. By 1850 he was troubled by melancholia and sleeplessness. Help was sought from the royal physician, Sir James Clark. The Queen wrote: "Clark admits that it is the mind . . . Diet has been of no avail."[54] At Balmoral Dr. Robertson often commented on the Prince's ready fatigue and small reserve of strength.[55] It is possible that his attempts to emulate his wife's rugged resistance to cold and wet may have weakened his constitution further.[56] In his last years he was beset by "English Cholera" and gastric trouble. His gums became inflamed and the nerves jumped in his cheeks. He said, quite freely, that he did not cling to life and that, if he developed fever, he would die.[57] So it was. Therein lay the mistake of Uncle Leopold and Stockmar. It needed a stronger stomach than Albert's to cope with Britain and Queen Victoria at the same time.

So to the man and woman together—Albert and Victoria— known at the fashionable dinner tables of London by the code names "Joseph and Eliza".[58] Their's *was* a great love. It was

* As a remedy, leeches were applied and the marks that they made on his skin remained until manhood.

égoïsme à deux. It was a love that never faltered—what tragic consequences would have come to the country if it had. Victoria would allow of no comparison with her marital bliss.[59] Yet all great loves are one-sided. There is always one who loves, and the other who suffers to be loved. After three years of close companionship with Lord Melbourne, Victoria was in love with love. Marriage was a physical necessity to her. She became the passionate lover, he the consenting mate.[60] Albert, having fought and conquered "a disordered unnatural fancy" for his tutor as a boy,[61] scarcely knew passion as an adult.[62] When her eldest daughter, the Princess Royal, became engaged to Prince Frederick William of Prussia, the Queen could not understand how this plump girl could arouse such passion in a man.[63] It was because she herself had never known passion in a man.

Albert was of the type who only become sexually dominant at times of power and success. Thus the two were happiest as lovers after Albert had disposed of Lord Melbourne and Baroness Lehzen in 1842. Victoria always leaned on men. When Albert took full command, she leaned on him too hard. She came to rely on him completely. Her giant strength lay dormant as she basked in the brilliance of his brain. Incapable of sorting out and throwing away the unnecessary trifles, he collapsed under the weight of business.[64]

Albert stole one vital gift from Victoria—her blitheness and her buoyancy.[65] Harriet Martineau said that she never saw the Queen before her marriage but that she was laughing. Between them, Albert and Stockmar took the zip and the tinkle from a fun-loving girl. "Thus the foundations were laid in the Queen of those stern views, that hard outlook on life, which with the years developed into the most regrettable intolerance."[66]

Who was Albert? The question of whether he was the son of Duke Ernest I has been discussed by many of the biographers who have dealt, in part or in the main, with his life. The majority have come down in favour of his legitimacy, the minority have stated (one categorically) that he was a bastard. Some of the majority have spoilt their case by obvious bias before posing the question.

It is difficult, if not impossible, to prove that a young man and woman slept together a century and a half ago. If they had so chosen it is probable that it could have remained their secret, and their's alone. Certainly in this case, as the female concerned was the wife of the ruler of a principality, all efforts would have been made to conceal the happening and false trails left to confuse the inquisitive. It is hardly likely that a neat confession would have been filed away for the benefit of some researcher much later in time.

If Albert's mother, the Duchess Louise, did stray in the closing weeks of 1818, it must have been a very clandestine affair—that much is certain. The ultimatum that, if a man's name be not produced, then she was innocent, is no real answer. In any case, a man's name was produced, that of Baron von Meyern, Chamberlain at the Coburg court at this time. He was described as a "handsome, cultivated man of Jewish extraction, much her senior . . ."[67] Max W. L. Voss stated that the Prince Consort "is to be described without contradiction as a half-Jew".[68] But the detailed researches of Hector Bolitho and D. A. Ponsonby produce no evidence of such a liaison and point to the fact that the Duchess did not start "to look outside her wedding ring" until Albert was three or four years old. On the other hand the research of Gerald Hamilton is to the contrary. In 1932 he was a guest at the wedding in Coburg of Princess Sybille of Coburg and Prince Gustavus Adolphus, son of the Crown Prince of Sweden. While in Coburg Mr. Hamilton renewed his acquaintance with ex-King Ferdinand of Bulgaria, a Prince of Coburg. Mr. Hamilton wrote of an event subsequent to the wedding:

. . . King Ferdinand took me, as a specially invited guest, to inspect the Ducal archives. His mind very naturally running on Coburg weddings at the time, he showed me the State documents concerned with Duke Ernest's separation from the Duchess Louise . . . the documents displayed before me and explained by King Ferdinand left me in no doubt that the Duchess had indeed had a liaison with the Chamberlain von Meyer before the Consort's birth, that the date of the Prince's birth coincided with such a calendar, and that, whatever the Duchess may have said about her marital happiness in correspondence with her friends in Gotha, she had not been sharing her husband's bed during those operative months in the autumn of 1818.[69]

The King explained that there were good reasons, personal and state, why Duke Ernest was prepared to acknowledge Albert to be his son.

Even if one chooses to dismiss the involvement of Baron von Meyern, or Meyer, there remain pointers to the possibility that some man, other than Duke Ernest, was the father of Albert. Firstly, the Coburgs were believers in large families and these arrived in succeeding generations. Duchess Louise stopped at two boys. Secondly, there is clear evidence that the Duchess had flirted prior to Albert's birth and that the Duke had not taken the aberration lightly. Thirdly, the Duchess made it very plain that Albert was her favourite child. This was so obvious that the boys' tutor, M. Florschütz, wrote: "Duchess Louise was wanting in the essential qualifications of a mother. She made no attempt to conceal that Prince Albert was her favourite child . . . He was, in fact, her pride and glory. The influence of this partiality upon the minds of the children might have been most injurious . . ."[70] Fourthly, there was the astounding gap in character and outlook between Albert and his father and his brother, a gap which even Stockmar said he would never understand.

In search of this elusive man, if man there was, a start may be made with the most elementary of clues. Albert was born on 26th August 1819. Who then was in company with the Duchess Louise nine months before that date? Was there a man on terms intimate enough to be allowed alone with her? Was there a man near her attractive enough to draw her attentions? Indeed there was. Chatting with her beside the fire was a man of twenty-eight, fitting neatly into the category of tall, dark and handsome. He was ambitious and he was clever and he was a seeker after power. He was a man without a woman yet a man who loved women. At this time he was sad, and pity leads to love.

Prince Leopold of Coburg was spending the winter with his brother and sister-in-law. A year had passed since his wife, Princess Charlotte of Wales, had died in giving birth to a stillborn son.

Strangely enough, Sir Theodore Martin, in his monumental five-volume life of the Prince Consort, determines that Prince Leopold was not in Coburg at this time, saying that he did not leave England from the time of the death of the Princess Charlotte until after the coronation of George IV in 1820.[71] Both Sir Theodore, and Queen Victoria who worked in close concert with him, knew better than that. In the short reminiscences which Leopold, King of the Belgians, wrote at the request of the Queen after the death of her husband in 1861, he thus dealt with the year 1818:

1818 was passed in retirement by Prince Leopold, who only saw some members of the Royal Family. . . . In September Prince Leopold went by Switzerland to see his sister to Coburg where he remained till the beginning of May 1819 . . . .[72]

Leopold was indeed in Coburg and the letters of Duchess Louise to her great friend, Augusta, are full of reference to him. She was impressed by his importance, considered him handsome and found him intelligent, friendly and kind in conversation:

His sorrow lies deep in his soul and shows itself in his whole manner . . . he tries to recover from it at parties, and he is happy with those who are happy; but at times the sorrow bursts forth with great force and drives the brief spells of happiness away . . . he still feels, with fervour, what it means to be happy and to be loved.[73]

After Augusta had seen Leopold at Gotha, Duchess Louise wrote to her:

Tell me quite frankly, which do you think the most handsome, him or Ernest? I shan't tell anybody, and as I love them both— only in different ways—I shall not mind a bit what you say.[74]

The Dowager Duchess of Coburg made note of the doings of Leopold in her diary. For his birthday on 16th December a dinner was arranged, followed by the staging of a French comedy. This was slightly rewritten to allow Louise to recite, "very prettily", some verses about her brother-in-law.[75] Early in the New Year the old Duchess wrote that she saw little of Ernest now and looked back sadly to "the dear past" when the family spent their evenings together.[76] With Ernest away, or otherwise engaged, how did Louise and Leopold pass the time?

By a cruel blow of fate Leopold had lost at one time the wife who would one day have been Queen of England and the son who would have followed her as King. He had schemed and fought hard to gain this prize. The Marriage Race was on, the elderly sons of George III mating with unseemly haste and competing to be the first to produce an Heir. As yet none had been born.

Did the idea now come to him that here was the chance to

recoup his losses and sire a child who could one day, by careful arrangement, share the British Throne? On the face of it unlikely but, with a man of Leopold's character, possible. Ernest was sixteen years older than his wife and already tiring of her girlish enthusiasms. He had been discredited throughout Europe by his unsavoury affairs, particularly that with Pauline Panam. He was short of money. Leopold was an important and ambitious man, with an income of £50,000 per year. There is a price for all things.

It seems scarcely credible that, with Prince Leopold a guest in her house, Duchess Louise could have been taking Baron von Meyern as her lover. That would have been hard to hide from a man as astute as Leopold and he certainly had too many plans for the Coburgs to have countenanced it. So what, then, was the answer to the rumour that Melbourne only agreed to the marriage of Victoria and Albert when he learned that Albert was not the son of Duke Ernest?[77] Melbourne may have turned to Leopold for enlightenment. Leopold may have told half of the truth and used the name of the Chamberlain as a necessary convenience. Mayern was known to be fond of the ladies.

Strangely enough, whilst the letters of Queen Victoria to King Leopold were preserved for all other years, they were missing for 1862.[78]

While dealing with a case of doubtful parentage, Frederic the Great remarked that it was of no matter who put the pigeon in the pie provided that the eating was good. Certainly this pie tasted of industry and morality, efficiency and foresight, art and intellect. It is doubtful if history will rob Duke Ernest of his rightful responsibility. Yet Albert—and his times—would be more readily understandable if he had been half of Leopold, or even half a Jew.

CHAPTER TWO

Bids for Power

*T*HERE WERE many Alberts and Ernests of the House of Wettin before the deluge of World War One washed away the structure of old-time Germany. They were often known by adjectival labels, as indeed was Albert the Good, the sanctified companion of Queen Victoria, though no suitable description could be found for his brother Ernest, whose reputation for the devastation of women was so fearful that his sister-in-law would not allow diplomats with pretty wives to be accredited to Coburg.[1] In previous centuries the names on occasion carried opposite values, as in Ernest the Pious and Albert the Debauched.

Their story can well begin in 1423 when Frederick, Margrave of Meissen, was appointed Elector of Saxony, his authority spreading over the other possessions of Saxony, these including Thuringia. In 1485 his two grandsons, Ernest and Albert, finding themselves joint rulers, decided to divide the territories. Albert, having first choice, took the area which was to become modern Saxony, while Ernest had to be content with Thuringia. Thus originated the Ernestine and Albertine branches of the family, the former, and senior, being that to which the Prince Consort belonged.

Two factors contributed to the cutting up of Thuringia into many small principalities. The first was the custom of having large families. The second was that, on the death of a father, his estates and possessions were equally divided among all his children. The result was that the map of Thuringia came to look like Joseph's coat, and it was fast coming to the stage that one could not go for a walk without crossing a frontier. So, at the end of the seventeenth century, the law of primogeniture was introduced, with the proviso that the heir should make proper provision for his brothers and sisters.[2] The Ernestine families at this time were those of Weimar-Eisenach, Meiningen, Hildburghausen, Coburg-Saalfeld and

Gotha-Altenburg, all prefixed with "Saxe-" to show their link with Saxony.

Money was a constant source of anxiety to the family and by the sixteenth century the coffers were nearly empty. It was then realised that the only solution was to marry into rich ruling houses, the exile being responsible for sending home what moneys he or she could lay their hands on and preparing the way for further weddings in the next generation.

Thuringian eyes were first focused on England in the reign of Henry VIII. John William of Weimar, a member of the Ernestine branch, had an aunt named Anne, daughter of the Duke of Cleves. Anne of Cleves became the fourth wife of King Henry VIII. Known by her husband as "the Flanders mare", Anne was legal wife for but a few months and physical wife not at all. But this did not deter John William. Using the slight relationship, and his aunt's comfortable home in England, he put himself forward as a suitor for Elizabeth,[3] soon to be Queen. He failed, but the pattern had been set.

It was in 1714 that the German Duchies learned of the great prizes which could be won as a result of an appropriate marriage. The daughter of James I of England having married the King of Bohemia, and their daughter marrying Ernest Augustus, Elector of Hanover, the son of the last named couple was able to take over the British Throne. George I journeyed to his new land leisurely and in his own time. He was accompanied by a staff of ninety, two Turks, two mistresses and a dwarf. His wife was not with him as she was in prison for adultery.[4]

The families of Coburg and Gotha prepared to follow this profitable example and their first chance came twenty years later. In 1735 there was laid across the path of George II, by previous plan, one Augusta, the seventeen-year-old daughter of Frederick II, Duke of Saxe-Gotha.[5] The King was visiting the Herrenhausen, near Hanover, for two reasons, the first that he might enjoy the rapture of a mistress—which he did, in the person of Madame de Walmoden*—and the second that he might find a wife for his heir, Frederick, Prince of Wales.

Frederick was a most awkward young man and caused his father considerable anxiety, as have all but two Princes of Wales in the past two and a half centuries. He was known as

* Afterwards Lady Yarmouth.

34

"Fed", the "r" being omitted as in "Federic the Great". It was said of him:

If there had been dislike and disagreement between George the First and his son, the feeling of George the Second towards his son Frederick amounted to detestation. Nor was this profound aversion confined to the King. Neither his mother nor his sisters could long endure the society of the Prince of Wales, who never seemed to lose an opportunity of opposing his father, either by supporting the adverse faction in parliament, or by demands for money at the very time that he was acting with shameless animosity.[6]

Having decided that Augusta was the obvious choice for "Fed", the King said a tearful farewell to Madame de Walmoden and raced for home. He went so fast that the jolting of the carriage brought on an attack of piles.[7] He was therefore in poor humour by the time he reached Kensington, a humour that was further strained when he discovered that in his absence Queen Caroline and Lord John Hervey had changed the pictures. He demanded an immediate return of the old order, in particular that of a favourite of his known as "the fat Venus". He was in no mood to argue with "Fed" on matrimonial matters and the union with Princess Augusta was accordingly arranged, Lord de la Warr being despatched to Gotha to ask for the Princess's hand. He found himself a most welcome visitor, as Augusta was one of a family of eighteen, and her brothers and sisters jumped for joy at the news.[8] The bride-to-be was packed off to England without delay, reaching Greenwich on Sunday, 25th April 1736. "Fed" met her and, although she was pitted with small-pox, seemed delighted with his prize. They were married two days later, at St. James's Palace, at eight in the evening. At midnight they went to bed and made history. They were the last royal couple to be watched by the wedding guests during their bedding. It was reported: "About twelve the illustrious couple were put to bed, when *the king did the bride the usual honours, and the company were admitted to see them.*"[9]

The proceeding was so organised that there could be no repetition of the "warming pan" rumour, it then being said that Queen Anne's half-brother, James, the Old Pretender, was a supposititious child. The royal parents now resolved that the sexual cycle leading to the birth of a grandchild should be observed from alpha to omega.

Augusta was undressed by her sisters-in-law, suitably anointed, led from her dressing-room and deposited in the bed. Meantime "Fed" had been stripped by his brother, Cumberland, and his father. He was enveloped in a night-shirt and glorified with a dressing-gown of silver tissue, the whole being surmounted with a high nightcap of fine lace. He looked ridiculous and the company tittered as he made his solemn way towards his bride. The Queen whispered asides to Hervey and with difficulty restrained her laughter.[10]

Into Frederick's strange mind there crept a degree of annoyance at this circus. Ensuing domestic and financial disagreements with the King and Queen increased his discontent and he decided that his first child should not be born under his parents' roof and that, if he could possibly prevent it, his mother would not be present at the birth.

Fourteen months passed and the summer came again. Still no word reached the interested court, and public, that the Princess of Wales was in an "interesting condition". This was most unusual progress for an Hanoverian husband. To add to the talk, the Princess was kept out of view of prying eyes and no tell-tale signs could be noted.

It was less than four weeks before his wife's time was due when at last the Prince informed his mother of her pregnancy.[11] That was on 5th July 1737. Furious, Queen Caroline determined to keep the couple handy to her at Hampton Court, unaware that her son planned to disappear with Augusta when he considered the moment right. Inexperienced in natal matters, he set out for London with her several times, only to find that it was a false alarm and to return to Hampton Court. In the end he left it almost too late. The Princess began her labour on the evening of 31st July, yet, despite her distress, "Fed" would not admit of defeat. He half-carried her to a carriage and raced for London and St. James's Palace, cold and unprepared as it was. There a wee mite of a girl was born.

Blandly, the Prince despatched a courier through the night to inform his parents, and there followed a noisy scene at Hampton Court when the plot was learned. The King cursed the Queen for being a fool. The Queen said nothing, but dressed quickly and ordered a carriage, there being little doubt in her mind that a "chairman's brat" had been slipped into the bed and that another warming-pan scandal was about to shake the British Throne. But at St. James's Palace she saw enough to know that the child was Augusta's.[12]

The King ordered the Prince of Wales to quit St. James's Palace and foreign diplomats were requested not to visit him. In 1745 he was refused permission to command the British army against the Jacobites, his brother, "Butcher" Cumberland, being assigned to the job of staining Culloden Moor with patriot blood. Six years later the Prince died, having sired seven children. Horace Walpole wrote:

> *Here lies Fred,*
> *Who was alive and is dead . . .*
> *There's no more to be said.*

So ended the first attempt by the Wettins of Thuringia to share the British Throne. Her husband's early death had robbed Augusta of the chance of becoming Queen, but she had a consolation. The blood in her eldest son, George, Heir to the Throne, was half of Gotha, and she planned that the Sovereigns who came after him should have more than half. The lust for family power outweighed all other worldly values.

George, Prince of Wales, born in 1738, was physically most advanced for his age. By the time he was seventeen, when, as Macaulay says, "the mightiest of human instincts ordinarily arises from its repose", the instinct had arisen within him with a vengeance, a portent maybe of the porphyria which was later to overtake him. Noting this, the King, his grandfather, considered that the boy should marry. He had another, and a greater, reason. He wished to make sure, before he died, that the Dowager Princess of Wales did not marry her son into the Saxe-Gotha family, as he knew full well that she wished and intended to do. He proposed a Princess of Brunswick. Augusta reacted violently:

> Every secret art was employed by his mother to instil into the mind of the Prince of Wales a rooted dislike to his intended bride; depreciating all her personal attractions, and representing her as bereft of every amiable quality which could render the married state happy. On the other hand, the charms, the mental qualifications, the superior endowments, and the fascinating manners of a Princess of the house of Saxe-Gotha were the constant theme of panegyric, the diamond could not surpass her eye in brilliancy, nor the snow the whiteness of her skin.[13]

George II heard about this and put the veto firmly on

Gotha, remarking that "he knew enough of that family already". So the Dowager Princess of Wales decided to let the matter rest until the old King died, which he duly did in 1760. Meantime George, "the boiling youth" as he named himself, had to have a safety valve and he found one in the person of Hannah Lightfoot, the niece of a linen-draper in Covent Garden. With the assistance of his brother Edward, he would slip undetected out into the night. Then Hannah had a son. She was immediately married to a man named Axford, who disappeared after the ceremony.[14] In time the son, known as George Rex, became a nuisance and in 1796 was shipped out to Africa, the first town founded after the Cape came into British possession being named after him.[15] Tales of Rex abound in George today.

After Hannah came Sarah—Lady Sarah Lennox, sister of the Duke of Richmond—the great love in the life of George III. He could not sleep at nights for thinking of her and, when he did drop off, dreamed that she was sharing his Throne. It was Lord Bute who told him that this could never be, but it was the schemings of his mother which made certain that it did not, for, to Augusta, "her son might just as well marry a negress as marry outside the Royal Houses of Europe".[16]

The Princess Dowager was affected by this discovery no less powerfully than if she had been apprized of the sudden death of her eldest son. She had been for some time suspicious that the Prince was deeply engaged in an amour, but her pride repelled the idea that he had already plighted his faith to raise an English lady to be the partner of his throne. Rage—indignation—scorn—dismay—each by turn assailed her agitated bosom. . . .[17]

In time the love of George for Sarah became somewhat of a family joke. When his eldest son heard that the King had been chased out of a field at Windsor by cattle he remarked that it was not the first time that his father had been in danger from a *Lean Ox*.[18]

Soon after the death of his grandfather, George III instigated enquiries in Hanover to discover a German Princess, of pleasant disposition and no inclination to meddle in politics, whom he could make his wife. His mother ensured that the name of the Princess of Saxe-Gotha was at the head of the list. Little was known of her and the first brief report, that she was deeply interested in philosophy, did not please the King at all—he wanted no theorising in his private life. The next message indicated that she was pitted with small-pox and had *un defaut de taille*. At length the truth came out—not only was the Princess deformed, but it was extremely unlikely that she would be able to have children and, even if she did, it was probable that the deformity would be trans-mitted.[19] The Dowager Princess of Wales had to admit defeat, but her attitude, and her willingness to submit her son to such a fate, was indicative of the lengths to which the Wettins of Thuringia would go to capture the British Throne.

Meantime Augusta's cousins of Saxe-Coburg-Saalfeld had made a significant step up the social ladder. In 1749 Duke Ernest Frederick married Sophia Antoinette, daughter of the Duke of Brunswick and sister to the Queens of Prussia and Denmark. The principle of importing, as opposed to export-ing, in marriage did not prove altogether successful, as Sophia Antoinette's grandson, Leopold, wrote:

> She ruled everything at Coburg, and treated that little duchy as if it had been an empire. She was very generous, and in that respect did much harm as she squandered the revenues in a dreadful manner. The Duke stood very much in awe of his imperious wife . . . She was, in fact, too great a person for so small a duchy; but she brought into the family energy and superior qualities above the minute twaddle of these small establishments.[20]

This lady was largely responsible for the air of sometimes sickening superiority which emanated from later generations of Coburgs. It was said that the last Dowager Duchess died of shock when she received a letter from the newly formed German Republican Government addressed simply—"Frau Coburg".[21]

The social earthquake of the French Revolution and the campaigns of Napoleon condemned the members of the Thuringian Duchies to quarter of a century of turmoil and poverty, fighting and flight. Seated as they were at the centre of operations, ringed by warring countries, it seemed as if every time an army marched, Coburg was on the line of advance or retreat and, each time the columns passed, the Duchies were left the poorer. Some of the family, such as the Duke of Saxe-Gotha-Altenburg, admired, and openly backed, the French leader.[22] Others leaned towards Russia, Prussia or Austria, but the general policy was one of opportunism, the object being to find themselves on the winning side when the final battle came. At one point Napoleon shouted in anger: "Wherever I go, I find a Coburg in the ranks of the enemy."[23] Yet a Coburg Prince had begged the Corsican to make him an A.D.C. and it was the same self-seeking young man whose handsome face was to be seen smiling at the right people in the best places in London soon after Waterloo. Strangely enough, once Napoleon was safe on Elba, there were few recriminations about the varied course of these divided loyalties. Once again the all important question centred round who married who.

This tempestuous period coincided with the arrival on the scene of a brood of most ambitious and needy Coburgs.

Duke Ernest Frederick and Sophia Antoinette had one son, Francis—a family total strange in the Coburg story. Francis was a peace-loving and affable man and the strain of wars and financial hardship took its toll, his reign lasting only from 1800 to 1806. His energies were concentrated in a highly developed lust for women, and his blacksmith threatened that he would attack with a hammer if the molestation of the daughter of the forge did not stop.[24] Duke Francis married Augusta, daughter of Henry XXIV, Count of Reuss-Ebersdorf. They had a family of seven, three boys and four girls, and it was this brood which looked towards the palaces of Europe as the new century dawned.

It happened that Catherine the Great of Russia was searching for a bride for her grandson, Constantine, and, hearing good reports of the Coburg girls, she invited their mother to bring them to St. Petersburg. This was the kind of prize of which the Wettins dreamed. Princess Francis decided to offer as wide a selection as possible, loaded her three eldest into a carriage and set off on the long trail to Russia.

Unfortunately, in this so tempting offer there was a snag, of which the mother was either ignorant or chose to ignore. Grand Duke Constantine was a spoiled pig of a boy of sixteen, many of the worst characteristics of Peter showing clearly in him. He was cruel and sadistic and nothing delighted him more than to knock out the teeth and eyes of the soldiers under his command. A favourite trick was to march them into the river until they were up to their chins before giving the order to about turn.

Of the girls, Juliana, who was only fourteen, was chosen for the torture. Her husband demanded all sorts of favours from her in public, while his behaviour behind the bedroom door was said to be indescribable. Juliana stood it for seven years and then retired to lonely peace in Switzerland. Still, the Coburgs had gained the entrée to the Russian Court and waved aside the sexual extravaganza as immaterial in view of the advantages to be gained in the fields of power and favour.

The second girl, Antoinette, married the Duke of Würtemberg and was considered to have made a good match, although the only apparent good was the advancement of the family. The Duke was exceedingly ugly and a glutton. When Antoinette awoke at the end of the bridal night, she saw her husband sitting up in bed chewing a ham bone. Of their children, the elder son married Marie, daughter of King Louis Philippe, and their daughter, odd as it may sound, became the second wife of her uncle, the Prince Consort's father.[25]

The eldest girl, Sophia, went against Coburg form by marrying simply for love. Her husband was a charming French *émigré*, Count Mensdorff-Pouilly, and they were very happy. The youngest, Victoria Mary, known as Victoire, married the elderly Prince Emich Charles of Leiningen, who ruled over the poor territory of Amorbach in Lower Franconia. The Prince died in 1814, leaving Victoire with the Regency, two children—Charles and Feodora—and precious little money. She was therefore free, ready and willing to make an attack on the British Throne through the soft under-belly of the sons of George III as and when the chance came—as it did.

The name of the eldest son was Ernest, born in 1784. As the French were in occupation of Coburg at the time of his father's death, he did not assume responsibilities in Coburg until 1807. He inherited from Duke Francis a lust for women, and a visit to Paris to pay his respects to Napoleon proved his downfall. He liked his ladies young and became entwined with Madamoiselle Pauline Adelaide Alexandre Panam, daughter of a Greek. Although she was only fourteen, she was already known as *La belle Grecque* and obviously advanced for her age. Disguised as a boy, she returned with Ernest to his home. In her heart were dreams of one day becoming Duchess, or at least being accorded the dignity of official mistress. She was to be sorely disappointed.

Young ladies of the nineteenth century and of other lands who, through romantic liaison, found themselves embodied in the family circle of a German Grand-ducal court most often and quickly wished that they had stayed at home, even if they were to lie alone at night. The rehabilitation course conducted by the elders was aimed at reducing the newcomer to a state of subservience and impressing upon her that the indigenous way of life was inviolable and the only way. This was the lot of the newly married, and there were no exceptions, even the daughters of Queen Victoria. Pauline was neither married nor was she highly born. She became a prisoner and a slavey. Ernest's mother and sisters were forever accusing her of ensnaring him in a trap, of attempting to get money from him, of corroding his fine nature, of spoiling his chances in life. Pauline, a captive in her room, came to dread the clack-clack of the Dowager Duchess's heavy slippers as she advanced along the castle corridor to administer another session of accusation and reproof. Yet, when the desire came upon him, Ernest expected to rediscover the same transport of delight that he had experienced in Paris. Then regrets for the past and promises for the future poured from him, only to be lost without trace with the morning sun.

Pauline became pregnant. In an attempt to avoid a scandal, she was sent to stay with Ernest's sister, Victoire, at Amorbach. Queen Victoria's mother-to-be treated the girl with such harshness that she ran away. She had her baby in poor lodgings in Frankfort in March 1809. It was a boy and she named him Ernest, in defiance of instructions from Coburg. The father would not acknowledge the son. Financial promises made to Pauline, now known as Madame Alexandre, were not kept. Two objects now filled her life, to get recognition for her son and to make the Coburgs pay. She threatened that, if she did not get her terms, she would write her memoirs. She did write them, and in 1823 she played her ace of trumps and published them.[26]* The Coburgs emerged tarnished and rumpled. Soon, however, they were able to recoup their losses as they pointed with delight at the white flag of purity which fluttered over Windsor Castle and Albert the Good.

Pauline had proved a two-pronged thorn in the flesh of the Coburgs. Firstly, by demanding money, she had touched a

* *Mémoires d'une Jeune Grecque: Madame Pauline Adelaide Alexandre Panam, contre le Prince Régnant de Saxe-Coburg* (2 vols.).

vital spot. The Coburgs hated parting with cash—to them it was a commodity which flowed one way, towards and not away. The canniness persisted through the generations. Alfred, Duke of Coburg, charged Parisians and Americans five louis for an introduction to his brother, the Prince of Wales, and fifty for meeting him at lunch.[27] George V, who liked to have a small bet on a horse, could not bear to part with coins bearing his likeness and arrangements had to be made for him to wager on credit.[28]

Secondly, Pauline spoiled Ernest's chances in the matrimonial field. In 1808 a brilliant alliance had been arranged for him with the Grand Duchess Anna Paulowna, sister of Emperor Alexander of Russia. But the reverberations of the Panam scandal reached St. Petersburg and the engagement was called off. Thereafter there was a signal shortage of foreign brides with good prospects and in 1816, when Ernest was thirty-two, he decided to remain within the Wettin orbit. He drove over to nearby Gotha and became engaged to Louise, only child of Duke Augustus of Saxe-Gotha-Altenburg. She was half his age, gay, pretty and romantic. They were married in July 1817 and Louise seems to have found love all that she imagined it would be in the arms of her experienced husband, although her habit of expressing the wish that her girl-friend, Augusta, could be present to witness the happenings and her happiness must have proved rather tiring to so sophisticated a rake. A son was born to them on 21st June 1818, and he also was named Ernest. So, for a while, we leave the couple by the cot, to outward appearances, at least, content and happy and ready to produce a cohort of Coburgs.

The second son's name was Ferdinand. He was the wily one. He married Antonia Kohary, daughter of the Chancellor of the Austrian Emperor and the owner of over 300,000 acres of the best land in Hungary. Their son, Ferdinand, became King Consort of Queen Maria II da Gloria, Queen of Portugal, and a grandson, also so named, landed another kingship into the Coburg net when he was invited to rule Bulgaria, being thereafter known as "Foxy Ferdy".

After his marriage Ferdinand discovered that an unexpected obstacle prevented him from laying his hands on the Kohary millions. The estate was entailed in favour of the male line and, although his wife was an only child, she had

43

no right to succeed. A neat device was therefore adopted. The Emperor of Austria was persuaded to sign a filiation order which, in law, meant that Antonia was henceforward to have the standing of a boy and therefore could inherit. Not unnaturally, the male members of the Kohary family took exception to this piece of guile and one of them, a monk called Brother Emericus, took peculiar action. At midnight he crept from his cell and hurried to the churchyard where the founder of the family was buried. On the tombstone he lit seven oil wicks. As these flickered in the eerie darkness he intoned some most terrifying words from the *Manuale Exorcisorum* and thereafter called down a fearful curse upon the children of Ferdinand and Antonia to the third and fourth generation.[29]

By this time curses were considered to be somewhat outdated weapons, and the Coburgs laughed. Would they have done so if they could have foreseen some of the moments of sadness and horror which lay ahead for coming generations? Take the tragic story of the Royal Family of Portugal, from November 1861 when young King Pedro and two of his brothers died of cholera, to that terrible February day in 1908 when King Carlos and his elder son, Luis, were assassinated in the streets of Lisbon. Ferdinand of Bulgaria was more fortunate in that he escaped with abdication. On the personal side, consider the married life of Philip of Coburg and Louise of Belgium. On the wedding night Louise fled from her husband's bed and, naked but for nightdress, raced through the Palace gardens and was nearly shot by a sentry when, in her terror, she refused to stop. The bestiality of the Coburg husband ruined her health and he had her certified as mad. She escaped at last through the scandal of divorce in 1906. That same Philip was involved in the nightmare of Mayerling.

The climax of the curse came upon Philip's son, Leopold, of the third generation. On 17th October 1915 a volley of shots rang out from a first floor flat in Vienna. The police fetched a locksmith to force the door. There were two twisted bodies lying on the floor. The Hussar uniform of Leopold had been ripped by revolver bullets. There was a hole where an eye had once been. The flesh on his face had been eaten away to the bone. Camilla Rybika, his mistress, had fired five shots at him and then smashed a bottle of vitriol in his face. And yet he breathed and screamed. The last bullet she

44

had kept for herself. She lay, half naked, by the bed, shot through the heart.[30]

And so we come to the last of the brood of Duke Francis of Coburg and the Princess of Reuss. His name was Leopold and he was born in 1790. He was the ambitious one. The military campaigns in Europe gave him ample scope to exercise these ambitions. His sympathies lay with Russia and at eighteen he joined the staff of the Emperor Alexander, being given the rank of major-general. This annoyed Napoleon considerably and strong reactions against Coburg were threatened if he did not retire, which he accordingly did. For the next few years he travelled, appearing at any conference or family gathering where he could further the cause of the Coburgs. He popped up in Berlin and Berne, Paris and Carlsbad, Vienna and Munich, Dantzig and Prague. In 1813 he was back in the ranks of the Russian army and served through all the campaigns of that year, distinguishing himself in the battles of Leipzig, Lützen and Bautzen. In June 1814 he arrived in London in the train of the Emperor of Russia and the King of Prussia to enjoy the celebrations being staged in honour of the victorious Allied Sovereigns. The Emperor was footing the bill for the accommodation of his accompanying princes and generals and, to his chagrin, Leopold found himself in shabby lodgings at a greengrocer's in Marylebone High Street.[31] He was a very young major-general, handsome and much sought after by the ladies. Whether he was in London merely in the course of his duties or by clever pre-planning must remain an open question.

It so happened that this June was a crisis month in the life of an eighteen-year-old girl called Charlotte. She was the only daughter of George, Prince of Wales, by this time Prince Regent as his father was incurably mad. One would have thought that from a family as large as that of King George III it would not have been difficult to find an heir to the Throne in the second generation. Yet Princess Charlotte was the only legitimate grandchild. None of the many ladies who had shared the beds of her father and her uncles had the necessary qualifications and standing, except for one who proved childless.

Charlotte was strange, farouche and complicated. This was not surprising as there had been no lullabies in her childhood days, their place being taken by the strident storm

45

music of family quarrels. George, Prince of Wales, was drunk when he married Caroline of Brunswick on the evening of 8th April 1795, and spent most of the bridal night lying in a stupor in the bedroom grate. Charlotte was born in January 1796. In April Caroline received a message from her husband, which she translated thus: "I never was to have de great honour of inhabitating de same room wid my husband again."[32] Though cohabitation was over, the bitterness lingered on.

In 1813 the Regent decided that his daughter should marry. He brought over Prince William of Orange and Charlotte, snatching at any hope of escaping her domestic unhappiness, agreed to marry him. William was nicknamed "The Frog" and he grinned perpetually. He grinned so blatantly at her father, so obviously toadying to him at the expense of her mother, that Charlotte staged a quarrel and broke off the engagement. She did this at the time that the Allied Sovereigns arrived for the celebrations, thus preventing the Regent from punishing her by confinement to her quarters, as the guests would naturally have thought it odd that the future Queen of Great Britain was absent from the festivities. So it was that Charlotte met Leopold at a ball at Carlton House. She commented on his good looks and the words were passed on to him, as such words were apt to be. When the Emperor of Russia departed from London, Prince Leopold stayed on, moving to more impressive quarters. With infinite stealth he crept up upon his target Princess. If she drove in the Park, he would be certain to ride by, gravely bowing. If she looked behind her, it would be most likely that he would be in the group of riders who followed her. Charlotte was being most carefully watched by her irate father throughout those July days, yet the Russian major-general from Coburg managed to make his personality felt. And he made good use of the hours when he was not on her trail. He ingratiated himself with Lord Anglesey, Lord Castlereagh and the Duke of Wellington. Thus it came about that the suggestion was put to the Regent that, as the Orange engagement had fallen through, the young Prince of Saxe-Coburg-Saalfeld might fit the bill of husband to Princess Charlotte.

The Regent, furious that his daughter had broken her engagement, now thought that he had found the answer why. Remembering well the guile employed by his grandmother

Augusta of Gotha, he decided that Leopold had engineered the downfall of William of Orange so that he might take his place. Having been convinced that this was not the case, he went so far as to allow the Coburg Prince to be formally introduced to the Royal Family before he left for Germany. Yet George was a shrewd judge of character and, watching the young man's diplomatic behaviour and listening to his carefully chosen words, he dubbed him *le Marquis Peu à Peu*.[33]

Leopold was also shrewd and he decided that his best chance of success was to play hard to get. He also ensured that, by making friends with the right people and living a blameless life, only advantageous reports reached the Regent. His character was thus described by a contemporary author, words which could have been fitted exactly to Prince Albert twenty years later:

In his early youth, he manifested an excellent understanding and a tender and benevolent heart. As he advanced in years he displayed a strong attachment to literary and scientific pursuits, and even at that time all his actions were marked with dignified gravity and unusual moderation. His propensity to study was seconded by the efforts of an excellent instructor; and as he remained a stranger to all those dissipations with which persons of his age and rank are commonly indulged, his attainments, so early as his fifteenth year, were very extensive. His extraordinary capacity particularly unfolded itself in the study of languages, history, mathematics, music, drawing and botany, in which latter science he has made a proficiency that would be creditable to a professor.

The early part of the life of Prince Leopold was marked by vicissitudes, but they seem only to have contributed to preserve the purity of his morals . . .[34]

The Coburg information services were ever good and Leopold was able to keep himself well informed of the moves in the stormy relationship between the Regent and his daughter. He ensured that his own image remained fresh in Charlotte's memory by means of letters smuggled to her through her uncle Edward, Duke of Kent, who already had plans for discarding the comforts of his mistress, Madame Julie de St. Laurent, for the respectability of marriage with Leopold's widowed sister, Victoire. Then Napoleon escaped from Elba, the armies of Europe marched again, and Princess

Charlotte prayed for the safe return of the handsome major-general. In September the Regent, prompted by Waterloo and Wellington, sent him an official invitation to visit England. He was slow in coming, to the anger of the impatient girl who awaited him. He arrived in February, became engaged at Brighton, and on 15th March the Chancellor of the Exchequer announced the proposed marriage settlement. It was expensive: £60,000 was allotted for the Princess's establishment, £40,000 for the establishment of the royal household, and £20,000 for dresses and jewels for the bride. A most important item was that, if Leopold outlived his wife, he was to receive an annual income of £50,000 a year. As his existing income was but £400, this was generous indeed and Peter Pindar sang:

> *he himself maintained*
> *Upon one hundred pounds* per annum
> *With some assistance from his Grannum.*[35]

Prince Leopold and Princess Charlotte of Wales were married in the Grand Crimson saloon at Carlton House at nine o'clock on the evening of 2nd May 1816. All looked set that little Coburgs would arrive to inherit the British Throne. As a provincial newspaper was to say quarter of a century later:

Coburgs in France! Coburgs in Belgium! Coburgs in Portugal! and we verily believe that if the billionaires among the children of Israel should buy Jerusalem and all the land about Jordan, we should doubtless see all the machinery of diplomacy instantly at work with a Coburg King of the Jews.[36]

There was even to be talk of a Coburg being appointed to the headship of the United States of America.

CHAPTER THREE

Hunting for the Heir

*A*T ELEVEN O'CLOCK Leopold and Charlotte left
Carlton House on their way to honeymoon at Oatlands
Park, Weybridge, lent for the occasion by the Duke and
Duchess of York. The old Queen considered that it was highly
improper that the couple should be alone together so late at
night and instructed the bride's lady-in-waiting, Mrs. Campbell, that she should sit between them. This Mrs. Campbell
refused to do.[1]

Oatlands was a strange place for the couple to get to know
one another, since the eccentric Duchess of York lived as a
recluse surrounded by many monkeys and parrots and a
pack of forty dogs. Often she slept in a strange edifice which
had been erected in the garden. But at least they were away
from public gaze:

> The house is extremely secluded in the park from all intruders,
> so much so that it is difficult to find the way to it unless by applica-
> tion at either of the lodges at Walton or Weybridge, although a
> stage-coach going to Weybridge is allowed to pass through for
> the purpose of setting down passengers going to the house, or of
> leaving parcels there. On Friday, the day subsequent to the
> marriage, the royal pair amused themselves by walking in the
> delightful grounds and on the terrace, from which nine counties
> are to be viewed; and they afterwards resorted to the celebrated
> and largest grotto, bath, &c. in England, and, perhaps in Europe;
> the construction of which occupied a man and his son, with
> assistants, a great number of years, and the expense of which
> exceeded the purchase of the estate.[2]

The honeymoon suffered from a number of disadvantages.
Firstly, the rooms and corridors were impregnated by the
unromantic odour of their habitation by the Duchess's many
furred and feathered friends. Secondly, the weather was
appalling. Thirdly, Charlotte found that her trousseau was
too tight for comfort and she had to set about letting out the

seams. Fourthly, Leopold's health was far from good. He was suffering from the after effects of two campaigns and was thin as a rake, causing the Regent to prescribe a diet of punch and steak. Since landing in England he had been the victim of rheumatism in the head and ringing in the ears.[3] Peter Pindar thus described him:

> *His nose was long, his eyes were grey,*
> *His phiz was somewhat thin and sallow,*
> *His locks were brown—a lightish bay—*
> *His teeth irregular and yellow.*[4]

Charlotte found him "the perfection of a lover" but was not at ease with him when alone. This is readily understandable as they were antithetical. He thought carefully before he spoke—she said exactly what was in her mind. At a picnic lunch she was asked what she wanted to eat and shouted, "Cold roast beef—with plenty of mustard." That was not at all the reply that her husband would have given. His sense of humour was carefully cultivated and rather récherché. She laughed loudly at little things, whereat he would mutter, *"Doucement, ma chère, doucement."* His movements were graceful and strictly correct. She was apt to walk with her hands on her hips and roll like Henry VIII. She conversed with her hands behind her back, her legs wide apart and her bosom thrust forward, a stance which her husband considered to be unladylike. Neither did he approve of her habit of stamping her feet when annoyed. She prattled, while he liked to pontificate. Yet, when once they were settled in their country home of Claremont, Esher, they came to know and love one another. They made a rule that night must never fall upon a misunderstanding unsettled. It is nice to remember that this poor girl found one oasis of happiness as she walked hand in hand with Leopold round the paths of their Surrey garden.

Leopold's serious character could never provide the required quota of fun, but in this direction she was fortunate in finding a playmate, on hand, who would play hide-and-seek with her in the garden and slide with her along the polished corridors. It was said that the playmate fell a little in love with the Princess. His name was Christian Friedrich von Stockmar—"Stocky" for short. He was a doctor, aged twenty-nine and the Prince's physician.

Stockmar was a Coburg man, his father being a lawyer who had on a number of occasions helped the reigning Dukes with their problems. For five years he studied medicine and it was this training which, throughout his long political career, helped him to understand people and learn their motives. From 1812 to 1815 he ran a military hospital at Coburg, pioneering in his insistence on fresh air and cleanliness. Prince Leopold noted his potential and, on his marriage, asked Stockmar to become his personal doctor, an appointment which, not unnaturally, led to criticism in the British medical world.

A strange character, this young doctor. Inordinately ambitious— but with the ambition that has no wish for public applause, infinitely preferring to remain in the background and pull the strings that make the puppets dance. Intensely German and genuinely patriotic; thorough, painstaking, cold, critical and sceptical. Gifted, too, with a memory and power of observation possessed by few . . . Dyspepsia ruined his hitherto cheerful disposition and turned him into a hypochondriac. He was, like the average middle-class German, rough and unpolished, and his table manners were appalling. Like most Germans, he worshipped rank; especially princely rank.[5]

In May 1817 it was announced that Princess Charlotte was expecting a child in the autumn. In August Prince Leopold pinpointed 19th October as the likely day. Dr. Matthew Baillie was the Physician in Ordinary. Sir Richard Croft was appointed accoucheur. Dr. Sims was to remain handy in case instruments were required. Sir Richard was fifty-five, dictatorial in his manner and demanded complete obedience from his patient. He prescribed a weakening diet, which consisted in the main of bread and butter, bled her often and curbed "any excess of animal spirits".[6] He moved into Claremont three weeks before the birth was expected.

There was a fourth doctor in the house—Stockmar. Although he had treated Charlotte on occasions when Dr. Baillie was absent, he now informed Prince Leopold that he would have nothing—repeat nothing—to do with the pregnancy. Later he explained why:

I can only thank God that I never allowed myself to be blinded by vanity, but always kept in view the danger that must necessarily accrue to me if I arrogantly and imprudently pushed myself

51

into a place in which a foreigner could never expect to reap honour, but possibly plenty of blame. I knew the hidden rocks too well, and knew that the national pride and contempt for foreigners would accord no share of honour to me if the result were favourable, and, in an unfavourable issue, would heap all the blame on me. As I had before at various times, when the physician was not at hand, prescribed for the Princess, these considerations induced me to explain to the Prince that, from the commencement of her pregnancy, I must decline all and any share in the treatment . . . When I recall all the circumstances, I feel but too vividly the greatness of the danger which I escaped.[7]

As an example of the self-centred approach to life of the Coburg clique, this is unique. Regardless of his affection for the Princess and the warm reception to England that she had accorded him, forgetful of the debt that he owed his master, Stockmar let the politician in him overrule the physician. His attention was fixed on the fate which he had shrewdly avoided, not on the fate and suffering of the girl who was facing childbirth for the first time. He relented, and advised professionally, too late. If there was satisfaction in being wise after the event, that doubtful prize was his.

The Princess became so immense that it was thought she would have twins. She was taken ill on the evening of 3rd November. She said: "I will neither bawl nor scream."[8] It was not until 9 p.m. on the 5th that her son was born—dead and between ten days and three weeks overdue. Shortly after midnight the Princess had an attack of nausea and became ice-cold. She had had a severe haemorrhage. Sir Richard Croft plied her with hot wine and brandy and placed a hot water bottle on her stomach. His treatment was wrong— cold water should have been applied. Stockmar, at last aroused from his retreat, warned that the Princess was sinking and advised certain steps. Croft abruptly told him to mind his own business. Two hours later he saw that the German doctor's opinion was correct and summoned him to the dying woman's bedside. She recognised him and said: "They have made me tipsy." A little while later she cried out, "Stocky, Stocky," and was gone.[9]

Her aunt, Princess Augusta, wrote to Lady Harcourt:

The poor Angel was ill 52 hours, all *Patience*, all *Obedience*; and Her *Resignation*, when they foretold Her the child would be born dead, was quite Exemplary. The Decrees of Heaven are wise, just and unrevokable; but to us poor Mortals we can only humbly *submit* when we don't understand them, *still* being certain they are meant for our ultimate good . . . Dr. Baillie said *the last* two hours were like a *hurricane*; all was *so frightfull even to Him* as a Medical man . . .[10]

Shortly afterwards the news of another death was to reverberate throughout the country. Sir Richard Croft, while attending a birth in Wimpole Street, was found dead in the room allotted for his retirement. There were pistols in either hand, their muzzles still pointing at either side of his head.[11]

With the death of Princess Charlotte the question of the succession to the Throne became acute. Of the fifteen children of King George III, twelve survived. Of the five Princesses, three were married but childless, and two were elderly spinsters. Three of the Princes were bachelors and the other four married but without children.

No prize existed large enough to tempt George, the Prince Regent, to share again the bed of Caroline, the wife whom he hated. In addition the doctors were of the opinion that his mode of living had made it most doubtful whether he could ever become a father. So he was ruled out. Frederick, Duke of York, was married to the eccentric lady who lived with her animals at Oatlands. She was forty and the mere thought of a child joining the animals was ridiculous. The horrible Ernest, Duke of Cumberland, was married to a German widow. It was rumoured that she had murdered two husbands, while he, it was said, had cut the throat of his valet, Sellis. They lived mostly in Berlin and the Royal Family would not speak to them. Ernest has been described as being "vicious, incestuous, perverted, disgusting, tyrannical, reactionary and un-British".[12] In his case the prayer of the British public was— "To hell or Hanover"—a Queen, under Salic Law, being unable to succeed in Hanover. In 1817 the Duchess had a daughter who died at birth.[13]

Augustus, Duke of Sussex, had married Lady Augusta Murray in 1793, but the young alliance was declared void as it violated the Royal Marriage Act. Two children, barred to the succession, were born before the couple separated. At this time he was living with Lady Cecilia Underwood, was well content and had no intention of changing ladies even if Britain did look as if she would be short of a Sovereign.

Of the bachelors, William, Duke of Clarence, had a large

family by Mrs. Jordan, the actress, but this did not alter his legal status. Edward, Duke of Kent, had retained the same mistress, Julie de St. Laurent, for twenty-seven years, but had already considered jettisoning her for monetary reasons, his financial affairs being in a frightful state. Adolphus, Duke of Cambridge, was the genuine article, a bachelor unencumbered by mistresses or bastards.

The Royal Marriage Race began on the day after Princess Charlotte died. Edward of Kent, hiding from his creditors in Brussels, told diarist Creevey:

Independent of the regret which all must feel at the premature fate of the presumptive heiress of the throne, and so amiable and so generally loved a princess as my niece, her death is much to be regretted as a political event. To me it is perhaps more important than to any other member of the royal family. The country will now look up to me, Mr. C—, to give them an heir to the crown.

Edward was thinking in terms of the financial advantages of married life, before his eyes floating the magic figure of £50,000 which Prince Leopold was now to receive annually for doing nothing. His propaganda, aimed through a channel which he knew well would soon reach a wide audience, was well thought out. He stressed how he had preserved his health and manliness. He wiped a tear from his eye as he recounted the sadness he would endure at parting from his beloved Julie. No wonder that his sisters called him Joseph Surface.

Within a few days the *Ghent Journal* had the message: "It will not excite surprise if four nuptials and one divorce enliven old England . . ."[14] At home popular Peter Pindar joined the fun with a poem filling a sixty-page booklet, entitled:

HUNTING FOR THE HEIR
THE R———L H—MB—GS
or
LUMPS OF LOVE

Yoicks! the R—l Sport's begun
I' faith but it is glorious fun
For hot and hard each R—l pair
are at it hunting for the Heir.

On 7th May 1818 the Duke of Cambridge, who was living in Hanover as the representative of his father, married

Augusta, daughter of Frederick, Landgrave of Hesse-Cassel. On 29th May the Duke of Kent married Victoria Louisa Mary, widow of the reigning Prince of Leiningen. On 11th June the Duke of Clarence married Adelaide, daughter of the Duke of Saxe-Meiningen. It was a race to be first at the font. The fourth runner was Cumberland who, although he had the advantage of being already married, was handicapped by his wife's abortive effort in 1817. The betting was even, with a slight advantage to Cambridge as he was the youngest and had led a pure life.

Meantime Leopold staggered through the dark days at Claremont as if in a dream. He was prostrated by a mixture of emotions, shock at the suddenness of it all, grief at the end of a deep and genuine love, exasperation that all his hopes, his plans, his ambitions had come to nothing. Stockmar shared his bedroom, ready with sedatives and soothing talk when he awoke. While Charlotte lay in her room, he visited her constantly. When the mausoleum was built in the garden where they had wandered so happily, he and the doctor would spend long hours there, Stockmar pouring out worldly wisdom while Leopold fondled a marble likeness of his wife's head. Nothing of Charlotte's was moved—her watch still ticked where she had laid it down for the last time, her coat and hat hung casually on the screen where she had placed them when she came in from her last walk.[15] In the same way was Victoria to leave the belongings of Albert.

After the funeral Leopold wanted to return to the Continent, to visit his family in Coburg, his sister in Switzerland, and allow the interest of travel to calm his shattered nerves. But Stockmar would have none of this. The Prince must show Britain "how nobly a man could bear an incredible misfortune, caused by no fault of his own". The public would look upon his absence as ingratitude and a want of right feeling.[16] "It is in England that you must weep for your Princess," warned the doctor. "If you return to Coburg your position in this country will be forever destroyed."[17]

It was on the foundation of these words of Stockmar that the assumption has often been made that Prince Leopold did not leave England during the lifetime of George III. When Sir Theodore Martin said the same thing in his *Life of the Prince Consort*—and it was well known that Queen Victoria checked every paragraph of this work—the evidence appeared clear enough. Yet Leopold left England ten months after the death of his wife, and stayed away for eight months.

The reason for Stockmar's insistence that the Prince should stay at Claremont was the fear that, if he went away, his income might be the subject of a substantial cut. There were good grounds for this fear, as the *Morning Post* and other papers had been quick to urge that there should be a "magnanimous relinquishment". In May 1818 a story appeared in the Press that Prince Leopold had agreed to hand over to his sister, the Princess of Leiningen, one fifth of his income on her marriage to the Duke of Kent. A denial was issued from Claremont and the *Morning Post* hit out in a leading article:

> We do not hesitate to confess we feel most grievously disappointed, and, under the circumstances of the case we cannot, consistently with our public duty, avoid asking most seriously, whether under the present severe and unexampled pressure of our national affairs, his Royal Highness Prince Leopold really means to make no sacrifice whatever in alleviation of the crying distresses of the country from which he receives so enormous an income as £50,000 per annum besides his emoluments as a Field-Marshal and Colonel of a Regiment of Cavalry . . . Though lately made *Royal*, we repeat, his Highness has in fact no longer any immediate connection with our Royal Family . . .

The newspapers had not yet learned that it needed more than an appeal, or an attack, to extract money from a Coburg. Anyhow, sorrowing though he might be, Leopold was making good use of his income on his own account. Not only was he carrying out the improvements which he and his wife planned to do at Claremont, but he also had a "town residence" to keep up and adorn—none other than Marlborough House. Mrs. Campbell went to see him there and wrote to Lady Ilchester:

> He (Prince Leopold) has laid out a great deal of money in Marlborough House in painting and cleaning it—very handsome—carpets to the whole range of apartments, and silk furniture; and on my asking if the silk was foreign on one sofa he seemed quite to reproach me, and said I should never see anything that was not English in his house that he could help. There were magnificent glass lustres in all the rooms, etc. He has also purchased a large collection of fine paintings, which are coming over, and though that is giving money out of the country it brings value back . . .[18]

There was an uncanny likeness between the financial acumen of Leopold and Albert, Queen Victoria's consort.

In September 1818 the Prince slipped quietly away from England, on the excuse of pressing family business. After a short stay with his sister, Juliana, at Berne, he headed for Coburg. There he found a ripple of discontent on the waters of married life. Duke Ernest and Louise had just returned from Dresden, where the King of Saxony had staged a gay programme of entertainment. It seemed that it had been a little too gay for young Duchess Louise, for she had set the tongues a-wagging.[19] The most vicious of the tongues belonged to Frau von Senft, wife of an officer stationed at Dresden, who knew Coburg well. The Duchess wrote to her friend Augusta: "*La chère femme* has said a lot of nasty things about me when I was in Dresden *à cause de certain aventure*."[20]

Leopold was faced with a second domestic crisis. His sister-in-law developed chicken-pox and was looking anything but romantic when he came to her bedside. But in one of her chatty letters home she wrote how happy she was to be looked after by her angel of a husband and her kind brother-in-law. H.R.H. the Prince from England obviously impressed her very much. She considered him "a very famous, great man", admired his well made features, and described him as being friendly, intelligent, kind, religious, noble and trustworthy. Noting his sadness, she commented: "He still feels, with fervour, what it means to be happy and loved."[21]

Leopold, on the other hand, was less expansive in his correspondence. In a carefully worded letter to Mrs. Campbell, his late wife's lady-in-waiting, he wrote:

At first I did not derive the comfort of my stay here which I had every reason to expect; but the young and happy *ménage* of my brother's, as well as the sight of his fine child, gave me almost more pain than I had strength to endure. Time, which softens by degrees the most acute feelings, has kindly exercised its power on me; more accustomed to the sight of these objects, I enjoy now somewhat more tranquillity . . . I should already sooner have thought of returning to dear old England, but I greatly wanted quiet and retirement, fallen from a height of happiness and grandeur seldom equalled . . .[22]

Louise certainly gave her brother-in-law every reason and encouragement for not returning to "dear old England". The Coburg winter season was brilliant. There were dinners and balls, quadrilles and amateur dramatics, birthday and luncheon parties, tableaux and recitals, and sleigh rides in the snow. The driving force behind this round of entertainment was the young Duchess, admittedly intent on driving the gloom out of Leopold's life. In public she tossed him compliments from the stage and in private listened to the weepings of his secret heart. Early in December she became pregnant. In the New Year the Dowager Duchess complained that she did not see Duke Ernest in private any more—that things had changed. In May Prince Leopold travelled back to London via Paris.[23]

In "dear old England" conversation was restricted to baby talk. The favourite for the Royal Marriage Race had won by a tiny head, the Duchess of Cambridge having given birth to a son* in Hanover on 26th March. The same issue of *The Times* reported that the Duchess of Clarence had been delivered at Furstenhof of a daughter on the morning of the 27th. A later paragraph gave the news that the child had died. There were two runners still to come in. On 24th May a daughter—"as plump as a partridge"—was born to the Duchess of Kent at Kensington Palace, and three days later a son† arrived safely for the Cumberlands. The Kent child took the lead and it was now up to the Clarences to depose her.‡ On 24th she was christened Alexandrina Victoria. Fräulein Charlotte Siebold, the distinguished midwife who was also a qualified doctor and had brought the child into the world, now left for Germany where she had another appointment. On 26th August a second son was born to Duchess of Louise of Saxe-Coburg-Saalfeld. He was called Albert.§

* George, Duke of Cambridge (1819–1904).
† Prince George of Cumberland, George V of Hanover (1819–78).
‡ A daughter, Elizabeth, was born to the Duke and Duchess of Clarence in 1820, but died in 1821. She was followed by still-born twins.
§ The full names were Francis Albert Augustus Charles Emmanuel.

CHAPTER FOUR

Young Al

ALBERT WAS a love-child, and it showed. His mother made no attempt to hide that he was her favourite, and this bias might well have had an injurious effect on the elder boy. Albert took after Louise in looks and, because he was her pride and joy,[1] became outrageously spoilt. He was soft, sensitive and rebellious. The overpowering love of the mother for her son makes it difficult to understand why she agreed to part with him for ever when he was only five. Could she not have bargained that she kept the younger boy, and her husband the elder? Did the romantic attachment to a young officer prove so powerful that it entirely outweighed the great love she had for her son? Or does the great love make her subsequent actions easier to understand?

A strange point about the boy Albert was that, from very early days, he disliked females, both young and adult, though he made an exception of grandmothers. Even though she left him when he was five, one would have imagined that, with the love and understanding radiating from his mother, he would have taken a differing view. Yet he preferred men, and one in particular—Prince Leopold who came from England in 1821 to see how the boy progressed. Duchess Louise wrote:

Albert adore son oncle Léopold, ne le quitte pas un instant, lui fait des yeux doux, l'embrasse à chaque moment, et ne se sent pas d'aise que lorsqu'il peut être auprès de lui . . . Il est charmant de taille, blond, et yeux bleus . . .[2]

As Sir Sidney Lee said,[3] Leopold regarded the eventual marriage of Princess Victoria of Kent as within his peculiar province and he had chosen her first cousin, Albert, to be her husband as soon as the two were born. Thereafter it was just a case of careful planning and direction. He had been cruelly robbed in 1817. Next time he was determined that Coburgs should inherit the British Throne.

When he was only three Albert was transferred from the

59

care of Nurse Müller and handed over to a tutor, Herr Florschütz of Coburg. His grandmother feared that the step was being taken too early, but Albert, only too glad to be rid of the women, rejoiced at the change. Florschütz was a kind and understanding man and a very good tutor, and he supervised the boy's studies for the next fifteen years. Unfortunately there were born in Albert strange and unnatural feelings towards his mentor, and these had to be sternly suppressed. Thus it came about that, when he himself became a father and learned that his eldest son was sending affectionate notes to his tutor, that tutor was changed.

Albert was not only shy with girls and young women, but he actively disliked them. He would run to the furthest corner of the room, cover his eyes with his hands and refuse to move or speak. If interfered with, he yelled. His mother gave a fancy dress dance when he was five and he was garbed as Cupid. When his turn came to take the floor with a little girl, he refused to move and, on force being exerted from the rear, his screams echoed round every room in the *Schloss*.

In secret, he hatched up nasty little naughtinesses to annoy females. One of his victims was his cousin, Princess Caroline of Reuss. While she was guest at a dinner party, he filled the pockets of her evening cloak with a soft and soggy milk cheese. He waited in the cloakroom to help her on with it and screamed with delight as she flung the garment to the floor and wiped the cheese from her hands. Albert was too sensitive and spoiled to be clouted or chastised—which makes his harsh treatment of his own children difficult to understand. So Princess Caroline had to wait her chance to get even.

One summer's afternoon Albert found a frog in the garden. Intrigued, he picked it up and ran to show it to the grown-ups who were having tea on the lawn. The ladies cried out in horror. Their revulsion communicated itself to the boy. He threw it away and from that time forward had an unconquerable aversion for the frog family, toads in particular.

Some time later Princess Caroline walked round the gardens of the Rosenau with a basket, into which she placed all the frogs that she could find. She then crept up to Albert's room and emptied the basket into his bed.[4]

During his early years Albert suffered from two main handicaps—poor health, and the state of guerrilla war which existed between Duke Ernest and Duchess Louise. As to the first, he was slight, frail and anaemic and the lack of strength showed in his tiredness. When he was missing, he was certain to be asleep behind some curtain. He even dozed off during meals. The slightest upset, such as a touch of cold, would bring on severe, and often serious, attacks of croup, with accompanying temperature. The aftermath was a period of hoarseness. A number of remedies were suggested, including the passing of a hair through the boy's throat. Fortunately for him, this suggestion was turned down, although the more commonplace cure, the application of leeches—which was used—was in itself unpleasant enough. It was these attacks which caused the Dowager Duchess to regret that the boy passed so young from the care of his nurse to that of the tutor, as night care was essential. Florschütz long afterwards described these nocturnal crises, in words which reveal, not only the character of the boy, but the tutor as well:

I shall never forget the gentle goodness, the affectionate patience he showed when suffering under slight feverish attacks. His heart seemed then to open to the whole world. He would form the most noble projects for execution after his recovery—and though apparently not satisfied with himself, he displayed a temper and disposition which I may characterize as being, in thought and in deed, perfectly angelic.[5]

There was a broad gap between Albert at ten and the average British schoolboy. The gap was to continue throughout his life, accompanied by a mutual dislike.

The first shots in the war between the Duke and Duchess were fired when Albert was one year old. The marriage had been for purely dynastic reasons,[6] and love had run cold. For some time there had been obvious absences and suspicions, but the matter was brought to a head in the summer of 1820, when a lady-in-waiting informed the Duke that his wife was in love with the Court Chamberlain. Louise cleared herself, but only after a row and many tears. From then on Ernest watched her every movement.

The events of 1822/3 precipitated the end. The Duke of Saxe-Gotha-Altenburg, Louise's father, an amiable hypochondriac who spent many of his days in bed, died in May 1822. He was succeeded by his bachelor brother, Frederick, which pointed to the early demise of the Gotha establishment if he did not take quick marital action, of which there was no sign. That autumn Louise was ill: "I had an inflammation of the bowel, and as a result of this a haemorrhage."[7] In view of this, and a similar happening before her death, it has been suggested that the Duchess was a "she-bleeder", and that this was the reason for Albert's failure in health at so early an age.[8]

Early in 1823 the secrets of the love life of Duke Ernest and *la belle Grecque* poured from printing presses in Paris and London. Pauline Panam, alias Madame Alexandre, was tired of waiting for an acceptable offer of silence money. She wanted her revenge and she got it. Thereafter she married a rich man. She was free of the Coburgs now except for one blemish. Her son took after his father, and died early in dissipation.

To Duchess Louise there was a world of difference between hearing rumours of her husband's aberrations prior to marriage—such was the fate, in varying degrees of most wives in her category—and seeing those aberrations recounted in detail in print which was open to all to read. There was one unexpected shock in the pages. Pauline revealed that Prince Leopold had also been in love with her, telling how she had been forced to flee from him round a farmhouse to escape his attentions. The interesting point emerged that Leopold did not consider as untouchable the female attachments of his brother.

Now there was no longer any pretence of a normal relationship existing between Louise and Ernest. Letters to her girlfriend in Gotha were full of her romantic adventures. A courtier said of her:

The Duchess has indeed committed mad pranks with her lovers, and has by no means concealed them. She is possessed of wild *naïveté* and carries on with an artless, bold frankness what others conceal . . .[9]

In the summer of 1824 Louise fell violently in love with Baron Alexander von Hanstein, a lieutenant serving at Coburg. He was twenty-one, and thus two and a half years her junior. The attraction was mutual, and obvious. Thunder clouds gathered over the Thuringian woods and hills, yet week succeeded week and still the storm held off. When the first shaft of lightning struck, Louise was taken by surprise.

Since 1820 Ernest had been spying on her. For this purpose he had used the eyes and ears of his adjutant and adviser, Colonel Maximilian von Szymborski, a Pole who had been fifteen years in his service. Szymborski had become, or endeavoured to become, indispensable. He was disliked and mistrusted by the people who labelled him a "grinder of the peasants". Although he had accompanied the Duchess on a number of official journeys, she never mentioned his name.

As August drew to a close Szymborski asked to speak to the Duchess alone. He put to her a most strange proposal—that she should, "to some extent", separate from her husband. Louise's first reaction was amazement that a mere attendant should make such a suggestion to the wife of the reigning Duke. She assumed that he had been sent by her husband and accordingly went to see him. She found Ernest friendly but insistent on separation. It was fixed, finally, there and then, and sealed with tears. She later made the telling comment that she felt more sorry for him than for herself. She went to the Rosenau, the country house four miles from Coburg where Albert had been born. Ernest, with the two boys, drove to his mother's home, Ketschendorf, a short distance from the town on the other side.[10]

The news of the coming departure of Louise into apparent exile spread quickly through the Duchy. The people adored her and decided that the separation savoured more of a betrayal than a mutual arrangement. They laid their plans.

On Sunday, 29th August, a crowd, numbered in thousands, gathered outside the Rosenau, shouting for Louise to appear. When she met them, they insisted that she enter a carriage. A team of men with ropes pulled her away and at each village through which she passed the team was changed. Behind the carriage a long procession shouted and sang. Flags and bunting were out in the Coburg streets and the space before the *Schloss* Ehrenburg was packed. When Louise came out on to the balcony, a tiny figure waving and crying with emotion, and the vast burst of cheering had subsided, the crowd sang together "Now thank we all our God".

But this was only half of the required result. Off again went the carriage, under its eager manpower, to fetch Duke Ernest and the boys from Ketschendorf. There the Duke received a deputation, but at first refused to leave the house. In the face of overwhelming forces, he eventually agreed, but only on condition that he drove his own carriage. Between seven and eight that evening the Duke and Duchess, Ernest, aged six, and Albert, five, came out on to the balcony of the Ehrenburg together, to a rousing reception.[11] Thereafter, the task completed, the crowds melted away to discuss the day's events and to absorb copious tankards of the famous Coburg Brew.[12]

During the night the situation altered for the worse. Obviously there were many with private scores to settle with Szymborski and this was their chance. His house was attacked and stones thrown at his family. Reports of the day's happenings reached outlying villages, and doubtless became garbled and exaggerated on the way. Dawn saw parties of farmers and peasants, all armed with flails, making towards Coburg town. They gathered outside the Ehrenburg, where Szymborski had taken refuge, and it was clear that they were after his blood. When the ringleaders tried to force their way into the *schloss*, the Duke, magnificent in a long green coat and a white top hat, appeared and ordered them back. He was forced to make a hasty retreat. Furious, he decided to call out the Austrian cavalry, an order which the Commander refused to obey. It was left to the fire brigade and a company of archers to hold the entrances. The crowd jeered. Next, massed clergy tried their hand, but proved to have no more effect than the firemen. The outlook for the Duke's adjutant appeared dark indeed. Then guile was tried.

A carriage and four drove up to a side door of the *schloss*. The crowd sensed a trick and rushed towards it. They were informed by a footman that it was for the conveyance of the old Dowager Duchess, who was in a most upset state and must not be worried. But it was not the long nose of Augusta of Reuss which appeared slowly when the door opened, but the fast moving form of Szymborski, who made the leap from step to carriage in one. The horses galloped away, with cursing Coburgers behind them. Along the road cavalry were waiting and Colonel Szymborski was escorted across the frontier.[13]

Anticlimax came to Coburg. The people thought, maybe, that now the scheming Colonel had gone, the marital relationship of the Duke and Duchess would revert to normal. Of course, it did not. Louise signed the Deed of Separation. She went out for drives, and for ever after heard the echo of those last cheers. As the clock struck midnight on 4th September, she left Coburg and no one saw her go. She wrote:

The future is rather dim, but one must not lose heart . . . Parting from my children was the worst thing of all. They have

*Ernest I, Duke of Saxe-Coburg and Gotha. From a portrait by Dickinson
after Ruprecht.*

*Madame Pauline Alexandre Panam
and her son.*

*Louise, Duchess of
Saxe-Coburg-Saalfeld.*

Princess Charlotte. From the painting by Alfred Chalon.

Prince Albert at the age of nine.
From a portrait by Schneider, after Eckhardt.

Prince Leopold of Saxe-Coburg-Saalfeld.
From a drawing by Sir George Hayter.

*Lord Melbourne in 1838.
From the painting by
Sir George Hayter.*

*Prince George of Cambridge.
From a portrait at Windsor
Castle.*

The Queen at the kill in Windsor Forest.
From the painting by Sir Edwin Landseer.

The Duchess of Kent and Princess Victoria in 1834.
From the painting by Sir George Hayter.

Prince Albert at the age of
twenty. From a miniature by
Sir William Ross,
engraved by W. Holl.

*Prince Ernest of
Saxe-Coburg and Gotha.
From a portrait by
R. Thorburn.*

Prince Albert in the uniform of a field marshal.

*Queen Victoria in the robes of the Order of the Garter.
From the painting by F. Winterhalter, 1859.*

Numb. 19795.   2411

The London Gazette
EXTRAORDINARY,

Publiſhed by Authority.

SATURDAY, NOVEMBER 23, 1839.

HER Majesty being this day present in Council, was pleased to make the following Declaration, viz.

I HAVE caused you to be summoned at the present time, in order that I may acquaint you with my resolution in a matter which deeply concerns the welfare of My people, and the happiness of my future life.

It is My intention to ally Myself in Marriage with the Prince Albert of Saxe Cobourg and Gotha. Deeply impressed with the solemnity of the engagement which I am about to contract, I have not come to this decision without mature consideration, nor without feeling a strong assurance that, with the blessing of Almighty God, it will at once secure my domestic felicity and serve the interests of my country.

I have thought fit to make this resolution known to you at the earliest period, in order that you may be fully apprised of a matter so highly important to Me and to My kingdom, and which I persuade Myself will be most acceptable to all My loving subjects.

Whereupon all the Privy Councillors present, made it their humble request to Her Majesty, that Her Majesty's Most Gracious Declaration to them might be made public; which Her Majesty was pleased to order accordingly.

C. C. Greville.

Extract from The London Gazette *announcing the Queen's affiance to Prince Albert.*

Queen Victoria in robes of state. From the painting by Thomas Sully, for the St. George's Society of Philadelphia.

Royal art:

Islay and Eos, by Victoria.

three small etchings by Victoria, after originals by Richard Doyle

the Princess Royal, signed
"V R delt" and "Albert scult"

female head by Victoria.

The marriage of the Queen. From the painting by Sir George Hayter.

Baroness Lehzen.
From a drawing by Queen Victoria.

The Prince of Wales
in his sixth year.

whooping-cough, and they said, "Mamma is crying because she has to go away while we are ill."[14]

The departure of Duchess Louise from Coburg is cloaked in mystery. Both the suddenness and the fact that she made no terms are difficult to understand.

When Szymborski first spoke to her, he suggested a separation *to some extent*. This could be interpreted as divided sleeping accommodation. But after Ernest and Louise had talked together, the rift became final. The Hanstein affair could well have kept the couple to their own bedrooms, but was such an *aventure* sufficient grounds for sending Louise into exile and robbing her of her children? Ernest had given her every ground for being unfaithful, and lovers and mistresses were not uncommon at ducal courts. The people did not condemn her, and showed very clearly that they were on her side and wished her to remain. Later, in Paris, Louise summed up the situation in a few, somewhat odd, words:

> The Congress of Vienna, where the Duke of Coburg and Prince Leopold distinguished themselves, was a *cour d'amour*, and so was the Residence at Coburg.[15]

There must have been more to the affair than the romance with the young lieutenant.

The supposition has been made that homosexual relations existed between the Duke and Szymborski. This appears possible, as Szymborski took the first move and the public put the blame for the separation squarely on him. In a letter Louise referred to him as her husband's "darling",[16] and *Liebling* is a strong and telling word. She also said, after her critical talk with her husband, that she was more sorry for him than she was for herself. Revulsion may well have decided her that she could never again live under the same roof.

But (a) would Louise have agreed to leave her children in the care of a man with homosexual tendencies, and (b) would Ernest have risked a show-down with his wife at this time, when the bachelor Duke of Saxe-Gotha-Altenburg obviously had not long to live and Louise was the sole heiress? Coburgs never rated moral behaviour as high as a good inheritance. Yet Louise made no stand over leaving her children, though it must have torn her heart out to part with Albert, and, in the event, she allowed Gotha to pass to Coburg, although she could have used this as a card.[17]

It would therefore appear that Duke Ernest held a trump and his wife could not match it. Let the case be put that he revealed that arrangements were well in train for Albert to marry Princess Victoria of Kent, by this time all set for British Queenship, and that, as her consort, would win a position which Prince Leopold had described as "a grandeur seldom equalled"; that, if Louise did not comply with his demands, he (the Duke) would reveal that he was not the father of Albert. It was obvious that the British public would not allow their young Queen to marry a bastard, and a penniless bastard from Coburg and Gotha at that.

So, if Louise had refused to obey, she was faced with a grim alternative. Not only would her son lose the chance of a future of unrivalled brilliance, but she would be damned as a lost woman. There was a vast difference between mere flirting and being the mother of an illegitimate child. There could be only one answer.

Prince Leopold made interesting reference to the tragedy which began and ended so quickly. He said that he arrived at Coburg "too late to prevent some painful events".[18] The inference is that, if he had known earlier, it would have been in his power to prevent the separation. From her exile, Louise wrote to Stockmar: "Speak sometimes with Prince Leopold about me. I would not like him to forget me completely."[19]

There is another possibility—that Duke Ernest had discovered that Louise was pregnant. Such a situation would fully account for her abrupt disappearance into obscurity. Claim has been made that a daughter was born in 1825 and lived into old age.

One last, strange point. Queen Victoria, who froze at the mere mention of divorce and remarriage, was very kind about Duchess Louise. She wrote a pretty little obituary about her, just to put the matter straight. She placed flowers on the grave of Albert's mother and even named her fourth daughter Louise.[20] She did not do this at the expense of Duke Ernest, with whom she remained on affectionate terms, weeping copiously at his death. So it would appear that she considered neither guilty. Perhaps she thought that anything to do with Albert was beyond the judgment meted out to ordinary mortals. Perhaps she knew more than she gave away. Probably she did not learn the whole truth until after Albert was dead.

CHAPTER FIVE

Prelude to Victoria

*A*LBERT, AT FIVE, lived in a world of men and was never allowed to see his mother again. Women were strangers to him, and so continued to be throughout his life. If he had had sisters, he would have been very different. Florschütz regulated his days with a set programme of lessons, organised recreation and rest and, although children were invited round to play on Sundays, they were always boys. He had no maternal aunts. Of his father's sisters, the three eldest arrived on occasional visits, but the youngest, the Duchess of Kent, stayed firmly in England, intent on watching over the interests and future of Princess Victoria. So the feminine touch was restricted to two "grandmamas"—the Dowager Duchess of Coburg and Duchess Louise's step-mother who lived at Gotha. They cared for him and spoiled him but, when it came to companionship, could not bridge the age gap.

Duke Ernest, contrary to that what might have been expected, proved an excellent father. He was kindly and understanding and yet had complete control. He insisted that the boys joined him for breakfast each morning and, as he varied the location for this meal, choosing one of his shooting lodges or, if the weather permitted, a spot in the woods or gardens, Florschütz found that his carefully prepared programme for the day was put out of gear. But Duke Ernest was often away, on official duties or following his fancies. Then Albert's letters to him show clearly his affection, and also how he missed his mother. He ended all his letters in the same strain: "Think of me with love, your Albert"; "Think of me very often, and bring me a doll that nods its head, Your little Albert";* "Keep your love for your Albert".†[1]

Duke Ernest, with treats and presents, added a touch of

* 1825.
† 1828.

lightness to the routine of the schoolroom. The organising mind behind this routine was Prince Leopold, who arrived on annual visits to see how the training was progressing. He soon noted how bright and receptive was Albert's brain, how he loved to learn and cried when a problem was too much for him, how he quickly caught up to his elder brother's educational standard and how, although he was the more frail of the two, he was the leading spirit. The boys were so different that Florschütz wondered, as later Stockmar was to do, how sons of the same parents could be so far apart.[2] Yet they were essential to one another and miserable if parted.

Later Prince Albert was to tell Queen Victoria that his childhood days were the happiest of his life,[3] which might appear to be a back-handed slap on the cheek for the woman who gave him all her love, a regular supply of healthy babies, bi-annual holidays and a princely income. Yet he was speaking the truth. A sheltered regularity suited best his constitution and the domestic crises which have already been recounted, or are yet to be, were kept from him. If he had not been prodded by Prince Leopold and Stockmar, and had occupied his manhood with minor duties in his native Duchy, he would have been more content in his mind and undoubtedly lived longer. But the true source of his childhood happiness lay in the green pine and leaf-wood forests, the hills and the villages, the meadows and the streams of the Thüringerwald. There he left his heart when he drove away to share a double bed at Windsor.

Fresh air was an essential to Albert and in cities he suffered from a feeling of claustrophobic restraint. He lived only when he felt the wind on a hill-top, looked out over a wide picture of wood and water and heard the bird-song come up from the valley. When, much later, he law the lakes of Killarney, he marched up and down saying to himself: "This is sublime! This is perfectly sublime!"[4]

The Thüringerwald lies between Coburg and Gotha and there Albert found all the beauty and excitement that a boy could ask for. At the southern edge lay the Rosenau and at the northern the shooting lodge of Reinhardsbrunn, the summer months being divided between these two homes. The tutor took his charges on occasional walking tours lasting as long as ten days, with nights spent at the tiny villages where a warm welcome awaited the Duke's children. Both were keenly interested in natural history and brought home specimens with which they started their own museum.

Not all their occupations were so idyllic. When chemistry was added to the curriculum, Albert became a nuisance. He managed, with his instructor's help but not connivance, to fill a number of small glass vessels with sulphuretted hydrogen. These were in his pocket when he attended the Coburg theatre that night. In the interval they were hurled into the pit and boxes, causing mild chaos and considerable discomfort among the audience.[5] But he was the Duke's son, and Victoria's Albert, and thus biographers have interpreted this piece of nastiness as a sign of winning cheerfulness, endearing amiability and love of fun.

Meantime life was proving difficult for poor Duchess Louise. She had gained a man and lost her children, and there were consequent heartaches and bitterness. She made her home at St. Wendel, a small town in what is now the Saar, and took the title of Countess Pölzig und Baiersdorf, after estates which she had inherited. So cut off was she that when her uncle, the Duke of Gotha, died in 1825 she was not allowed to attend his funeral. Gotha was her inheritance and, after much family wrangling, it passed to Duke Ernest, so the House of Saxe-Coburg and Gotha began.* In great style, Ernest, his two boys behind him, rode into his new possession.

On 31st March Louise was divorced and six months later she married Alexander von Hanstein, who had been created Count von Pölzig by the Duke of Hildburghausen.[6] The marriage was happy and Louise's interests turned towards music and the stage—she even offered to appear in Paris.[7] But her gay life did not decrease her longing to see Ernest and Albert again. Dressed as a peasant, she went back to Coburg at a time of festival and watched her boys from the crowd[8]. Her stepmother knew of her longing and wrote to Duke Ernest:

The thought that the children have quite forgotten her, worries her deeply. She wishes to know if they talk about her. I told her that it was impossible for them to forget their mother, but that they were not told how much she suffered, as that would make them suffer too.[9]

* In consideration of the acquisition of the Duchy of Gotha, the Duke of Coburg ceded that of Saalfeld to the Duke of Meiningen, who also received Hildburghausen. The Duke of Hildburghausen took the Duchy of Saxe-Altenburg and assumed that title.

But there was no mercy in that Coburg heart.

In February 1831 Louise travelled to Paris with her husband to consult a specialist. A few weeks later, as they watched Maria Taglioni dance at the Opera House, she had a haemorrhage. She was suffering from uterine cancer and died on 30th August.[10] Her body was embalmed.

Shortly before she died Louise expressed the wish, in writing, that she should be buried near her husband's home, either at St. Wendel or wherever he chose to live. She had been happy with him in life and she wished to be near him in death. It was a very natural wish. But the most extraordinary rumours began to appear in the German Press. It was said that, wherever Count Pölzig went, his wife's body went with him, and that, to make the cortège less conspicuous, the body was hidden in a grand piano.

Various reasons were given for this strange behaviour. One was that, by Louise's will, the annuity which she had given to her husband would cease if he was parted with her body for even a single night. Another was that Count Pölzig believed that he had a right to the Duchy of Gotha, through Louise's claim, and that, to have any chance in this direction, he would have to produce the body. One practical point emerged—these newspaper reports would obviously prove most distressing should they be seen by the dead woman's sons. By the time that it became clear that Albert was going to marry Victoria, it was most unfitting, and even a danger to the marriage, that rumours should be rife that the mother of the husband of the British Queen was being trundled round Europe in a grand piano. The idea was reminiscent of some ghastly side-show. The next story revealed that the body had been stolen. It was said that men of Coburg had raided Count Pölzig's house, chloroformed him and taken away the coffin. Thereafter poor Louise was located lying in a grave near St. Wendel. The rest was fact. Her son, Duke Ernest II, arranged for the remains of his mother to be moved to the ducal tomb at Coburg in 1846. In 1860, when a new mausoleum was completed, there was another move. Then Louise lay beside her first husband, and not by her second, as she had wished.[11] Queen Victoria tip-toed in and laid her offering of flowers, and peace and understanding came at last.

Duke Ernest's divorce was not the only marital upset in

the Coburg family as young Albert studied in his schoolroom. There was the extraordinary case of Prince Leopold's "mock marriage".

After Charlotte's death Leopold had become hypochondriacal. He was forever complaining about the dull, wet weather of England, a country to which he was tied by his lavish income. He had not enough to do to occupy his ambitious mind and his only hope of a brighter future lay in the early demise of King George IV and his brothers, when there might be a chance that he would be made Regent. He aged quickly, just as Albert was to do, but he was still handsome, an impression helped by a dark wig, a feather boa, and three-inch soles to his shoes.[12] The dash had gone from him and he rode a pony so that, in the case of accident, there was not so far to fall. His lethargy was Stockmar's despair, as the doctor, now promoted Baron, watched his master for ever waiting for the resurrection of the vision of Princess Charlotte. It was not physical love that he required, but the recapture of a dream of romance, the detail of which was fast fading away.

Leopold found his resurrection on a September evening in 1828 in a private theatre at Potsdam. Stockmar's niece, Caroline Bauer, was acting there. His heart raced at the moment that she walked on to the stage, for she was the exact replica of Princess Charlotte. He made immediate offer of a morganatic marriage, promising to give Caroline and her mother financial independence and a house in London.

The actress, complimented, found the offer tempting enough. Stockmar approved, considering that the liaison would give new life and interest to the Prince, but he warned his niece that she would find him phlegmatic, that in London she would be kept hidden from the social world and that, in the event of Leopold accepting the current suggestion that he should become King of Greece, separation must follow.

In May 1829 Caroline and her mother arrived in London. They found a delightful house waiting for them in Regent's Park. There was only one essential missing—and that was Prince Leopold. When he did arrive he was muffled to the ears and dragging his feet. He said nothing for a time and then commented that it was a pity that she had allowed herself to become sun-burned on the journey. The flame, which had burned so brightly in Potsdam, had gone out. He was flat again.

Caroline soon realised that the romantic role which she had pictured for herself was non-existent. She was merely there to read aloud and play the piano—just someone whom Leopold could visit when he had nothing else to do. But others saw the matter in a very different light. The King of Prussia wanted to know why one of his favourite actresses was being held in London as Leopold's mistress. The Duchess of Kent was outraged and kept her daughter well out of the way. Society laughed. The result was that the Bauers rebelled and Stockmar offered to escort them back to Berlin.

This suggestion had the most extraordinary effect on Leopold. He became revitalised overnight. The drooping hypochondriac switched into an ardent lover. He took Caroline's hand and walked with her in the garden, as he had walked with Charlotte in the long ago. Caroline, who was rather a simple girl, thought that her dreams, though late in coming, had begun to take shape at last. The two went through a form of marriage in the Regent's Park house on 2nd July, the contract bestowing on Caroline the title of Countess Montgomery.

There followed a few happy weeks of honeymoon, at the end of which Leopold announced that he must visit Germany on business. He arranged for his "wife" and her mother to stay in an hotel in Paris. After a while he joined them there, but stayed at a different hotel. The flame had gone out again.

Unloved, Caroline tried to escape, but Leopold would have none of it. He brought mother and daughter back to England and installed them in a dreary villa near Claremont. Caroline was not allowed to visit him in the "big house", but he regularly came to her, talking little but seemingly content to hear her read or play. Frau Bauer grew near to hysterics and constantly reached for the smelling salts. How long Leopold intended the arrangement to go on was not apparent and the Bauers prayed for the news that he had been elected King of Greece. On this point Leopold vacillated and argued, and at length in May 1830 turned the proposal down, one of his reasons being that George IV was on his deathbed and there might be better pickings at home. The end came over the one value that Coburgs put above all others— money. Caroline's "naughty" brother became involved in a scrape and financial aid was essential to avoid a scandal. Caroline asked for that aid. Not only was it peremptorily refused, but a volley of insulting epithets was fired at her. The Bauers quickly packed and set off for Berlin. With her from Claremont Caroline took Princess Charlotte's grey parrot, Coco, aged but still capable of screaming rude words in German. Leopold seemed glad to see the bird go. Thus, in bitterness, ended another Coburg romance.[13]

William IV liked Leopold no better than had his brother George, and the Duchess of Kent was named as Regent in the event of the King dying before Princess Victoria became of age. It seemed, therefore, as if Leopold's lethargic life would continue until Albert was old enough to marry Victoria. But in 1831 came a change of fortune. The Belgians and the Dutch were at loggerheads and in January it was decided, at the London Conference, that Belgium should become an independent State. A King was required and Leopold's name was put forward. He accepted and in July became the King of the Belgians. Thus began the main chapter of his life, his place in history. The job suited him and he did it well. He became the "Mentor of Europe", the "Nestor of Sovereigns". Contentedly he strolled the gardens of the Palace of Laeken. "The State is myself," he said. "I am the Atlas . . ."[14] He was happy at last.

The promotion entailed the taking of certain steps. For reason of politics, it had been suggested that he should marry into the family of Louis Philippe, King of the French. For reason of succession, it was necessary for him to have children, who must be Catholic. For reason of relations with Britain, it was necessary for him to give up the income granted to him on the death of Princess Charlotte.

France decided to sacrifice the King's eldest daughter, Princess Louise d'Orléans. She was twenty, against his forty-two. She was shy and mild, sweet natured and entirely inexperienced. The arrangement appalled her, but nobody took any notice. The wedding in July 1832 was very grand but as melancholy as a wet afternoon in February.

Step one safely over, Leopold began on step two. Here matters proved more difficult. The son born in 1833 died in infancy and the shock deprived the father of his new-found energy. He decided that he would sire no more, but beneath his dark gloom lay a streak of bright cunning. He suggested that his successor should be young Albert of Coburg. This neat trick for advancing the family fortunes was firmly negatived, as the French wanted no more recruits from Germany. So back Leopold returned to his nocturnal labours. He ended up with a family of three, two boys and a girl. The elder of the sons, his namesake, gained for himself a reputation for cruelty and scandalous behaviour unrivalled in the royal records of the nineteenth century. The daughter, Charlotte— for what else could she be called—married the Emperor of Mexico. He was executed—she went mad. Much unhappiness would have been avoided if Leopold had adhered to his wish and slept alone.[15]

The third step, concerned as it was with financial sacrifice, was the one which Leopold found the hardest to face. He had received some three-quarters of a million pounds from British funds since his marriage to Princess Charlotte and had given few services in return. He had merely "drizzled"* away the years. On being elected King of the Belgians, it was generally accepted, and firmly hoped, in Britain, that he would no longer accept the £50,000 per year which had been granted to him. The wily Stockmar sensed the public feeling and, before Leopold left for Brussels, an announcement was made that arrangements had been concluded regarding the pension. The general relief was short-lived. It emerged that Leopold would still receive the full amount but would return such sum as remained after he had paid existing commitments in England, these including the upkeep of the Claremont estate, contributions to charities and pensions to the needy and, most telling of all, after he had paid off his English debts. As Leopold was considered to be a most parsimonious chap, it was at first thought that this total amount would not be high. Then came the shock. It emerged that the debt figure was £83,000 and the annual commitments totalled £20,000. Rumblings of discontent were heard in Parliament when no money was returned in 1832. They grew louder when the same thing happened the following year. In 1834 the storm broke and Members made charges which reflected on the honour of the King across the Channel. Stockmar saw that time had come for action and shortly afterwards a token sum,

* "Drizzling" was a craze of the period. Into little boxes, often highly ornamented, were placed gold and silver tassels and baubles. On the turning of a handle, interior wheels ground the metal from the materials, the competitive angle of the occupation being to see who could obtain the most precious dust. Prince Leopold "drizzled" daily and the noise from his whirring machine had driven Frau Bauer near to hysterics.

amounting to a few thousands, was paid back. Thereafter repayments became regular, but Leopold remained a pensioner of Britain to the tune of some £20,000 a year until the day of his death.[16]

The years of 1831-2, during which time his mother died and his uncle became King of the Belgians, brought other changes to the life of young Albert. The Dowager Duchess of Coburg survived Duchess Louise by only two months. She had been the sole feminine influence in his upbringing for the past seven years and both boys were devoted to her. Duke Ernest put the balance back in 1832 when he gave them a stepmother. He married his niece. She was Princess Marie of Würtemberg, daughter of his sister Antoinette. It was not a romantic union and there were no children, but at least there was a woman to take her place in home and court life and someone to whom Albert could turn and call "Mama."

It was now considered necessary that travel should become part of the boys' curriculum and what better initiation could there be than a visit to the King of the Belgians. So, in 1832, they travelled to Brussels, met their new aunt and, more exciting, were allowed to inspect the outposts of the Belgian army during the siege of Antwerp. They returned fired with thoughts of liberalism and revolution. In contrast, the atmosphere at the court of Mecklenburg-Schwerin was mediaeval. At Mayence they swam three miles down the Rhine to Biberich. In Berlin, in the rôle of poor relations, they bowed to the King of Prussia. In Vienna their reception was distinctly frosty. They accompanied their Kohary cousins on excursions into Hungary and Moravia.[17] They saw Prague and Pesth and were thus experienced travellers by the time their turn came to visit London in 1836. But this journey posed one hurdle which as yet they had not faced—the crossing of the sea, and the adventure figured more prominently in their young minds than the meeting with King William IV and Princess Victoria, or seeing Windsor Castle. The journey from Mayence to Rotterdam by Rhine steamer took three days, the boys taking the opportunity of brushing up their English by talking with British passengers. From Rotterdam Albert wrote to Duchess Marie: "Ernest and myself are well, and only afraid of sea-sickness."[18] He always was.

CHAPTER SIX

First Sight

MANY TELLERS of the royal story of the last century
pass on the impression that, from baby days, Albert
was meant for Victoria, Victoria for Albert, and that the
little girl who, at twelve, was told that she would one day be
Queen, reached that grand state without query. That may
well have been the confident belief and hope in Coburg.
After 1861 the Coburg view was enshrined, and thus it was
written:

At the little ducal Court of Coburg there was the perfect young
prince of all knightly legends and lays, who fate seemed to have
mated with his English cousin from their births within a few
months of each other. When he was a charming baby of three
years the common nurse of the pair would talk to him of his little
far-away royal bride. In all probability these predictions would
have come to nothing had it not been for a more potent arbiter
of the fortunes of the family. King Leopold ... was deeply
attached to the niece who stood nearly in the same position
which Princess Charlotte had occupied twenty years before.
Away in Coburg there was a princely lad whom he loved as a
son ... Look where he might, and study character and chances
with whatever forethought, he could not find such another
promising bridegroom for the future Queen of England.[1]

In the event the existence of Albert was scarcely known in
London. He lived in a penurious duchy the size of Stafford-
shire, five days' journey away. While the names of Coburg
and Gotha were known throughout the land, owing to the
antics of George III's mother and the financial acumen of
Leopold, that of the boy was not. Few dreamed that another
take-over bid would be attempted from the same office and,
although there had been considerable speculation about a
mate for Princess Victoria, Albert had not been included
among the likely candidates. In addition, in 1836 it had not
been finally accepted that the Princess would succeed, and no

subject was being more fiercely discussed round the royal and fashionable dinner tables than that of the Hanoverian succession. The two people most concerned about it were King William IV and the Duke of Wellington. Under Salic law Victoria could not succeed to Hanover and the old King dearly wished to preserve the bond that tied Britain to the land of his forefathers. There was one obvious way out of the impasse. If Victoria were to marry Prince George of Cumberland, who would become King of Hanover on the death of his father, the marriage would preserve the union of the Crowns. Unfortunately Prince George was blind, a blow received while at play having accelerated an inherited weakness.

Emily Crawford, a writer who contrasted strongly with the lady quoted above, dealt with the matter in some detail. A journalist, Paris Correspondent of *The Daily News* and *Truth*, Emily Crawford possessed an unrivalled store of handed-down information. Drawing on tales which had come to her from a member of the household of the Duke of Sussex, she wrote in 1903 of the Hanoverian succession:

It agitated Clarence House, where the Cumberlands then lived, Buckingham Palace, Kensington, and disturbed the even-tempered Duchess of Gloucester. The King wavered a good deal. He was one day for the union of the Crowns by a marriage between his niece and the blind Prince; another day he inclined to break through any survival of the Salic law. Then he thought it would be a shame to force a blind husband on Victoria. His sense of fairness and his kindness of heart led him to think he must not deprive his afflicted nephew of his heritage. But what he considered patriotic considerations were strongest . . .

William took the opinion of international jurists . . . A rescript, of which I can find no trace in any English history, was drawn up by the King's orders to settle once and for all the doubtful points in regard to the Hanoverian succession. It did not entirely cut off the heiress-presumptive to the British Crown, but provided that she was to inherit only in the event of extinction of heirs male. The feminine rights were to be determined, not by proximity to the last King, but by seniority of line, and the Brunswick male heir was to have seniority over the females of the English Guelphs or elder line. Once united, Brunswick and Hanover were to remain indissoluble. Princesses on attaining the age of sixteen, and in every case on marrying, were to renounce all rights under this rescript.[2]

But opinions were divided, interests crossed, and the King was old. By the time the rescript was promulgated in December, he had but a few more months to live. Leopold, aided by Stockmar, had spent many years planning the game and, when Albert was deposited in the courtyard of Kensington Palace in May 1836, checkmate was not many moves away.

Leopold hid the real aim of the introduction of the Coburg Princes by camouflaging it as merely a family visit—one of a series. Victoria's cousins of Würtemberg, Alexander and Ernest, had already been guests and, when they left, the lonely girl had confided to her diary that she was "VERY UNHAPPY" and missed them every moment of the day.[3] In March 1836 came the sons of her Uncle Ferdinand, Ferdinand and Augustus, little older than herself. Ferdinand had been married by proxy to the Queen of Portugal the month before —Augustus had been promised to a daughter of King Louis Philippe.[4]

Queen Maria da Gloria, so young a widow and to whom re-marriage was said to be a physical necessity, appears to have been in some danger during the London visit of losing her "husband". Victoria, starved of men, set her cap at him. Creevey listened with delight:

> The town at present is kept in perpetual motion by the Duchess of Kent, everybody going to her *fêtes* at Kensington to see the young King of Portugal, her nephew. Lady Louisa (Molyneux) tells me that he is an innocent looking lad of 20 and that he never seems happy but when talking to his cousin Victoria, and that then they seem both supremely so. What wd. I give to hear of their elopement in a *cab*! . . .[5]

The Princess made no attempt to hide her feelings:

> I think Ferdinand handsomer than Augustus, his eyes are so beautiful, and he has such a lively, clever expression; Ferdinand has something *quite beautiful* in his expression when he speaks and smiles and he is *so* good. They are both very handsome and *very dear*! Ferdinand is superior to Augustus . . .[6]

If it had been in King Leopold's mind that this visit would titillate his niece's interest in men before he placed his *pièce de résistance* before her, he was certainly taking a risk, for the Coburg boys who followed on 18th May were not in the same category as the older Ferdinand. Ernest, "tainted with the hereditary disease of the House",[7] could not be classed as handsome and was already showing signs of desiring to follow his father into the mere of dissipation. Any sign of Albert being "a young prince of all knightly legends and lays" was at this time entirely invisible. A fat, studious, self-centred boy of sixteen, he was recovering from a severe bout of seasickness* and about to enter a session of biliousness. He could not dance, fell asleep on his feet after ten o'clock in the evening, and actively disliked girls.

Leopold and Stockmar made one very wrong assessment about the visit, neither anticipating the strong opposition that the news would arouse. In fact it brought forth a violent outburst of anti-Coburg propaganda in the public press[8] and caused King William to become choleric. William disliked Coburgs in general, and the Duchess of Kent and King Leopold in particular. He considered that the Duchess had been disrespectful to him, ungrateful to Queen Adelaide and downright rude when referring to his children by Mrs. Jordan as "bastards". Apart from anger at interference in a matter which he considered to be his concern, William disliked Leopold because he only drank water.[9] To scotch the plan, he immediately invited over the young Duke of Brunswick and the Prince of Orange and his two sons, selecting the younger, Alexander, as Victoria's future husband. He announced, and loudly, that no other marriage than this should take place and that the Duke of Saxe-Coburg and his sons should not be allowed to land but go back whence they came.[10] As Queen Victoria was later to admit, this action and tirade caused her uncle to be "amazingly frightened". He vented his feelings in a letter to the Princess:

I am really *astonished* at the conduct of your old Uncle the King; this invitation of the Prince of Orange and his sons, this forcing him upon others, is very extraordinary . . . Not later than yesterday I got a half-official communication from England, insinuating that it would be *highly* desirable that the visit of *your* relatives *should not take place this year—qu'en dites-vous?* The relations of the Queen and the King, therefore, to the God-knows-what degree, are to come in shoals and rule the land, when *your relations* are to be *forbidden* the country, and that when, as you know, the whole of your relations have ever been very dutiful and kind to the King. Really and truly I never heard or saw anything like it, and I hope

---

* He wrote home: "The journey to England has given me such a disgust for the sea that I do not even like to think about it."

it will a *little rouse your spirit*; now that slavery is even abolished in the British Colonies, I do not comprehend *why your lot alone should be to be kept, a white little slavey in England,* for the pleasure of the Court, who never bought you, as I am not aware of their having gone to any expense on that head, or the King's even having *spent a sixpence for your existence.* I expect that my visits in England will also be prohibited by an Order in Council. Oh consistency and political or *other honesty,* where must one look for you![11]

Leopold had strong reason to be worried, on two counts. Firstly, the Dutch and the Belgians were still very much at loggerheads. Secondly, the Prince of Orange was none other than 'Young Frog', the suitor for the hand of Princess Charlotte whom Leopold had displaced twenty years before. Now the Orange Prince said of his hated rival, "*Voilà un homme qui a pris ma femme et mon royaume.*"[12] The outlook seemed black for the Coburgs until the King was informed, to his great disappointment, by Lord Melbourne that the Orange alliance would not "be a good thing". William had, therefore, to make the best of the Coburg invasion, but the undercurrent continued to flow. At the instigation of Queen Adelaide, the boys were invited to Windsor. The Duchess of Kent replied that they were busy that day—it later transpired that they had gone to the Zoo.[13] When they did arrive, the King showed his disinterest by falling asleep at dinner.[14]

To Albert, the introduction to London was not an overwhelming success. To begin with, he had language trouble, as he had only recently begun to learn English.[15] The evenings were too long and his stomach gave up the unequal struggle. He wrote to his tutor:

> I feel very strongly that we are not leading at all a normal life here . . . On the 24th, my dear cousin's birthday, the King gave a great ball at St. James's Palace, the one at which my partner and I fell, and I was taken ill and had to go home . . .[16]

The programme was certainly a strenuous one for a sixteen-year-old. A levée was followed by a dinner at Court and concert, at which he had to stand until two a.m. The next day there was a Drawing-room at St. James's, when 3,800 people filed before the King and Queen, followed by another dinner and another concert. The fancy dress ball given by the Duchess of Kent at Kensington Palace lasted until dawn. There were excursions to Sion and Claremont, a service at

St. Paul's and a luncheon at the Mansion House. Then there were people to meet, among them the Duke of Wellington, sailor-novelist Captain Marryatt and Benjamin Disraeli, whom Albert dismissed as "a vain young Jew with radical opinions".[17] Other personal assessments expressed by the adolescents were that the British King was an insignificant old man, while Princess Victoria had to be content with an 'amiable'. Complaint was made that there was not enough room in their apartment at Kensington Palace, though this was mild compared to their condemnation of their accommodation in Paris, their next port of call, which Albert described as "most horrible".[18]

Cousin Victoria adopted a very different line towards Albert and Ernest. In her diary, and in her letters to Uncle Leopold, she heaped upon them "handsome, kind, honest, intelligent, beautiful, sweet, fine, delightful, clever, good, dear, merry, natural, well instructed, affectionate, gentle, amiable, agreeable, sensible, reasonable, gay, happy, witty and attentive".

When the adjectival flow dried up, she would borrow from the outpouring of the previous day, adding one or two "verys" to merry and a "so very" to good.[19] The ultimate step to which she resorted to avoid repetition was to underline, which provided her with a multitude of alternatives. Her words, to be so widely quoted in after years, were indicative of very little. As Sir Sidney Lee said of the Princess at this time, "Her views were uncoloured by sentiment—her personal inclinations hardly entered into her estimate of the position of affairs." She knew that her diary would be read by her mother. She knew that Uncle Leopold wanted her to like her cousins. She wrote accordingly. That she cried when Ernest and Albert left is readily understandable—she had done the same in the case of the departure of Ferdinand and Augustus. She was desperately lonely and longed for the company of young people. She was almost a prisoner and only when visitors came was there a chance to escape into the outside world. And, most important, the cruel campaign, which was to make her eighteenth year the most unhappy of her life, had already begun against her.

The issue behind the campaign was completely simple. If William IV died before Victoria's eighteenth birthday, the Duchess would become Regent. If he survived that birthday,

Victoria would become absolute Queen. Only a change in the Hanoverian succession could alter this.

It had been thought that William would not last until that vital date of 24th May 1837. When it became apparent that he would, those who stood to benefit by a Regency became desperate and without scruple. There was so much to gain— wealth, possessions, honours, power and the chance to get revenge and settle old scores. The greatest of these was wealth.

It was therefore suggested that a Regency should be in force until Victoria was of a more mature age. "A short time" was mentioned, but the plan was that the Duchess of Kent and Sir John Conroy should hold the reins of power until Victoria was twenty-one. That would give them ample time to do all that they wanted to do.

Conroy, Comptroller of the Duchess's Household, was the evil genius and chief of staff behind the campaign. In her Journal Queen Victoria referred to this Irish adventurer and schemer as a "monster and demon incarnate". Not only did he blight her girlhood, he was a confounded nuisance during the early years of her reign. Conroy was in the Regency plot primarily for money—he needed it badly. Extravagant to a degree, the fault lay to a certain extent with the family whom he served. For the last ten years of the Duke of Kent's life, Conroy had been his equerry and, on the Duke's death in 1820, had been appointed an executor of the estate—if estate it could be termed, as the debts amounted to some £50,000. Kent's life had been marred by a series of acts of financial insanity, as he was apparently under the impression that the income provided for him by the British public should equal the amount that he spent. Thus Conroy's apprenticeship in royal service could hardly be described as sound financial training. Having caught his master's disease, he was entrusted, not only with the care of the income of the Duchess of Kent but also that of Princess Sophia, spinster daughter of George III and a permanent inmate of Kensington Palace. After 1829 he kept no accounts. All told, he swallowed some £60,000 of the Duchess's money, while Princess Sophia's wealth at death was only £1,600, despite a large annual allowance and parsimonious habits.[20] But this information was not available in 1836. If, at this time, Conroy could have brought about a period of Regency, himself occupying the posts of Private Secretary and Keeper of the Privy Purse to Victoria, he would have been able to extricate himself.

The Duchess of Kent—"a short, stout, foolish woman, rustling self-importantly about in velvet and ostrich plumes"[21] —was left in a very invidious position when her husband died. Not yet having conquered the English language, she had very few friends and a great many enemies, jealous of her daughter's prospects. It was only natural that she should turn for guidance and comfort to the man who had served the Duke for a decade. The two were of an age—thirty-four in 1820. Because they were so much together, the gossips took it for granted that they were lovers. According to Greville, the Duke of Wellington thought that they were so, and Melbourne also, but they were the kind of men who would themselves have undertaken that rôle if they had been in the same position. Most men would have done in those lusty days, but Conroy was different. Sex did not have a high priority rating. It must be remembered that his wife and children were mostly on the scene and that the Duchess of Kent slept each and every night in the same room as her daughter, two factors which would have made a serious affair most complex. Wellington was convinced that the Princess hated Conroy because she had witnessed some act of familiarity between him and her mother.[22] This may well have been—Conroy may have considered that a kiss and a cuddle were expected of him and helped his cause—but, on evidence,[23] it appears that he did no more than paddle.

Conroy and the Duchess had strong supporters behind them in the pushing of the Regency plan. Princess Sophia was used as a spy at Court, reporting back on what was being said and done in the Family circle. Charles Leiningen, the Princess's stepbrother, was taking the line dictated by his mother. Lady Flora Hastings, Lady of the Bedchamber, was hand in glove with the Irishman. Beyond the Palace Conroy relied on the backing of Mr. Abercromby, Speaker of the House, and Lords Durham and Duncannon.

Victoria had but one militant ally—her governess, Baroness Lehzen. There were many who could have come in to rescue her if they had known the full story, but bullied, imprisoned, only seventeen, she could not get the truth through to them. Lord Melbourne admitted later that he would have "blown up" if he had known. Uncle Leopold was too deeply occupied with the affairs of newly born Belgium to give the matter the close attention that he should have done and it was upon his shoulders that Queen Victoria was later to lay the blame for her troubles. The one supporter who did see the whole matter clearly was the King, and he was hampered by age and illness and the lack of a channel of communication. William hated Conroy. He called him "King John" and asserted that he had no right to the uniform that he wore. He also hated the Duchess and stood up and lambasted her in front of his guests at his last birthday dinner at Windsor. Later he said: "The real point is that the Duchess and King John want money."[24]

Many means were adopted to promote the Regency plan, one of them being to keep the Princess as inexperienced as possible, thus making it difficult for her to escape the Kensington influence.[25] Inside the Palace, Conroy was rude, disrespectful and sarcastic, and barged into her room without knocking. When he tried to extract a signature from her when she was ill in bed, his methods savoured of third degree. He referred to the Heir to the Throne as the "Little Woman" and described her as being "arch, sly and artless".[26] He accused her of being as mean as her grandmother, Queen Charlotte, who was, in truth, exceeding mean. He said that, facially, she resembled her uncle of Gloucester, when everybody knew that that Duke was the double of a cod, his nickname being "Slice".[27] He labelled her family in general as "hogs from Low Germany".[28] He intercepted her mail and despatched answers without consulting her.

Outside the Palace, Conroy whispered the words that the Princess was sullen, stupid, mentally unstable, backward for her years and that her mind was occupied only with fashion and frivolities. He added that she was only too well aware of her imperfections and herself desired a Regency.[29] By May 1837 it became clear that the King was failing and in desperation Conroy and Lady Flora Hastings stepped up their ill-treatment of the girl. Still she defied them, still she refused to sign. Conroy tried to persuade the Duchess to shut Victoria up in a room and "keep her under duress" until she had extracted an agreement regarding the Regency from her,[30] but the Duchess was beginning to show signs of weakness.

At last Leopold awoke. He admitted that there were happenings taking place in London about which he was uninformed, but he was so concerned about 'the schemes and intrigues of those who would exert all their power to entrap

the almost isolated young Princess',[31] that he despatched
Stockmar post haste. The Baron arrived on 25th May, with
the usual open mind upon which he prided himself. After
listening to Victoria, his mind quickly became one-sided and
he hurried round to Lord Melbourne to explain what was
going on. The Prime Minister, who had been hoodwinked,
was "struck all of a heap".[32] Yet Conroy and the Duchess
had still one advantage—they had the body of the Princess
safely secured at Kensington Palace.

This was not the only royal home in which secret con-
ferences were being held and plans laid. One midnight at
Windsor Queen Adelaide knocked on an equerry's bedroom
door. She told him that the King wanted to see him. The old
man, weak and ill, propped up in his chair, handed the
equerry an envelope and told him to deliver it to the Duke of
Wellington. He was to take his pick of the horses in the Castle
stable and start at once on the twenty-three-mile ride to
London. He was to go across country, as there was a possibility
that he might be stopped on the high road. A nobleman in the
close confidence of William took the equerry to the stables,
unlocked them and saw him off into the night. The rider did
as he had been bid and kept to the quiet lanes, at times taking
to the fields. Even so, at half-way point, he heard the sound
of galloping hooves behind him, but the King had made sure
of the quality of man and horse, and the pursuit died away.

Apsley House was in darkness when the messenger arrived
and a night porter said that the Duke was asleep. The equerry
ordered him to be woken and five minutes later was shown
into an apartment as bare as a barrack-room. Wellington was
sitting up in his truckle-bed and read the message without
even troubling to say good morning. Having discovered that
the equerry knew nothing of the contents of the letter, he told
him to sit down, hold his tongue and not to fidget. The Duke
then wrote a few lines, enclosed them with the King's letter
and sent the man off to Lord Melbourne, ordering him to
return in six hours with the reply.

Melbourne, whose habit it was to keep very late hours and
eat meat and drink wine before he finally went to bed, was
looking out of the window at the early light when the equerry
rode up. A more compassionate man than the Duke, the
Prime Minister gave the tired rider a drink and put him
straight to bed. That afternoon the equerry, having called at

Apsley House, retraced his rural route to Windsor.[33] He was never to learn the contents of the envelope that he carried—and only three men ever knew. Yet it is a safe guess that the names of Cumberland and Conroy appeared on those secret sheets.

On 15th June Lord Liverpool saw the Princess, alone, and also the Duchess of Kent and Conroy. He was convinced, as Stockmar had been, that the girl needed no Regent. He reported to the Duke of Wellington and Lord Melbourne.[34]

Conroy came to his last ditch and summoned his remaining supporters. Charles Leiningen overheard a conversation with Abercromby in which the word 'coercion' was used. So she was to be compelled to obey and the compulsion was to be by force! Victoria was in isolation in her room, eating alone, seeing no one but Lehzen. The threat was too much for her half-brother and he spoke quickly to his mother in German so that the others would not understand. He begged the Duchess "not to lock her up".[35] Conroy saw that she had weakened.

On 20th June King William IV died and "King John" was defeated. But the bitterness lingered on.

In the excitement and sadness of the year that was past there had been little time for Victoria to dwell on the progress, the hopes and the ambitions, of a German student—Albert of Coburg. Nor was there place in the hectic days of the girl new crowned with Empire to ponder on the daily round of a penurious cousin. Odd letters were exchanged, and sketches arrived from Switzerland.[36] But three and a half years passed between Victoria's first and second sightings of Albert. It would have been a simple matter to ask him to spend a few days at Windsor, as much of his time was spent at Brussels and Bonn, yet no such gesture came from the Queen. When, at long last, she did agree to invite him, it was, firstly, because King Leopold turned on the pressure and, secondly, because she realised that the only way in which she could cut herself completely clear of Mama and Conroy was to have a man about the house. No other suitor had shown the willingness and the strength to undertake the job.

CHAPTER SEVEN

Lovers from far ...

*T*HE BIT OF A GIRL of just eighteen who was transformed early one June morning in 1837 into the Queen of Great Britain, was to have many admirers and prospective husbands before King Leopold tied her firmly to Albert.

The Princes and the Dukes (plain and grand) came from Prussia and Russia, Denmark and France, Holland and Hanover, and all the corners of Germany. Palmerston wrote when she was seventeen:

> There seems to be a flood of German princes pouring over us; the Duke of Brunswick, the Prince of Solms, two Dukes of Württemberg, and the Prince of Reuss-Loebenstein-Gera have all been seized with a sudden desire to see England.[1]

These hopeful young gentlemen were candidates for a marriage of national convenience and the advantage of love was not considered. On the occasions when the young Queen showed portents of budding affection, Duke Ernest of Coburg, tipped off by Brussels, popped up unexpectedly in London,[2] talking of family ties and the progress of his dear boys. Fortunately for the Duke, little passion burned in the hearts of the Continental rivals and it was left to the indigenous admirers to show that Victoria could light a flame. Yet the time had not yet come for such an alliance and not since Mary, youngest daughter of Henry VII, married the Duke of Suffolk in 1515, had a Princess married, with the Sovereign's official sanction, outside the confines of a reigning house.* In this case Victoria could have given the sanction herself, but she did not want to. She discussed the matter with her Prime Minister:

> Lord Melbourne said it was a difficult subject, the marriage of the Royal Family; marrying a subject was inconvenient, and

---

* The couple in fact first married privately, without official permission. Later, on agreeing to pay Henry a large sum of money, they were openly married at Greenwich.

there was inconvenience in foreigners. "It was very often done" (marrying subjects); "Kings did it; and I don't know there was any harm in it," said Lord Melbourne. Anne Hyde was the last who married a Prince who became *King*,* and that was considered a dreadful thing.[3]

Melbourne's real objection was that he considered that such a marriage would lead to jealousies between the Whigs and the Tories. Victoria feared that it would embroil her in having to marry the whole family, leaving the way open to odd aunts and cousins being able to equate themselves with the Sovereign.[4]

On the reverse side, any young man of the British élite contemplating a union with Victoria would have been called upon to make considerable sacrifice—freedom, inheritance, way of life. While there were some who were unquestionably in love with the Queen and whose heartbeats quickened as they watched her gracefully act her way through great occasions, would their feelings have been the same when closeted with the Woman, some of each day and all of each night? When Queen Victoria later attempted to find native husbands for her younger daughters, there were few takers. The one case which did materialise ended, sexually, in catastrophe.

Then there was only five feet of her, which might well have been considered a disadvantage by some. And, in the linear perspective, there were already signs of robustness fore and aft, pointing to the dimensions which she might, and in fact did, attain in the afternoon of her life. Yet she moved with absolute balance and lightness, seeming almost to float. She was very proud of this and when her eldest daughter reached the same state of plumpness, unkindly reprimanded her for "waddling when she walked".[5]

Victoria suffered from being an only child and starved of the company of children of her own age. This showed in many small ways, not least being the absorption of Germanic habits and customs from her mother and Baroness Lehzen. "I" was her firmament—"I want" her creed. When an equerry arrived at Kensington Palace with a little dog, she said "I want"—and got it.[6] She was never taught to share. As she had never been integrated in a covey of girls, she had learned none of the tricks of the trade of life. If she was attracted to a man, she put on her "I want" look and her eyes followed him

* James II.

as do the eyes of a child follow a shopkeeper as he fulfils an order for sweets. She lacked polish, for example, in her eating habits. Victoria ate as fast as Louis XVI. She crammed food into her mouth, a habit which some of her children inherited and she tried her best to eradicate.[7] She picked up bones in her fingers and gnawed them.[8] She was very fond of mutton chops. When dining with her uncle of Sussex, she was asked if she liked the lamb cutlets. She replied: "Oh, the chops are not bad."[9] She was a glutton with soup. A Frenchman with romantic ideas watched her demolish three large platefuls and was completely disillusioned. She could consume hot buttered toast in vast quantities. This intrigued a German newspaper, which described the strange dish as "slices of bread roasted on the coals and buttered hot".[10] But she was weak on breakfast, preferring to have it alone in her room, although this gave her a guilty conscience. She favoured special wafers which Uncle Leopold sent to her from Brussels.[11] A glass of hot water drunk daily at ten put her digestion back to rights.[12]

But to those from across the sea who looked upon Queen Victoria as a career, an advancement for their family and, most likely, a source of income, minor habits and characteristics were of no matter. In any case, such affairs rarely passed the planning stage. Typical was that of Prince Christian of Schleswig-Holstein-Sonderburg-Glücksburg. He was a nice young fellow, a year senior to Victoria, full of good qualities but poorly educated and not intellectual.[13] He was the nephew of the King of Denmark, but not very Danish and not very royal. As he was poor and his prospects appeared to be limited to an army career, his chances were not highly rated. But he had his dreams and, although this particular one did not materialise, others did. He became King of Denmark, his son King of Greece, one daughter Queen of Great Britain and another Empress of Russia.

On Queen Victoria's accession the Danish King decided to send Christian to London as the bearer of his congratulations. Both Blome, Danish Ambassador in London, and Browne, English Chargé d'Affaires in Copenhagen, realised at once that this would lead to marriage rumours, and London warned Copenhagen to expect a chilly reception from the Duchess of Kent.[14] Christian arrived early one morning and woke the Ambassador as he had no money to pay the cab. Blome took one horrified look at his outfit, and particularly his hat, and sent him off to a tailor. He emerged transformed.

Christian was trembling as Lord Palmerston led him in to meet the Queen, but "eighteen" and "nineteen" soon found their age level and plenty to talk about. She asked him to lunch and he took her in, talking long into the afternoon. It was quickly noted that she treated her visitor "with much distinction", and invitations poured in upon him. He was booked for every meal and danced far into every night, which fatigued his companion, the Ambassador, considerably. If Christian was to oust the Coburg, as most people hoped he would, it was politic to make a good impression from the beginning, and he was warmly received at every house but one. At Kensington Palace the Duchess of Kent was polite but icy.

Christian returned home brimful of hopes and dreams, thrilled by the gaiety of London and half in love. But no sooner was he out of the way than King Leopold arrived to see his niece. Blome guessed the reason for the visit but still advised that the Prince be sent over as the representative of the King of Denmark for the great occasion of 1838.[15]

Christian's problem was to find sufficient funds to cope with the pomp of Coronation. Coaches, lackeys and liveries all had to be provided. At last it was decided that £1,000 would cover his four-week visit, but this was only a fragment of the sums which larger nations were expending. There was therefore considerable ambassadorial pique when, at a Court concert, the Queen sent the Lord High Chamberlain to bring Prince Christian to the chair beside her. This was a triumph, but tragi-comedy was to follow. After the representatives of the various Courts had introduced themselves to the Queen, they were called upon to retreat across a wide floor, making three deep bows in the process. Christian omitted to note the position of a sofa which stood on the floor. As he was about to make his second bow, his knees went out beneath him and he landed on the sofa. The Queen saw the funny side of the incident, but it hardly helped the matrimonial stock.

By now the Press had scented romance and articles appeared forecasting that the Queen would choose the Danish Prince. Christian confided his hopes to the Duchess of Cambridge, a relative on his mother's side. This was not altogether wise as the Duchess's son, George, obviously had a prior claim but had shown violent opposition to sharing his life with cousin Victoria. The Duchess much preferred Christian to Albert, but still hoped that George would come to his senses. When she saw Victoria showering favours on Christian, she became jealous, and that was dangerous.

At the end of July the time came for Christian to return to Copenhagen. He said his goodbyes to Victoria at a Court Ball and people whispered that they were in love. Ambassador Blome heard all the rumours, but in August reported back:

As for the projected visit to London of the King of the Belgians, I learn on good authority that the Government do not want him and are taking measures to prevent his coming. The object of his visit is first his own interest, then the wish to improve the relations between mother and daughter which are growing steadily worse, and finally to set the seal on an alliance that has long been half-and-half arranged, which would put an end to the last hopes of our young Ambassador Extraordinary (Christian).[16]

So ended the dream of a Prince who would have suited Victoria well. He lost because he lacked backing and the cold, calculated judgment of the Coburgs. When next he saw the Queen, Albert was dead, and his daughter was about to marry her son.

Some early suitors gave in without a struggle. The Duchess of Kent received the following letter from the English Minister in Berlin:

MADAM,—Would it be agreeable to your Royal Highness that Prince Adalbert of Prussia, the son of Prince William, should place himself on the list of those who pretend to the hand of H.R.H. Princess Victoria?

Your consent, Madam, would give great satisfaction in Berlin.

The Duchess's reply showed a degree of tact which was so often missing from her spoken words:

. . . The undoubted confidence placed in me by the country, being the only parent since the Restoration who has had the uncontrolled power in bringing up the heir to the Throne, imposes on me duties of no ordinary character. Therefore I could not, compatible with those I owe my child, the King and the country, give your Lordship the answer you desire; the application should go to the King. But if I know my duty to the King, I know also my maternal ones, and I will candidly tell your Lordship that I am of opinion that the Princess should not marry till she is much older.

I will also add that, in the choice of the person to share her great destiny, I have but one wish—that her happiness and the interest of the country be realised in it.[17]

This facile reply appears to have nonplussed Berlin, where it was considered that any candidate put forward by Prussia would automatically go to the head of the list. The King ended the matter by refusing Adalbert permission to visit London.

Some parents would not take "no" for an answer. When the Prince of Orange was told that his son Alexander, despite the backing of William IV, was not suitable for Victoria, he went direct to the Prime Minister to ask if he or his Government had any objection to such a marriage. Melbourne replied, in his laconic way, that personally he had no objection to Alexander, "no more than to any Prince in Europe", but he went on to point out that the Orange dominions were so situated that they would constantly be involved if war were to break out. There was no answer to that.[18]

There was one bachelor in Europe whom it was universally hoped would be kept well away from Victoria, and that was Charles, Duke of Brunswick. The nephew of Queen Caroline, if the sons of George III had begat no children, he would, in all probability, have succeeded to the Thone. Brought up in London under the supposed care of George IV, he became one of the most reckless of the "dandies". His behaviour bordered on the insane. Such was the guest whom William IV, to spite the Coburgs,[19] asked to Windsor at the same time as Albert and Ernest arrived at Kensington Palace. Fortunately the Princess was well protected. In after years Charles was a regular attender at the Paris Opera House, "with a brilliantly-painted face, a black wig, and a shirt-front and fingers blazing with diamonds".[20]

Claimants with a much stronger chance were the sons of Louis Philippe. The King of the French had been a friend of the Duke of Kent, his daughter was married to King Leopold and plans were being laid for further marriages between the Orleans and Coburg families.* That Louis Philippe planned so seriously to make the English Queen his daughter-in-law made matters very difficult for King Leopold. He therefore, cannily, kept Albert's candidature a secret from the Orleans family, with the exception of his wife whom he swore to

* Marie married the Duke of Würtemberg; the Duc de Nemours, Victoria of Coburg-Kohary; and Clémentine, Augustus of Coburg-Kohary.

secrecy.[21] When later Louis Philippe was accused of double-dealing over "the Spanish marriages", it must be admitted that he had certain grounds for his behaviour.

The first son to try his luck was the eldest, the Duke of Orleans. He came to England to inspect Victoria in 1833. He was very tall and told his sister, the Queen of the Belgians, that, although her darling little niece was a rosebud, she was so short that if she were to be put into a riding boot, she would scarce be able to see over the top. He feared that the people of Paris would rock with laughter if they were to see the two standing side by side. As his suit was dependent on no child being born who would oust Victoria from succeeding to the Throne, he handed over to his brother, the Duc de Nemours.[22]

Louis Nemours, gay, irrepressible and a much coveted bachelor, was also tall and slender and Victoria found him *delightful*. But when she chatted to him at dinner who should be at her other side but Uncle Leopold,[23] watching points. Louis Philippe rated the chances of his second son so highly that he sent Nemours as his representative to the Coronation. It was this attractive Frenchman that the Queen disillusioned by downing three plates of soup in quick succession. Some thought it a pity that romance had not dawned. Percy Colson wrote:

Had Victoria married le Duc de Nemours, all would have been so different. One feels very much inclined to wish that she had. Perhaps the moral character of the young man was less admirable than that of Albert, but how much more agreeable a country to live in would England have been, had it come under French, instead of German, influences![24]

The first tremor of passion to shake Victoria coincided with her twentieth birthday. The experience quite upset her values and her feelings. It left her with the desire to spend more time with young people, because, as she said, she had lived so much with those much older than herself that she often forgot that she was young.[25] Melbourne and Uncle Leopold both showed signs of crustiness.

The man in the case was a Russian. Marriage was impossible, as he was the Cesarewitch, the Hereditary Grand Duke Alexander, heir of Emperor Nicholas. In an age when Grand Dukes were two-a-penny, to Victoria he was *the* Grand Duke and beside him, she said, "no one is seen to advantage".[26] He came to England in 1839 when the spring flowers were blooming and, although the posy of elation that he handed to the young Queen lasted little longer than those flowers, his memory has been resurrected annually ever since. The Cesarewitch, the Autumn handicap run at Newmarket, was named after him. Greville wrote:

> Yesterday the Grand Duke Alexander went away after a stay of some three weeks, which has been distinguished by a lavish profusion—perhaps a munificence—perfectly unexampled; . . . he has scattered diamond boxes and rings in all directions, subscribed largely to all the charities . . . and most liberally (and curiously) to the Jockey Club, to which he has sent a sum of 300*l.*, with a promise of its annual repetition.[27]

The first half of 1839 brought a series of crises into Queen Victoria's life. As she was later to admit, her inexperience and obduracy were in part to blame. In January her mother's lady-in-waiting, Lady Flora Hastings, was rumoured to be pregnant, the assumption stemming from the state of her figure. The Queen assented to a proposal that she should be examined by the royal physician, Sir James Clark. In the event Lady Flora was suffering from a tumour on the liver and died in July. The Hastings family, ably assisted by the Tory press, demanded a royal apology. The Queen's popularity slumped. She was hissed at Ascot and cries of "Mrs. Melbourne" came from the stands.

Early in May the Whig ministry lost its hold on the House of Commons and Melbourne resigned. It was a moment that Victoria dreaded and she burst into tears. The Duke of Wellington having refused to serve, she summoned the Conservative leader, Sir Robert Peel. The Queen disliked the Tories and found no *rapport* with Peel. When he insisted that some of her Ladies in higher posts should be exchanged for others of his political leaning, she dug in her toes and refused. Melbourne came back with a reformed, but still weak, Whig ministry. In the midst of this maelstrom of feuds and misunderstandings, tragedy and abuse, the Grand Duke Alexander arrived. Victoria could not have had a nicer birthday present.

From the moment that he was introduced to her at Buckingham Palace Victoria made no secret of her liking for him. She found him natural, merry and "so easy to get on with".[28] In one crowded London week they were together at two balls, two theatres, a concert and a reception. They rode together. "Quite deliberately she watched herself falling in love with him."[29]

It was as the visit drew to a close that she made plain her feelings—too plain for some, Melbourne among them. There was a house party at Windsor, with all the usual names— Argyll, Erroll, Albemarle, Paget, Bentinck, Cowper. It was the 27th May and the Queen was in her bedroom preparing to change for dinner. She moved over to the window, looking at the bright, green evening and the grey Castle walls. She knew the exact minute to be there—twenty minutes to seven. She noted it down. Alexander's carriage came up the hill. He must have known that she would be waiting for him, for, of all the many windows, he found hers and bowed. An hour later dinner was served in St. George's Hall. 'The Grand Duke led me in . . . I really am quite in love . . ."

Weippert and his band played for dancing in the Red drawing-room. In the opening quadrille the Queen partnered Alexander. She sat out a Valse with him, as Queens didn't waltz. Supper at midnight and then . . .

After supper they danced a Mazurka for ½ an hour, I should think nearly; the Grand-Duke asked me to take a turn, which I did (never having done it before) and which is very pleasant; the Grand-Duke is so very strong, that in running round, you must follow quickly, and after that you are whisked round like in a Valse, which is very pleasant . . .

Two dances later . . .

After this we danced (what I had never even seen before) the "Grossvater" or "Rerraut", and which is excessively amusing; I danced with the Grand-Duke, and we had such fun and laughter . . . It begins with a solemn walk round the room, which also follows each figure; one figure, in which the lady and gentle- man run down holding their pocket-handkerchief by each end, and letting the ladies on one side go under it, and the gentlemen jump over it, it is too funny. This concluded our little ball at near 2 o'clock. I never enjoyed myself more.[30]

Victoria was in bed before three, but she could not sleep. The music echoed on, the feet tapped and the strong arm was still around her. It was five o'clock and Windsor Castle was in the early light before at last her eyelids closed.

Only a few hours later the two were talking together again. He told her of his appreciation of his fine reception in England: *"Ce ne sont pas seulement des paroles, je vous assure, Madame."* He told her that he would never forget her, upon which Victoria commented in her diary: "which I'm sure *I* shall never also, for I really love this amiable and dear young man, who has such a sweet smile."

They danced again, until three in the morning. Then they had to say goodbye. Alexander came to her in the Blue room, next to her dressing-room. He took her hand and pressed it:

He looked pale and his voice faltered, as he said, *"Les paroles me manquement pour exprimer tout ce que je sens"*; . . . He then pressed and kissed my hand, and I kissed his cheek; upon which he kissed mine . . .[31]

They had their own tune—*"Le Gay Loisir"*. Next night the band played it over and over again—"which made me quite melancholy, as it put me so in mind of all, and I felt sadly the change". The music played, and the sadness and the longing were mingling together as only they can when one is twenty and in love.

... and near

QUEEN VICTORIA was a man's woman. It has been said of her that, if she had been born into a different stratum of the social structure, she would have had many lovers. The men whom she liked best were strong and imperturbable men who made her laugh, maybe with a touch of the rascal about them. Laughter was a physical necessity to her—without it she became morbid and introspective. Melbourne knew this, and so did the Ponsonbys, but many of her Household and Family, Princess Beatrice in particular, never understood. She liked men like Lord Rosslyn who, bland and unimpressed, would retail the latest *risqué* stories until the Queen was "shaking like an agitated jelly".[1] Or Lord Fife, whom Lady Ely used to say was one of the few men who could, with impunity, get the better of her.

At dinner at Windsor, when old Fife was mopping up his soup with much noise, he suddenly paused, looked up and said in his very broad Scotch: "Yer Majesty will be pleased to hear that I've given up brandy and sodas!" "I'm glad to hear it, Lord Fife," said the Queen. "I'm sure you'll be the better for it." "Thank you, Ma'am, I think I shall; and besides I find Scotch whisky and seltzer an excellent substitute!"[2]

Fife's son, Macduff, Duke of Fife, was another favourite, although his language on occasion was "Billingsgate at high tide". At a servants' ball at Balmoral he persuaded the Queen to dance a reel with him. He chose one which was reserved by custom for sweethearts, hands locked across the bosom, "and danced it in rather an improper way".[3]

Despite Napoleon III's lurid career with the ladies, the Queen was immediately attracted to him when she met him in 1855 and, despite the political differences which later came between the Emperor and herself, her letters to him were always in the cordial strain which had existed then. She

97

confided to her diary that there was "something fascinating, melancholy, engaging, which draws you to him". Here was a mixture of the mysterious and the mountebank. "It was one of Victoria's strangest idiosyncrasies to be fascinated by such men."[4]

Suitors of this calibre did not poach into her life during her early years as Queen. In any case they would have been outshone by Melbourne, chased off by the Duchess of Kent and outpointed by King Leopold. There was chat in the gossip columns of budding romances with eligible young men like Lords Eglinton, Mulgrave and Elphinstone, but they were only part of the backcloth, occasional dance partners or companions out riding. A certain amount of unrest did arise in the Tory camp over the case of the Hon. William Cowper.*

Cowper was Melbourne's nephew and secretary, and also Groom-in-Waiting to the Queen. It was the belief that the Prime Minister was scheming to unite his family with the Throne that contributed to his unpopularity with the Opposition. Greville commented with bitterness that the Groom dined four nights a week with the Queen but, although the couple certainly had long conversations together, the subject was usually Melbourne—his past, his character and his humorous ways. In any case Victoria had her very special young nobleman. When Count d'Orsay encouraged his nephew, the Duc de Guiche, to try his luck at winning the Queen's favour, he returned dejected from Windsor, saying that her eyes were so firmly fixed on Melbourne and Lord Alfred Paget that she could not see anybody else.[5]

There were so many of Lord Alfred's relations at Windsor that it became known as the "Paget Club House". Their number included Lords Clarence, George and Henry, Ladies Adelaide, Eleanora and Mary,† Miss Matilda, and Lord Uxbridge.‡ The Queen's friendship with the family began when she was thirteen and lasted until her death. In 1832 she was on holiday in Anglesey, staying at the Bulkeley Arms at Beaumaris. An outbreak of cholera caused the Duchess of Kent some anxiety and she gratefully accepted the offer of the Marquess of Anglesey to stay at his nearby home, Plas Newydd.

* Afterwards Lord Mount-Temple.
† Countess of Sandwich.
‡ Afterwards 2nd Marquess of Anglesey.

William Henry, second Earl of Uxbridge and first Marquess of Anglesey, was a brilliant soldier and one of the most picturesque men of his time. At Waterloo he was in command of the united British, Hanoverian and Belgian horse and he led the charge of the British centre which in part routed d'Erlon's *corps d'armée*. He was standing by Wellington when a round-shot hit his right knee. "By God, sir," he remarked, "I have lost my leg." To which the Duke replied laconically: "By God, I believe you have." The limb was amputated and an obelisk erected over its last resting place. His matrimonial career was also exciting. Having run off with Lady Charlotte Wellesley, a niece by marriage of the Duke of Wellington, the memorable Double Divorce followed. The deserted wife married her admirer, the sixth Duke of Argyll, and Anglesey married Charlotte. In all he had eighteen children.

"The Paget family eschewed from life all that was sombre or tedious: they shone with lustre in an atmosphere of sparkle and brilliance."[6] Melbourne said that the Paget educational system was never to learn anything.[7] Good looking and well built, their clothes were always a perfect fit and the envy of London, even of George IV.[8]

Lord Alfred was the second son of the second marriage and three years older than Queen Victoria. He was appointed to be an Equerry and soon after her accession she noticed him:

Dressed, in a habit of dark blue with red collar and cuffs (the Windsor Uniform which all my gentlemen wear), a military cap, and my Order of the Garter, as I was going to review the Troops. At 2 I mounted Leopold, who was very handsomely harnessed; all the gentlemen were in uniform, that is to say Lord Hill, Lord Alfred Paget (who looked remarkably handsome in his uniform of the Blues) . . .[9]

It was generally agreed that Lord Alfred adored the Queen. There were signs that the feeling was returned, but, as she often told Lord Melbourne, she was dead set against marrying a commoner. The newspapers depicted Paget as the lovesick swain and there were rumours of an engagement.[10] One of them accused him of "haunting" her and, on the arrival of Albert, put forward as one advantage that Victoria would now be able to appear without her shadow.[11]

Lord Alfred carried a portrait of Victoria on a chain around his neck and a miniature of her was on the collar of his dog.[12]

Maybe he thought that this was a way to Victoria's heart, as he well knew how fond she was of animals. The dog in question was a cross Newfoundland-retriever bitch called Mrs. Bumps and was a great success when presented at Court. She made a fuss of the Queen and then lay down at her feet. Melbourne commented that dogs knew how to behave as well as men and, added, perhaps pointedly, "*better* than some".[13]

Lord Alfred lacked the power of the Grand Duke Alexander and the influence and intelligence of Albert, and stepped back into the shadows of the Windsor stage. He went to the musical accompaniment of a song which became a hit:

> *The Lady I love will soon be a bride,*
> *With a coronet round her brow:*
> *Oh, why did she flatter my boyish pride?*
> *She is going to leave me now!*

Certain members of the Royal Family wished to see Victoria marry a male cousin, for obvious reasons. But the choice was small, and so were the chances. She showed tender interest in Prince George of Cumberland after the accident to his eye, but that was born of compassion.[14] Despite the Duchess of Cambridge's assurances, prompted by the wish to thwart Albert,[15] that the boy would be cured, Victoria and her advisers knew better. As she later pointed out, three generations of blindness and double relationship ruled out the Cumberlands on health grounds.[16] She was ever apt to put obvious signs of ill-health or physical deficiency as a barrier to marriage—on one occasion she objected on the grounds that the man had "feminine hips"—but was inclined to ignore the hidden dangers such as haemophilia and venereal disease.

In theory the undoubtedly attractive and amusing Fitz-Clarences, the plenteous offspring of William IV and actress Dorothea Jordan, had no chance with cousin Victoria, but in practice the attentions of one of them was feared. The Fitz-Clarences were fortunate bastards. Their father loved and spoiled them and on his accession gave all of them, excepting those who had already achieved that height, the rank of the younger children of a Marquess.[17] They occupied the best jobs at Windsor—Ranger, Governor, Housekeeper—and let everyone know that they were the sons and daughters of the King. Queen Adelaide accepted and favoured them, receiving patronisation in return, as an actress of world-wide renown was considered by them as good as any Princess from Germany, They remained unimpressed by anyone. Queen Victoria. glancing into a mirror, saw one of them pulling a snook at her behind her back.[18]

The son whom the Duchess of Kent feared was "Gus", the rollicking Rector of Mapledurham. Lord Augustus began life in the Navy, and there lay his heart. But for financial reasons his father transferred him to the Church, for which he was completely unsuited. He was given a good living and a Canonry at Windsor, and in time became Chaplain to the King.[19]

"Gus" took after his father in many ways—in his love of the sea, his strong language and his unorthodox behaviour. On an early train journey an old lady entered the carriage which he was sharing with a friend. "Gus" wanted to be rid of her and accordingly pretended that he was a lunatic and that the friend was his keeper. But his alarming and ribald imitation stirred the old lady not at all. She sat looking out of the window as if he did not exist. When she reached the station at which she was to dismount, she turned and castigated the Rector, comparing him very unfavourably with his talented mother.[20]

Lord Augustus also inherited his father's appetite for women. As a sailor-Prince, William had the reputation for taking, by fair means or foul, any young woman who attracted his fancy—this practice having led to him being attacked by an irate father in Mountain Street, Quebec, in 1787.[21] "Gus" was no less powerful. At Kensington Palace Sir John Conroy saw him looking at Victoria in a certain way and warned her mother that he was just the kind of man who would fling way his surplice and bolt to Gretna Green with the Princess. The Duchess of Kent was distraught with alarm at the mere thought and closed the doors on the FitzClarences, an action which acerbated the already troubled relations with the King.[22]

Last, but certainly not least, on the list of Victoria's suitors comes George, her cousin of Cambridge. He was the obvious choice. King William and Queen Adelaide wished the two to marry, and so did the Tories and the Established Church, and Parliament would not have cut the royal husband's allowance if they had. He was slightly older than she, brought up in England at the King's Court, and was very good looking. The snag was that George did not like Victoria.

His father, Adolphus, was the youngest son of George III. In 1815, when Hanover was raised to the rank of kingdom, he was appointed Governor-General and, later, Viceroy. It was a sinecure and a well paid one. He was an amiable and affable man, whose hobby was music, in which field his enthusiasm outstripped his talent. In elder life he became somewhat odd—Wellington described him as being "mad às Bedlam". He was the kind of man who shone at school speech days, City dinners, military inspections and charitable meetings. Under the parasol of royalty he deigned to be democratic, which pleased many people. He wore a blond wig over a completely bald head and was partially deaf.[23] He shouted when he spoke and repeated everything three times, presumably to give time for his mental machinery to operate. Conversing with him was to be likened to throwing a ball against a wall of mental cement, remarks returning, in query form, to the originator. Thus to his neighbour at dinner at Windsor:

Where do you *habitually* reside, Ma'am? Oh, Hagley—you *did* live there. I see, I see—your son lately married—how long? a few months? I understand. *Now* where do you mean to live? At Richmond for the winter? Oh, I see! Where have you been since your son's marriage? Leamington? Why to Leamington? Oh, your brother—I understand! Your brother, Captain Spencer! I remember—I perfectly recollect. A naval man, I believe. Yes, I saw him in 1825 at your father's in the Isle of Wight. Yes, yes, I know—Frederick Spencer, to be sure! *Your* father-in-law, Mr. Poyntz? No, surely not so, Ma'am. Oh, *his* father-in-law? Oh, I see, I see . . .[24]

The old Duke was best remembered for his Church performances. Not only did he act as master of ceremonies, counting the schoolchildren to see that none were absent, and noisily finding the places for those whose attention had wandered, but he engaged in a cross-talk act with the officiating clergyman. Owing to his status and bull-like voice, he stole the limelight. On the congregation being invited to pray, he would reply, "Certainly", and on a request being made to the Almighty for rain, some caustic comments about a change being necessary in the existing direction of the wind before that was possible, echoed round the Chancel. Some aberration must have been troubling the Duke's mind on the occasion when, after the Commandment was delivered, "Thou shalt not commit adultery", he replied: "Quite right, quite right, but very difficult sometimes."[25]

Young George spent his early childhood at the Royal Palace at Hanover and, as the only son of the Viceroy, was accorded regal treatment which he fully absorbed. At the age of eleven he was sent to England for British training. For six years he lived with King William and Queen Adelaide, who came to look upon him as their adopted son. It was some consolation to the Queen for the children whom she had lost. She spoiled him.

There was little of the Hanoverian toughness about the Cambridge boy. He was frightened of horses and the kick of a gun, but in his priggish diary constantly urged himself on to better things.[26] Not unnaturally, as he occupied the best rooms in England and Hanover, he came to have a very good opinion of himself, whilst the Palace cabals in which he was immersed can but have prejudiced his outlook.

The King was prone to attacks of over-excitement, especially in the spring, and there were those about him who believed that he would end his days in a straitwaistcoat. At such times he would hold forth, in picturesque and vituperative manner, against those whom he disliked, and there were signs of relief when he fell asleep after his second glass of port.[27] Among the targets for his invective were the Duchess of Kent and her adviser, "King" John Conroy.

The Queen was a mild and domestic minded woman, but unfortunately she had very little control over her Ladies. On one occasion she was noted driving round London with a female leg protruding from the window, the owner having complained that she had cramp. Conversation round the meal table was trivial and vulgar, even bawdy if the Fitz-Clarences were present, and the favourite subject was the flirtations and aberrations of members of the Household, and who would marry who.[28] Naturally Prince George came in for his share of badinage and he took it hardly. When Maria da Gloria, the young Queen of Portugal, came on a visit to England, he was told that "she had come to fetch him". Whereupon he turned as red as a radish and declared that he would seek refuge in America.[29]

Prior to the death of George IV the Duchesses of Kent and Clarence had been close friends, jabbering away together in

German like two sisters. When the daughter of the former became Heir and the latter became Queen, the relationship took a drastic change. The Duchess of Kent was transformed. She was formal, secretive and at times downright rude. As a result Princess Victoria saw the King and Queen only at Birthday Receptions and State Balls. At such times she sat between the King and Prince George and opened the dancing with her cousin. It must have been obvious to him that the King intended him to marry her, but he was unimpressed. He had been Heir Presumptive before she was born, he lived with the King and Queen and his father ran Hanover. The Kents were poor relations, the subject of constant criticism, who occupied restricted quarters in Kensington Palace. His diary comments on Victoria were certainly not ecstatic.

"A nice countenance and greatly improved" was his assessment of her after the Birthday Drawing Room of 1834. Another thought was: "What a very disagreeable thing it must be to be a king! May I never be one . . ." Thereafter his tutor urged him to improve his manners in society and to speak to people in a more pleasant way.[30] George made a detailed list of relatives' birthdays that he wished to remember, but Victoria was not on it. When she sent him a complete silver dressing-case for his birthday, he consigned it to the end of his list, adding, "I apologise for not having mentioned her before."

In 1836 Prince George returned to Hanover for military training, but was back again in London after the death of William IV, as his father's halcyon days as Viceroy were over and the "terrible" Duke of Cumberland reigned there as King Ernest. Duke Adolphus made his headquarters at Cambridge House, Piccadilly, in after years to become the Naval and Military Club—the "In and Out". George— "the Adonis boy",[31] as he has been described—made the few steps necessary to join the social round. "I am now quite a gay young man, and leading a regular London life, in a quiet sort of way nevertheless. Really, pleasure sometimes becomes quite a business . . ."[32]

At nineteen he was cynical and easily bored, with unmistakable signs of the snob. His criticism of the Queen's first ball, a most important night for her, was that "the thing was kept up too late, for almost everybody was gone before the Queen retired". His had been the honour: "I opened the Ball with Her Majesty, and I thought she danced really very nicely, and seemed to be very much amused."[33]

"Her Majesty" had indeed been amused. "I never heard anything so *beautiful* in my life as Strauss's band . . . I did not leave the ball-room till 1om. to *four*!! and was in bed by ½p. 4, —the sun shining. It was a lovely ball, so gay, so nice . . ."[34]

At the Birthday Drawing Room the Prince noted that, of the 2,200 guests, "there was a considerable collection of ugly ones". At the Cambrian ball a few days later "there were a great many extraordinary and, at the same time, vulgar looking people present".[35] George had already become a connoisseur of pretty ladies and so was to remain all his life. His flirtations did not escape the sharp eyes of the Queen and she had a chat with Melbourne on the subject. He was non-committal. "Lord Melbourne said that his age was a very awkward one, and he remembered it well himself; that living only for amusement in London was very tiresome, if you had no pursuits besides."[36]

Charles Greville, Clerk to the Privy Council, was more precise and outspoken when, at a later date, one of the Prince's romances got out of hand. He wrote:

Fortunately he is a very timid, unenterprising youth, not unwilling to amuse himself, but by no means inclined to incur any serious risks, as he has abundantly shown on other occasions. His vanity prompts him to make love to the ladies whom he meets in his country quarters and, as princes are scarce, his blood royal generally finds easy access to rural and provincial beauties, but when he finds these affairs growing serious and the objects of his admiration evince an embarrassing alacrity to meet his flame with corresponding ardour, I am told that he usually gets alarmed and backs out with much more prudence than gallantry.[37]

To the Duchess of Cambridge there were no flaws in the jewel of her only son. She had sacrificed six years of his companionship so that he might be impregnated with the ways of British Royalty, taking it as read that George was being groomed to be King Consort to Victoria. By the spring of 1838 it appeared that matters were not moving smoothly in this direction. She decided to exert some pressure and looked around for an ally. Having little experience of England or the royal intrigues of Windsor and Kensington, she made a fatal mistake: she enlisted the help of the Duchess of Kent.

The Duchess of Cambridge was a very large German from

Hesse. Her face was coarse and heavy and decorated with thick black eyebrows. Her hair shone black from its dressing of perfumed pomatum and her broken English was guttural in the extreme.[38] Friends were few, but on the day that she chose her compatriot, the widowed Princess of Leiningen, as her confidante, she began a series of Cambridge intrigues and feuds which continued until "May" and "Georgie"* came together in the nineties.

Relations between Victoria and her mother were at their worst. The Duchess, somewhat understandably, found it hard to accept that she must no longer enter her daughter's room without prior leave and knocking. When she did, the Queen halted her by "holloaing out", at which rough reception "Ma" begged pardon and retired.[39] The Duchess of Cambridge had the same failing, even trying to read the papers on the Queen's table. When the Duchess of Kent, out of spite, joined the Duchess of Cambridge in pressing George's suit, the Palace became even more sharply divided.

Victoria soon guessed what was afoot and, as usual when she had a problem, she talked with Melbourne:

> Spoke of George who I said I did not like—though had nothing to say for himself and was particularly stiff with me; but that I believed his parents teased him about me, and that Ma got into the Duke and Duchess's favour, by saying she would promote a match between us; all of which Lord Melbourne thought very likely.[40]

Shortly afterwards the Duchess of Kent played her ace. She suggested, with the connivance of the Cambridges, that the Queen should ask George to stay with her at Windsor.

Such a visit, *tout seul*, could lead to only one conclusion by the public. The newspapers were watching very closely for a lead on the Queen's matrimonial intentions, and this would be it. So once again the Queen turned to her Prime Minister for guidance. Melbourne was not polite about the Cambridges, classing them as "foolish people". After consideration, he advised against the invitation. As a result, when next he met the Duchess of Cambridge, she shouted after him down the corridor: "*Da geht mein grösster Feind.*"[41]

For George, the danger loomed altogether too near for his liking and he put into practice the plan which he had pro-

* King George V and Queen Mary.

posed at the time when he believed the eyes of Queen Maria da Gloria were looking in his direction. In September he bolted. After a few months of military service at Gibraltar he whiled away the summer of 1839 by exploring the Mediterranean and visiting friends and relations on the Continent. Of course, everybody said that he had gone away to escape from the Queen, and this did not please H.M. at all. The Prince made matters worse by reappearing in London as soon as he had heard on the family grape-vine that Albert has been accepted.

Victoria fumed in her fury at being scorned. She gave her opinion that George was "an odious boy", both "ugly and disagreeable". She denied that she had ever even thought of "taking him".[42] In the field of personal abuse she made unfavourable reference to his complexion. Her final thrust was that Albert "disliked him very much", but the pretences had to be on when the two met.

The Cambridges were not told of the engagement until a month after Victoria had done her proposing. George greeted the news (of which he had long been in possession) with a sigh of relief. "Nothing could have given me greater pleasure than this intelligence."[43] He was able to seek safety in numbers, as on the 18th November he travelled to Windsor to offer his congratulations in company with his father and mother and sister Augusta. For once, the old Duke's ceaseless flow of conversation was a blessing. The Queen confided in a note to Lord Melbourne:

> They were all very kind and civil, George grown but not embellished, and much less reserved with the Queen, and evidently happy to be *clear* of me.[44]

But she was not going to let George escape as lightly as that. In January she sent for him and saw him alone, and alone was underlined. Her only comment was that he was courteous.[45] Two years later she got her revenge when the Cambridges played into her hand over the scandal of George and Lady Augusta Somerset. The strange point was that Victoria really liked her cousin, as she made amply clear in after years. She forgave him many things.

On the night of 10th February 1840, when the marriage was over and Albert and Victoria grappled with their initial problems at Windsor, George of Cambridge attended a full dress party at the Duchess of Sutherland's—"a very handsome affair".[46] It was there that he met lovely Louisa Fairbrother, a pantomime actress from Drury Lane. From that meeting resulted the family of FitzGeorge.

May and October

*M*ANY PEOPLE thought that Queen Victoria would marry William Lamb, second Viscount Melbourne, her first Prime Minister. That expert on Palace affairs, Princess Lieven, remarked: "I for myself cannot help imagining that she must be going to marry him."[1] Lady Grey wrote to Creevey: "I hope you are amused at the report of Lord Melbourne being likely to marry the Queen. For my part I have no objection."[2] There were cries of "Mrs. Melbourne" from the stands when the couple arrived together at Ascot. A cartoon depicted Melbourne as landlord of the Windsor Arms, the Queen looking down at him from a bedroom window.

When she came to the Throne, the Queen was eighteen, Melbourne was fifty-eight. The obvious handicap of this disparity in age was somewhat offset by the contemporary example of Mr. Coke of Norfolk, that legendary figure from Holkham who was created Earl of Leicester in 1837. In 1822 Coke had married his goddaughter, Lady Anne Keppel, when he was sixty-eight and she nineteen. The couple were blissfully happy and six children had been born to them.

But Melbourne had not the resilience of Coke. In the spring of 1837 he was ready for the fall of the Whig Government and the end of his own political career. "The strain of accommodating himself to the King's temper and what he called 'Peel's low creeping policy' was becoming more than he could bear."[3] Then, in the early hours of 20th June, William IV died, and with the dawn began the *annus mirabilis*—for him and also for the girl-Queen by whose side he was to be for many hours each and every day.

It is unlikely that thoughts of marriage entered the minds of either the Queen or Melbourne. Such a step would have been almost beyond the boundary of feasibility and only a series of exceptional circumstances could have led to this result. The critical moment came in the spring of 1839 when the Whigs went out of office. Then the thought of losing her mentor and her companion overpowered Victoria in a deluge of emotion. It was the loneliness and the vulnerability that she feared in a life without him. She wrote: ". . . the thought of ALL ALL my happiness being possibly at stake, so completely overcame me that I burst into tears."[4] They were words which, two years later when in the clasp of love, she was to regret. But, by her action, Melbourne came back into power and the moment passed. Then, in the dances of the spring, the touch of a handsome Russian's hand set in train a new form of emotion.

The relationship of Victoria and Melbourne cannot be paralleled with that of father and daughter, or even teacher and pupil. He found love at a moment when he had considered that loving was over, and thus he clung to it, and revelled in it, as the evening settled in. For her the dawn had been cold and drear among the icy webs of intrigue and restriction and when the sun came out she gave all her imprisoned love to the man who made it so. It was characteristic of both of them that they loved intensely—a woman's man and a man's woman. To both, a lover was essential. So they played their parts, like characters in a story book, without the earthiness of reality, in defiance of time. It was a short, but vital, chapter which they wrote together. No sweeter and rewarding relationship has ever existed between sovereign and statesman. It was a relationship which annoyed the Coburgs immensely.

Melbourne fashioned Victoria into the great Queen that she became. The advantages were his. He was indigenous. He was beyond ambition for power or wealth. He was beside her during her formative years when her mind received little but the doctrine of the schoolroom. His knowledge was encyclo-paedic and he was the mentor born. Albert, in his time, was to teach her how to reason, how to work, even, as she admitted herself, how to rule, but he could not give her humanity or wisdom from the past.

Deep down, Melbourne was a solitary and pensive man. He described himself as a "quietist". He hated *dissensions*. He heartily disliked those who resorted to a broadside of verbal phons and personal abuse to win an argument, regardless of whether they were right or wrong. He considered that bishops died simply to irritate him, thus forcing upon him the task of choosing their successors. Stockmar described him as "weak and careless" and, although some truth could be attached to each word, the label was based on German hostility and non-understanding. Melbourne could be very strong and often when he was careless it was because he was bored. He was too wide-thinking a man to be contained by one party, and at times appeared more of a Tory than a Whig. When he received important visitors in his bedroom, shaving or lounging in a chair in his dressing-gown, the obvious impression was one of a lack-a-day, but the truth soon emerged that the Premier had been up half the night studying his subject.

Melbourne had been prodded up the political ladder by the two-tine fork of his energetic mother. He would have been content to devour books or stroll with a gun round the fields about his Hertfordshire home of Brocket Hall. Reading and a retentive memory were the backbone of his brilliant conversation.

This richness of talk was rendered more piquant by the quaintness and oddity of his manner, and an ease and naturalness proceeding in no small degree from habits of self-indulgence and freedom ... He was often paradoxical, and often coarse, terse, epigrammatic, acute, droll, with fits of silence and abstraction, from which he would break out with a vehemence and vigour which amused those who were accustomed to him, and filled with indescribable astonishment those who were not.[5]

He also talked to himself and fell asleep at the most inopportune moments.

In view of the chastisement that Queen Victoria meted out to matrimonial sinners in her later years, it is seemingly strange that she should have given her complete love, friendship and confidence to a man who had twice been involved in divorce proceedings and whose marriage had ended in legal separation. Widows who were spurned because they sought solace in remarriage must have pondered on how great was their sin when they considered the lurid career of Melbourne, or the love story of Prince Albert's mother, or even that George of Cambridge was given the prize of Commander-in-Chief when everyone knew that he had long lived in sin and had two bastard sons. The truth was that Victoria accommodated all her life, and that much of her prudery was a mere tape recording of Albert. Yet at eighteen she assured Melbourne that she would not marry a man who had slept

with another woman. He said that it did not matter unduly—
but it certainly put him in the clear. The assertion can be
attributed to adolescent egoism and the proud intent of
"H.M. the Oneness" that she would not share anything with
anybody. In the case of her own daughters, she certainly did
not apply the chastity test to their husbands.

Of the two ladies with whom Melbourne had become
entangled, lovely Lady Branden, who had delighted his Irish
evenings in 1828, had disappeared into the shadows. But the
other, Mrs. Caroline Norton, was still very much alive and
kicking—she had kicked the Prime Minister's hat high into
the air at a diplomatic function shortly before the death of
William IV.[6] Mrs. Norton was one of the remarkable Sheridan
sisters, granddaughters of the dramatist, the others being
Lady Dufferin and Lady Seymour, afterwards Duchess of
Somerset and Queen of Beauty at the Eglinton Tournament.
When Melbourne met her in 1830 his impression was one of a
beauteous blur of black hair and long lashes, bare shoulders
and olive skin. A contemporary male summary was: "A
superb lump of flesh, looking as if made of precious stones,
diamonds, emeralds, rubies and sapphires."[7]

Mrs. Norton was ambitious, temperamental, flamboyant,
egotistical, clever, amusing, sometimes human and always
short of money. She was married to a brute of a husband who
was not above bruising such parts of the olive skin as his boot
could reach. Melbourne saw much of her—too much. She
made him laugh and he was easy in her company. Gossip
raged, but the two were not lovers, both rating passion low.
Mr. Norton, out of spite and greed, went to law, and lost.
It was an undignified affair, yet the Queen did not appear to
mind, and often discussed the Sheridan sisters with her
Prime Minister. After her marriage, she received Mrs. Norton
at Court. Melbourne, it seemed, could be forgiven anything.

The one chapter in his life that the two did not discuss
concerned the other Caroline—"Caro" Lamb, née Ponsonby,
his wife. This romantic tragedy intrigued the young Queen
and she discovered all that she could about it from other
sources.

Caroline the elf was fourteen when William Lamb first met
her. She hypnotised him and, six years later, when he was
twenty-six, he married her. She was impossible. Mentally
ill-balanced, her mind flicked from the brilliant to the primi-

tive in a second of time. She adored those who agreed with her and attacked with fists and nails those who did not. Tiny of frame, she liked to dress as a boy. It was reported of her that at a dinner party she changed places with the boar's head and appeared stark naked when the meat cover was lifted. For a few years William and "Caro" were happy, as if in a prolonged honeymoon, while the grand passion lasted and there was fun in discovering the many secrets of the other's heterodox mind. Thereafter William attempted to curb his wife's impetuosity and turn her thinking into the way of commonsense. The result was the opposite to that which he intended, for there was no place for reason and normality among the twisting paths of fancy and emotion which made up the maze of her brain. The ordinary bored her. Children would have helped, but only one survived, a boy named Augustus, and he was mentally backward.

In 1812 Caroline met Lord Byron, then riding high on the wave of *Childe Harold*. For two years *poseur* and *poseuse* loved and fought, cried and made up, whispered and screamed, until even Regency society grew weary of their tantrums and their scenes. William smiled sardonically in the background, awaiting the explosion. This came when Byron, worn out, decided to retreat. At a ball at Lady Heathcote's "Caro", in a temper, broke a tumbler and proceeded to cut her bare arms with the fragment. While being held down, she attempted to do further damage to her body with a pair of scissors.[8] Her family finally came to the conclusion that she was mad and hurried her off to the country. There she wrote a novel—*Glenarvon*—the story of William, Byron and herself. After its publication, society was finished with her.

William was urged to take the step of legal separation. In this, after many scenes, he succeeded, but he never ceased to care for his wife and was by her side when she died in 1825. Despite all that he had suffered, he said of her: "She was more to me than anyone ever was or ever will be."[9] For the rest of his life, the mere mention of her name would cause his hand to shake and tears to well up in his eyes. To add to his sadness, his son died in 1835. He was therefore very much alone when the time came for him to take Queen Victoria under his wing.

On the day in June 1837 when they came together as Queen and Prime Minister, the bond was made. Both were transformed. Straightway he disposed of the rake image, forsook the set amongst which he had dallied with Mrs. Norton, curbed his language. Old friends scarcely recognised him, and some seldom saw him. She who had known no real friend but a German governess found her strength in the new sensation of confidence and trust which he imparted. By September they were in love. To him there flowed back all the intimacy and excitement that he had known with "Caro" over thirty years before—two girls so very different but equally compelling. She found romance in his eyes and his elegance, his vitality and his wit, his smile and his experience. All her thoughts were centred on him.[10] Her eyes never left him and, when he moved from the room, a sigh escaped her lips[11] as if she had been holding her breath while he was near.

The two spent more of the day together than is the case with many married couples—between four and six hours, and more than that on the occasions when they sat chatting together on the same sofa late into the night. While she was at Buckingham Palace, Melbourne talked State matters with her for two hours each morning, rode out with her in the afternoon and was her regular partner at dinner. He was so often at Windsor that he came to be looked upon as master. He wore the Windsor uniform. When the business of the House called him unexpectedly back to London, Victoria lamented: "I am *very* sorry to lose him *even* for *one* night."[12] He only of her Ministers she saw alone in her private sitting-room.

It was a high tribute to the character of Melbourne that there was little criticism of, or objection to, the close intimacy that existed between the Queen and himself in the early days of the reign. Amongst the few carpers was the Duchess of Kent, who considered that her daughter saw too much of him. When Victoria told Melbourne this, he commented that the Duke of Wellington had said that, if he was Prime Minister, he would establish himself in the Palace. To which Victoria replied: "I wish you would."[13]

After a visit to Windsor the Hon. George Villiers told Greville that

...he had been exceedingly struck with Lord Melbourne's manner to the Queen, and hers to him: his, so parental and anxious, but always so respectful and deferential; hers, indicative of such entire confidence, such pleasure in his society. She is continually talking to him; let who will be there, he always sits next her at dinner, and evidently by arrangement, because he always takes in the lady-in-waiting, which necessarily places him next her, the etiquette being that the lady-in-waiting sits next but one to the Queen. It is not unnatural, and to him is peculiarly interesting. I have no doubt he is passionately fond of her as he might be of his daughter if he had one, and the more because he is a man with a capacity for loving without having anything in the world to love.[14]

In her, there were many signs of the embryonic amoret. She was jealous. She was jealous of the Duchess of Sutherland,* accusing her of monopolising the conversation when she sat next to the Prime Minister at dinner. She was jealous of Lady Holland, "Old Madagascar" who was seventy, and constantly quizzed him about her. On an evening when Melbourne dined at Holland House, she wrote: "I WISH he dined with me!"[15]

Lady Holland was invited to be a guest at Brocket Hall, but the Queen was not. Melbourne explained that it was a small house and would hold no one else but him. "No one else?" she asked.[16]

She always sought his opinion when she changed her hair style or wore a new dress, wanting his approval while finding his views somewhat whimsical:

Asked Lord M. if he liked my dress, a cherry-coloured silk with a magnificent old lace flounce. "It's very pretty," he said, "I like those bright colours; it's very handsome." The dress I had on the day before, a striped one, he didn't think ugly, but said it was like the pattern of a sofa.[17]

They had their tiny tiffs and misunderstandings. On an April afternoon in 1838 the Queen rode out from the Palace to Hanwell through Acton and home by Castle Hill. She was due back at four to see "Lord M". But the sun was shining and the route was long and she was a few minutes late in returning. Melbourne had not waited. On being told at the gate that the Queen was still out, he said "Very well", and rode away. She sat for an hour in her riding habit waiting for him to come back. He did not. So she sent a note to him by messenger. In her diary she wrote: "It is all my own fault..."[18]

When the demands of politics kept them apart, they wrote

* Mistress of the Robes.

to each other two or three times a day.[19] She was not complete without him. For example, at her first ball:

One *only* regret I had,—and that was, that my excellent, kind, good friend, Lord Melbourne was not there. I missed him much at this my first ball; he would have been pleased I think![20]

Unwittingly, Melbourne encouraged her by his obvious attachment, care and attentions. He was the courtier, born and practised. As she came from her room for her afternoon ride, he was waiting for her at the head of the stairs. Pleasantly surprised, she asked him if he was going to join her. He replied that he was unable, but had left his work so that he might watch her start away. On another occasion she fell off while riding beside him. She bruised nothing more vulnerable than her backside. She jumped up and laughed, but he, she noted, "was much frightened and turned quite pale".[21] He said the right things at the right moment. After the Coronation: "You did it beautifully,—every part of it, with so much taste."[22]

He always treated her as Queen and kept the dignity. Only when the door of the private sitting-room closed behind them did he relax and seat himself without permission. Then, if a servant was wanted, it was the Queen who rang the bell.[23]

Lady Lyttelton, who was appointed a Lady of the Bedchamber in 1838, watched the Queen and Prime Minister closely during her first waiting:

I should think it would be hard to displace Lord Melbourne by any intrigue, constitutional or otherwise, while her present Majesty lives, unless he contrives to displace himself by dint of consommés, truffles, pears, ices, and anchovies, which he does his best to revolutionise his stomach with every day . . .[24]

Meals and months—those were the dangers to the idyll. And it was months, rather than years, that were the measure of time running out, for it was a family failing in the Lambs that they declined quickly after reaching sixty. In 1837 Melbourne could, and did, race any young lady-in-waiting down the long corridor. By 1840 Lady Lyttelton was to describe him as looking "as old as the hills".[25]

Diet was largely to blame. In being great eaters, Queen and statesman were birds of a feather, and therefore a danger to one another. But while Victoria rationed herself to broth only for lunch when she found her dresses becoming too tight, Melbourne trenchered on. Victoria said to Lady Cowper:* "He eats too much, and I often tell him so. Indeed I do so myself, and my doctor has ordered me not to eat luncheon any more." "And does your Majesty quite obey him?" "Why yes, I think I do, for I only eat a little broth."[26]

Melbourne was certainly in need of reprimand, for his menus were horrific. After a late sitting in the House, at four in the morning he demolished a pike, chicken, peas, a raspberry tart and a bottle of Madeira.[27] "He has eaten three chops and grouse for breakfast," Victoria deplored on one occasion.[28]

The unclouded happiness of Victoria and Melbourne lasted for two years. At the end of that time he had poured into her the knowledge of a full life. So many precious evenings on the sofa together, with no one to witness what they said—just Islay, the Scotch terrier, asleep at their feet or begging to be given Lord M.'s spectacles to play with.[29] They talked of many things—of mothers-in-law and marriage ("the happiest marriages are those where the woman's taken by force"); of why marriages break up ("Why, you see, a gentleman hardly knows a girl till he has proposed, and then when he has an unrestrained intercouse with her he sees something and says, 'This I don't quite like.'");[30] of vaccination and amnesia; of the punishment of children and extraordinary goings-on at Eton; of cannibalism and the behaviour of the English abroad—a hotchpotch of subjects which had never been discussed in the strict curriculum of Kensington.

He shed new light on history, a deep knowledge of the long ago switching to personal contact for the past half century. Those whom she had previously looked upon as saints or sinners on the printed page, he changed into human beings. One evening they looked together at *Lodge's Portraits*, he commenting on the short memoirs of the famous, ranging from Raleigh to Madame de Staël:

It is quite *a delight* for me to hear him speak about all these things; he has such *stores* of knowledge; such a wonderful memory; he knows about everybody and everything; *who* they were, and *what* they did; and he imparts all his knowledge in such a *kind* and agreeable manner; it does me a *world* of good . . .[31]

* Countess, sister of Lord Melbourne; afterwards Lady Palmerston.

In May 1839 came the moment that the Queen had long dreaded. On the 6th the Whigs, who in the last few months had been beset by increasing difficulties, were practically defeated on the Jamaica Bill. Early next morning she received a letter from Lord Melbourne in which he said that he had no alternative but to resign. Later he drove to the Palace.

At 10m. p. 12 came Lord Melbourne and stayed with me till 25m. to 1. It was some minutes before I could muster up courage to go in. "You will not forsake me." I held his hand for a little while, unable to leave go; and he gave me such a look of kindness, pity and affection, and could hardly utter for tears, "Oh! no," in such a touching voice.[32]

The Queen sent for the Duke of Wellington, but he declined to take office on grounds of age and because he considered the Prime Minister should be in the Commons. So, frigid, biased, fully prepared to fight to win back her friend and mentor, she faced the Tory leader, Sir Robert Peel. She took exception to his request that some of her Whig ladies should give place to those of Tory thinking. She gave not an inch, and cheated a little. Peel decided that, in view of the misunderstanding, he could not take office. Melbourne consulted his colleagues and thereafter agreed to take power again, this time with a reformed Cabinet. If the same political situation had risen four years earlier, he would gracefully and gratefully have retired to the library and fields of Brocket. But now he, and others with him, deemed it impossible to desert such a woman. There was a subsidiary reason. Melbourne had now passed the sixty mile post. He was over the age when he could have found full enjoyment in riding and shooting, and gossiping and philandering with the likes of Caroline Norton at Holland House. Ahead lay loneliness. He had never previously craved power, but he craved it now. Power was the only antidote to loneliness. His thinking was not unlike that of his colleague Palmerston, who said: "I don't at all conceal that I think it a great bore to go out; I like power, I think power very pleasant."[33]

So the same Prime Minister came back to sit with the Queen on the Windsor sofa. But he was not the same man, nor she the same woman. Nothing was ever to be quite the same again. It all appeared to be as before; his advice was as sound and his conversation as interesting; her trust and belief in him continued unabated. The change lay deep down in the complex of human relationship. Before he had been an admixture of father and lover. Now he was the benevolent grandfather.

The transformation in him was simple to understand. He had been under an unrelieved strain for months past and the climax of the fall of his Government had taken its toll. In addition he had seen the result of his handiwork. The child whom he had nurtured and taught, who had relied on him completely, had become an entity overnight. She had stood alone and growled. Men had drawn back from her and now she knew her strength. He was a little bit frightened.

The change in her was deep but natural. 24th May was her birthday—"This day I *go out of my* TEENS and become 20! It sounds so strange to me!"[34] She was beginning to feel quite old, and already she had been called upon to try her strength, and had won. Equally important had been the advent of Grand Duke Alexander. He had caused a new and strange sensation to flood her being. After the May balls she had climbed up to the roof of Buckingham Palace and watched the sun rise behind St. Paul's. She wanted a hand to hold at moments like these. She wanted to play with the young.

In addition she was having trouble with her health. Her complexion, people said, was becoming "muddy", and she was getting fat, weighing nearly nine stone. A stye made an appearance in her eye. She showed it to Lord M., which made him feel rather sick. She became lazy, dawdling in her bath at nights and skipping the brushing of her teeth. Her temper became unreliable and maids had a poor time. There were attacks of depression. Poor Melbourne had to carry the cross. He warned her against languor and the dislike of exertion, pointing out the dangers to "her business". He told her to do more walking. She said that it made her feet swell and that stones got into her shoes. He said that was because she did not do it often enough and that she must try. "No," she shouted at him. "Yes," he retaliated.[35] There must have been moments when he considered he was back with "Caro".

Inside herself, Victoria was becoming worried about romance and matrimony. Apart from an inferiority complex about her height, her plumpness and her inadequate eyebrows,[36] she was beginning to see rocks upon her way. On perusing with Melbourne a list of possible candidates for a husband, none was found suitable, while George of Cambridge's obvious antipathy was hardly complimentary or encouraging. There was also the question of competition to be considered. Union with a man who philandered would be disastrous, not only for her as Queen but also as a woman. She had to have a man who was proof against the charms and designs of many ladies of many courts. She had already had one small but bitter experience. At a ball she had come across Grand Duke Alexander and Princess Augusta, George of Cambridge's sister, together in the Gallery, and from what the Queen had seen the Russian was being more attentive than she cared him to be. There followed a "scene".[37]

Victoria and Melbourne frequently talked of marriage now, she revealing that her uncles Leopold and Ernest "pressed her much about it". "Lord M." made no secret of the fact that he was not keen on Albert or his family—"Cousins are not very good things" and "those Coburgs are not popular abroad; the Russians hate them."[38] In addition he was of the opinion that a man should not marry before he was thirty. Quick as a dart, she came back at him: "You did, at 26." "Yes," he answered, "I wasn't fit to be married . . . I was always ashamed of it."[39]

As a result of constant demands from Brussels and Coburg, Ernest and Albert had been invited to visit England in the autumn.

Talked of my Cousins Ernest and Albert coming over,—my having no great wish to see Albert, as the whole subject was an odious one, and one which I hated to decide about; there was no engagement between us, I said, but that the young man was aware that there was the possibility of such a union; I said it wasn't right to keep him on, and not right to decide before they came; and Lord M. said I should make them distinctly understand anyhow that I couldn't do anything for a year; I said it was disagreeable for me to see him though, and a disagreeable thing. "It's very disagreeable," Lord M. said . . . Talked of Albert's being younger. "I don't know that that signifies," said Lord M. "I don't know what the impression would be," he continued, "there's no anxiety for it; I expected that there would be." I said better wait till impatience was shown. "Certainly better wait for a year or two," he said; "it's a very serious question." I said I wished if possible never to marry. "I don't know about *that*," he replied . . .[40]

In August the newspapers carried reports that the reason behind the visit of the Coburg Princes was that the Queen was about to choose a husband. Melbourne declined to contradict the rumour, which strengthened it. The Queen asked him point blank whether he was against such an alliance. He laughed and did his best to opt out of giving an answer, but she insisted and at last he said, "I don't like it very much."[41]

In October Albert came and at lunch time on the 14th Melbourne chatted with the Queen. The first subject lay around the suggestion that had been made that he should marry again, and they laughed together at the mention of likely candidates. There was a pause. Then she blurted out that she had made up her mind—she did not have to say what about and the decision was in the happiness on her face. "I'm very glad of it," he said. "I think it is a very good thing, and you'll be much more comfortable."[42] She took his hand. She saw the tears welling from his eyes, falling as the brown leaves come from the tall English trees in October time.

CHAPTER TEN

The Student Prince

*T*HE THREE and a half years which separated the first and second meetings of Victoria and Albert formed a contrast in experience. She had learned how to fight and how to win, to walk through great occasions with grace and dignity, to bear calumny and to make decisions. She was a Queen. He emerged from the period no more than an itinerant student. His head was crammed with a mass of data about higher mathematics and the Law of Probabilities, science of government and the arts, but he had faced none of the realities of life. By restricting the location of his studies to Brussels and Bonn, he had been purposefully saved from exposure to the profligacy and intrigues of Berlin and Vienna. He knew nothing of the rude words and rough actions of the licentious soldiery or the physical hardships of military service. His travels had been restricted to escorted tours of Switzerland and Italy and he had crossed no sea wider than the English Channel, and that in trepidation. He had not experienced the comfort of the double-bed, or even the rough and tumble of the chaise longue. As Prince Hohenlohe was to say of him twenty years later:

In his whole attitude of mind there is something distinctly doctrinaire, and I thought how unfortunate it was for the Prince that he should come straight from a German University to his present position, after a course of superficial study, without having had the corners rubbed off by contact with the practical world.[1]

"Contact with the practical world" could well have included the descent of a British coal mine, where he could have seen children of five pushing trucks along tunnels only three feet high; girls of up to twenty-one, naked to the waist, carrying heavy sacks up interminable ladders through pitch dark shafts, with the ever present danger that one would lose her burden and sweep the climbers below to a certain death; of nude miners hacking at the coal face; of rats so fearless that they stole the lighted candles and caused explosions; of the stench of excreta; of imbecile adolescents who saw the light of day only on Sundays.[2]

Such dark subjects were excluded from the curriculum of the German Prince. For this his mentors must bear the blame, as in later years many urgently needed reforms received his strong backing. But for the moment Albert remained a supercilious and self-opinionated young man, ready to take over the post of husband to the British Queen, but not prepared to stand any quibbling from her; and valuing himself at £50,000 per annum, a sum equal to the total emoluments of 150,000 indigenous manual workers.

In view of the weepings and wailings of aged relations and retainers which accompanied Albert's departure from Coburg to marry the British Queen, the impression might be gained that he had been seldom away from the Duchy and that a great personal sacrifice was being made. In the event he was there for only short periods between the ages of sixteen and twenty.

After leaving London in 1836 he went first to Paris, to be introduced to the Orleans family. Despite the wars and revolutions which had rocked the French capital in recent years, he remained unimpressed. He complained bitterly about the noise in the streets and it was with relief that he settled down to a period of study in a secluded little house in Brussels, under the care of a Governor and, of course, King Leopold. Learning was everything and the teachings of M. Quetelet on mathematics and the Rev. Mr. Drury on English literature filled the day. So absorbed did he become that he was unwilling to take a holiday at Christmas. The Duke of Coburg had, very naturally, suggested that the boys should come home, but Albert would have none of it. Duke Ernest received the following reply:

Dear Papa,—We should be so glad to accept your invitation to go to Coburg for a few days, and to spend Christmas there. But if we are to profit by our stay here, I am afraid that we must deny ourselves that pleasure . . .[3]

Not only does it appear unusual that a father should issue an "invitation" to sons of school age to come home for Christmas, but also that the younger one should do the declining. Perhaps he was already beginning to wonder where his real home was.

In April the brothers moved on to Bonn University, living in a small detached house near the Cathedral, with splendid views of the hill-top Convent of Kreuzberg and the *Sieben Gebirge* (Seven Mountains). Their way of life was watched over by their Governor, Baron Weichmann, and their tutor, Herr Florschütz. While the possibility of nocturnal escapades on the part of Albert was infinitesimal, the same could not be said for Ernest. The story is still to be heard in Bonn that Queen Victoria visited Albert at this time and that the two spent romantic hours in the garden bower. She did, in fact, visit the house, but not until 1845, on the occasion of her first trip to Germany.

Bonn University was comparatively modern, with forward-thinking lecturers. It suited Albert exactly and the eighteen months that he spent on the Rhine were probably the happiest of his life. He gorged himself on international law, the science of government and philosophy and in his happy haze of learning did not bother to read the newspapers. His royal connections gave him status and he joined the "Borussia", a select students' corps which in after years was to count the Emperor Frederick and Emperor William II among its members.[4] On the lighter side he fenced with distinction and took part in concerts and amateur dramatics, but was best remembered by his contemporaries for his gift of mimicry of elderly professors, a somewhat hurtful form of humour which was inherited by certain of his descendants.

In the long vacation the Princes were treated to an extensive tour of southern Germany, Switzerland and northern Italy. The question must be posed as to whether this was financed from the meagre coffers of Coburg or included among the "charities and pensions" which King Leopold charged up to the British public. In fact it was Leopold who was the instigator of the plan and the details of the journey were already settled by the time Albert informed Duke Ernest, who was again robbed of having the boys home for the holidays. The underlying reason for Leopold's suggestion was that reports were about that Queen Victoria was contemplating an early marriage with Albert and the Belgian King thought it best that the young Coburgs should disappear for a while.[5] He wanted his candidate to have more muscle and manliness, more experience of places and ladies, before he produced him. The time was not yet.

On 28th August Ernest, Albert and Herr Florschütz set off up the Rhine, reaching Basle in five days. Then by carriage, boat and on foot, they subjected Switzerland to a minute inspection. They climbed the Rigi, crossed the Furka in a storm, trudged through snow two feet deep on the Mayenwand, reached the summit of the Faulhorn and climbed part way up Mont Blanc under the guidance of Balmat, son of the first man to reach the summit, in 1786.

Touchingly, or tactfully, Albert posted back to Cousin Victoria views and mementoes of each place that he visited. It was fortunate for her that, in the midst of her occupations with State and the Prime Minister, she kept them, for after the marriage Albert asked for them and expended much care in sticking them into an album and dating them.[6] As a result, twenty-seven years later his son, Arthur,* was sent on a similar tour. It is interesting to note that by 1865 the character of the country had changed, due to "the facilities of modern travel and the consequent overwhelming flood of annual tourists".[7]

Next Herr Florschütz took his charges to the Italian Lakes, Milan and Venice—"heavenly", Albert thought. Then back they went to Bonn, via the Tyrol, Innsbruck, Munich and, for a short stay, Coburg. Considering the tears that later were to be shed at his grandmother's death, it seems strange that Albert, after so long an absence, arrived to visit her late one night and left before eight next morning. She commented:

It is, no doubt, good for *them* to devote so much time to their studies, but it is very bad for *us* to see so little of them.[8]

Nor was Coburg favoured with a Christmas visit, Albert's eyes turning more readily towards Brussels. It was at Laeken early in 1838 that King Leopold informed him officially of the plan of which he had known unofficially since a child—that it was proposed that he should become the husband of the British Queen. Leopold reported the outcome of the talk to Stockmar, in London:

I have had a long conversation with Albert and have put the whole case honestly and kindly before him. He looks at the question from its most elevated and honourable point of view. He

* Duke of Connaught.

considers that troubles are inseparable from all human positions, and that therefore, if one must be subject to plagues and annoyances, it is better to be so for some great or worthy object than for trifles and miseries. I have told him that his great youth would make it necessary to postpone the marriage for a few years . . . I found him very sensible on all these points. But one thing he observed with truth. "I am ready," he said, "to submit to this delay, if I have only some certain assurance to go upon. But if, after waiting, perhaps, for three years, I should find that the Queen no longer desired the marriage, it would place me in a very ridiculous position, and would, to a certain extent, ruin all the prospects of my future life . . .'[9]

King Leopold and Duke Ernest were by this time both worried and disappointed men, Leopold at the thought that his cherished dream might not become a reality and Ernest at the delay in achieving the financial advantage that his son's marriage would ensure. Victoria, her head full of the Coronation and her eyes full of only Lord Melbourne, appeared disinterested in matrimony and even more so in her Coburg cousin. In the spring the brothers jointly turned the pressure on the young Queen and, as has been noted, she informed Lord Melbourne of this. Leopold was under the disadvantage of not being able to deal with the matter at source, his unpopularity in Britain being such that the mere mention of a visit raised an outcry in the Press, and was responsible for his absence at the Coronation. But Duke Ernest, less known and less suspect, did arrive. He was placated with the Order of the Garter. Victoria, cornered by him, said, "with some slight embarrassment", that her intentions were still the same but nothing could be done about it for two or three years.[10]

Although Leopold was unable to speak to his niece himself, he had control over a voice to which she listened daily—the voice of Baron Stockmar. Stockmar had been with her since before her accession and she had reason to be grateful to him. He kept his own establishment in London—first in Davies Street, then in Holles Street—but he was seldom there, inserting himself into Court life and moving back and forth with the Queen from Buckingham Palace to Windsor.[11] His policy was to be tactful and popular, ever ready to help and advise those who wished to draw on his vast knowledge of European politics. He won the esteem of Melbourne and

Palmerston, Aberdeen and Peel. He kept clear of Palace cabals. He was the most diplomatic, entirely unofficial, ambassador of Coburg. As regards the British public, his wish was to remain invisible, but the wish did not come true. Comment on his close contact with the Queen began in the confines of the Court and spread in ever widening circles throughout the country. The newspapers reported that the Queen had a German as a Private Secretary and that she was being pressured into foreign and unconstitutional views, and so loud did the clamour become that Melbourne was forced into making a public denial. It was therefore advantageous to both sides that the Baron should quit England for a time and so the plan was laid.

He discussed with the Queen the question of her cousin Albert's future, humbly putting forward a plan which was already cut and dried. The first step, he said, was that she should write to King Leopold and this she did:

> There is another *subject* which I wish to mention to you, *et que i'ai bien à cœur*, which is, if you would consult Stockmar with respect to the finishing of Albert's education; he knows best my feelings and wishes on that subject . . .[12]

Leopold, of course, replied that he was delighted that she had made Stockmar her commissary-general, that he had already consulted him and that the plan was that Albert and the Baron should make a lengthy visit to Italy. Meantime he was calling the young man over from Bonn to brief him on developments.[13] When Albert heard of the fate that was in store for him in Italy, he did not like it at all. He wrote to Florschütz:

> I am to go into society, learn the ways of the world and vitiate my culture with fashionable accomplishments, the last of which would appear to be an extraordinarily good testimonial in V's eyes. And I will do it . . . I shall suffer sometimes when I look at myself in private; but I hope it will be only a veneer which will not corrode the kernel.[14]

He went on to say that he heard that Victoria was stubborn and obstinate, delighted in Court ceremonies and trivial formalities, went to bed late and got up late. The danger that he saw in delaying the marriage was that Victoria's bad habits might harden to such a degree that by the time that they came together he might not be able to put them right. What a shock that boy of eighteen would have received if he had been able to overhear the conversation of Victoria and Melbourne chatting on the sofa together late of an evening. Yet, in the mirror of his self-contentment, he had envisaged himself moving straight from university into that boudoir of the British Queen, reaching her before her ideas and character were set, so that he might mould her like plasticine into the image that he considered a Coburg *Frau* should be.

His matrimonial plans being upset, Albert had to rearrange "his mode of life" and decided to spend another term at Bonn, reading political science and modern languages. Thereafter the brothers repaired to Coburg, Albert fretting at the enforced idleness and Ernest preparing to begin military training in the Saxon service at Dresden. The brothers had never been separated for even a night and both were deeply upset at the parting. Albert, who throughout his life was apt to over-state with the written word and understate with the spoken, poured out his feelings to the Duchess of Gotha:

I must now give up the custom of saying *we* and use the *I*, which sounds so egotistical and cold. In *we* everything sounded much softer, for the *we* expresses the harmony between different souls, the *I* rather the resistance of the individual against outward forces, though also confidence in its own strength.[15]

It is a strange coincidence that the same words should appear in a letter written a year later. They formed part of the congratulatory message which Queen Victoria received from Prince Ernest on her engagement.[16] It would therefore appear that Albert assisted his brother in its compilation, indulging in an opportunism which he little guessed the years would uncover.

Early in December Albert met Stockmar at Munich and they set off on their journey to Florence, travelling, in reverse, the route which Queen Victoria followed fifty years later on her way to Berlin to speak with Bismarck and say goodbye to her dying son-in-law, Emperor Frederick. In 1838 the two men were ten days upon the road—in 1888 the Queen covered the same distance overnight. Owing to the Baron's dyspeptic condition the daily stage had to be short and the snow was so deep in north Italy that at one time the carriage was drawn by six horses and two oxen.[17] Florence was eventually reached on Christmas Eve.

This, then, was Albert's introduction to Stockmar, the doctor and politician who was to mould his life and thoughts, who was to whisper his words and guide his pen, who was to convert him into the phrenetic worker who was, so tragically, to collapse under the weight of business placed upon him. A brilliant psychologist, backed by medical knowledge, Stockmar radiated a magnetism which ensured control. His eventual aims were the unification of Germany, the ascendancy of the House of Coburg, and fame for himself reflected back from the achievements of others. He cared not for humanities.

It is said that a man does not know a man until he has travelled with him. Stockmar wished to get to know Albert, every thought in him, every strength and every weakness, and what better chance could he have had than spending the daylight hours alone with him in a carriage, ploughing slowly through an endless field of white, and sitting together by the inn fire in the evening. He quickly made his summary.

Albert, he reported, had much in common with his mother —an assessment which cannot have been popular in a certain quarter. He had the same quickness of mind, the same over-ruling desire to appear amiable to others, the same tendency to *espièglerie*, to be droll, and the same habit of quickly changing the subject. Not one point did Stockmar find in common with Duke Ernest.

Healthwise, the doctor was not optimistic. The constitution was not strong, but careful diet might cure this. He noted that Albert looked pale and exhausted after any strain. "Great exertion is repugnant to him, and his tendency is to spare himself both morally and physically."

In character, though full of the best intentions and noblest resolutions, Albert fell short in their application. It was a matter of regret that he took not the slightest interest in contemporary events and never read a newspaper. He received bad marks for social graces and his approach to women—too little *empressement*, too indifferent and retiring.[18]

It was clear that Stockmar had much work to do and many alterations to make during the Italian interlude. Fortunately for him, in February King Leopold sent him an assistant, Lieutenant Frank Seymour,* a young British officer whose apparent task was to guard the Prince from vice—a revelation which later considerably upset Queen Victoria, who once

* Afterwards Major-General Sir Francis Seymour (1813–90).

again trotted out her piece about "the lily of a blameless life"—but in reality was there to impart a degree of English outlook and way of life. Lieutenant Seymour was to get a distinct shock, for never before had he encountered such purity.

Albert's days were simple—at least when he had control of them. He was up before six, studying by his student's lamp. After breakfast he read English with Seymour and then played the piano or composed, or practised the organ in the "Badia". There followed a feast of pictures—"I am often intoxicated with delight when I come out of one of the galleries." Dinner was at two, a simple meal which he rushed, giving as his reason that eating was a waste of time. His drink was water. More playing and singing and then a long walk through the countryside, the hours which he liked best "Now I can breathe—now I am happy." Tea was at seven and there followed conversation with Stockmar. Albert, if he was allowed to be, was in bed and asleep by nine.[19]

But he was not always given his way, Stockmar ejecting him into the social whirl of Florence. Albert wrote to Prince William of Löwenstein, a friend of his university days:

I have danced, dined, supped, paid compliments, have been introduced to people, and had people introduced to me; have spoken French and English—exhausted all remarks about the weather—have played the amiable—and, in short, have made "*bonne mine à mauvais jeu*". You know my *passion* for such things, and must therefore admire my strength of character, that I have never excused myself—never returned home till five in the morning— that I have emptied the carnival cup to the dregs . . .[20]

In March the trinity moved on to Rome, a testing experience for Albert in view of his Lutheran mind. Throughout his life he maintained a horror of the Catholic dominion and, after attending a Catholic wedding, announced that the rites followed were "perfectly ridiculous" and that when one got among the believers "all the nonsense becomes apparent". To a certain extent he instilled the bias into his wife, but this proved one of the rare points on which she parted from his preaching, with the passing years reaching a sphere of tolerance and understanding, largely through the influence of the Empress Eugénie.

It was teeming with rain when they reached the Holy City and Albert was not impressed. He told Duke Ernest that, but for a few beautiful palaces, it might just as well be any town in Germany. The only ceremony of Easter week with which he was not disappointed was the blessing of the crowds by the Pope from the Vatican balcony, "amidst the ringing of bells, firing of cannon and military music", though he added a rider that what followed "savoured of idolatry".[21]

The Prince had the honour of being granted an interview with Pope Gregory XVI and the old man and the boy talked together for half an hour in a little room:

We conversed in Italian on the influence the Egyptians had had on Greek art, and that again on Roman art. The Pope asserted that the Greeks had taken their models from the Etruscans. In spite of his infallibility, I ventured to assert that they derived their lessons in art from the Egyptians.[22]

Albert had a knack of putting people right, as statesmen in England were soon to learn.

There was a critical turn in events when the time came for the party to withdraw from the Vatican. Their guide, a devout Catholic by the name of Plattner, decided that the visit would not be complete without a kissing of the Pope's feet. Flinging himself to his knees, he made in that direction. Not noticing this manoeuvre, His Holiness took a step backwards so that he might pull the bell rope as a signal for the door to be opened. The retraction caused Plattner to lose his balance and he landed flat on his stomach. Undefeated, he crawled forward and grasped the raised foot. Now the Pope was a stout and heavy man and entirely unaccustomed to such physical exercises as balancing on one foot. He therefore struggled to regain his normal pedestrian security and in so doing landed a series of sharp kicks on the lips outstretched to kiss. This was too much for the English sense of humour and the vibrations of Frank Seymour indicated that he was about to dissolve into fits of laughter. Stockmar, the perfect diplomat, pushed him sharply out through the door.[23]

Naples was the next port of call, but Vesuvius was white with snow and the bay was dull and grey. Pompeii was interesting. Then the slow journey home, calling at Sienna, Milan, Turin and Genoa. The party split up and by early June Albert was home in Coburg and preparing for his coming-of-age celebrations. There were great fêtes and he became a man.

On reaching London Stockmar submitted his report to his master. Having perused it, King Leopold issued an ultimatum to his niece that she must inspect Albert in the autumn.

Victoria, shaken by political and palace strife, still hearing the echo of the tune to which she had danced with the Grand Duke Alexander, regarded marriage, and the visit of the Coburg boys, as an "odious thing", and was wondering whether she had been coerced, or tricked, into giving more apparent encouragement to Albert's chances than had been her intention. The pressure on her had been both strong and clever. So thus she wrote to her uncle:

Though all the reports of Albert are most favourable, and though I have little doubt I shall like him, still one can never answer beforehand for *feelings*, and I may not have the *feeling* for him which is requisite to ensure happiness. *I may* like him as a friend, and as a *cousin*, and as a *brother*, but not *more*; and should this be the case (which is not likely), I am very anxious that it should be understood that I am *not* guilty of any breach of promise, for *I never gave any.* I am sure you will understand my anxiety, for I should otherwise, were this not completely understood, be in a very painful position. As it is, I am rather nervous about the visit, for the subject I allude to is not an agreeable one to me.[24]

Meantime Albert, wearied of travel, planned to spend a peaceful period at the Rosenau, studying English literature. But that was not to be. Duke Ernest had also read Stockmar's report and noted the Prince's indifference to, and failure with, women. The maestro on sex therefore decided that he himself would make an attempt to break through the barrier and see if he could get an answer to the siren's song. Albert wrote sadly to Prince William of Löwenstein:

On the 13th (July) I shall accompany Ernest to Dresden, and stay with him for about fourteen days. Then I must go to a place that I hate mortally, that charming Carlsbad, where Papa is taking the waters, and much wishes me to be with him.[25]

Ernest had now been away from the company of his pious brother for some eight months and his subsequent actions showed that his outlook to life, and its pleasures, had undergone a considerable change. It was doubtless hoped that in his company, and that of fellow officers of the Saxon army, Albert might be induced to paint some small portion of Dresden red. It was a natural surmise—when twenty years later "Bertie", Prince of Wales, was left in the company of the officers of the Guards, he was smartly into bed with Nellie Clifden, the actress. But no such adventures apparently came to Albert. He wrote to Stockmar that the thought of going on to Carlsbad made him shudder, admitting that he knew full well that the idea was that he must learn to pay more attention to the ladies, which, "as an occupation", he thoroughly disliked. And so he joined "Papa" at his waters.

Dresden and Carlsbad—both held so many memories for Duke Ernest. It was at Dresden that Louise had had an *aventure* just prior to meeting Leopold. It was of the ladies of Carlsbad that Louise had been jealous in her early married days. Albert left no record of his activities in this gay resort. Did Duke Ernest succeed in overcoming the youth's aversion to ladies? Quite possibly. Shortly after the marriage one Countess Resterlitz made her way eastward towards London, her known intention to "urge some past friendship upon the Prince". She was stopped at Calais.[26] This, and a story that Albert was once caught staring at the bare legs of a kilted Scottish girl going upstairs,[27] appear to be the total of sexual aberrations in his debit account—omitting the case of the Empress Eugénie, which was different. Quite remarkable.

CHAPTER ELEVEN

The First Moment

*I*N THE SUMMER of 1839 the fear gripped King Leopold that he, and the Coburg family in general, were becoming increasingly unimportant to the Queen of Great Britain. Correspondence was spasmodic and impersonal, the rift between Victoria and her mother was as wide as ever, and Stockmar, abroad on other business, had been unable to maintain the balance of power. While the consensus of opinion in the country which paid the Queen was that the more the German influence was submerged the better, this smacked of heresy to Leopold. The atmosphere would be distinctly to the disadvantage of the messiah for whom he had prepared the way. He therefore planned a Coburg invasion of the southern shores of England, in order to soften up resistance prior to the landing of Albert.

As commander-in-chief he realised that he must himself take part in the landing and endure with fortitude the brickbats which, it was certain, would be thrown at him by the gentlemen of the Press. He decided to go in with the second wave, making his headquarters at Ramsgate, a place which not only afforded a convenient route of escape but also provided a useful excuse, that he was there only to enjoy the sea and the sands at holiday time.

The first wave was to be made up of younger and gayer troops, armed with fun and games and family anecdotes and chattering German. It consisted of his brother, Ferdinand of Coburg-Kohary, three of Ferdinand's children—Augustus,* Leopold and Victoire†—and Alexander Mensdorff-Pouilly, son of his sister Sophia. They landed at the end of August.

Windsor Castle was quickly taken over. The corridors rang with German laughs and German jokes and Victoria was

* m. 1843, Princess Clementine, 3rd daughter of Louis-Philippe, King of the French.
† m. 1840, Louis, Duc de Nemours.

delighted. It had been a tiring summer and the British public had dealt hardly with her over the Lady Flora Hastings affair. Now she was able to relax and laugh again. The cousins all called one another by their christian names, there were long, fast rides in the afternoons and games in the evening, including the thrill of "teetotums". She complained that, in the usual way, she had no young people to play with, at which one of the male cousins made a pointed joke about Lord Melbourne, which made everyone laugh.[1] Although his lordship did attempt to join in by demonstrating how to play cup-and-ball, he could not understand a word that anyone was saying and was rather bored by the whole proceeding—the sense of humour being somewhat in contrast with that to be tasted at Holland House.

Then King Leopold and sad Queen Louise arrived and so thick were foreign royalties upon the Windsor ground that mere English Dukes looked quite insignificant.[2] "Dearest Uncle" soon re-established himself in his niece's affections and the task was over, the battle won. But there was one small snag—Victoria was showing too much interest in Alexander Mensdorff. This young officer in the Austrian army was exceedingly handsome. Victoria thought so and Melbourne, maybe out of mischief and wishing to rock the boat, agreed with her:

"Nice hair *he* had," he said, looking at Alexander, "I'm glad he's a Frenchman; I knew no German could have such hair." I said I admired his eyebrows so. "Beautiful eyes and eyebrows," said Lord M., and I said I had been drawing him.[3]

She partnered him at small dances and persuaded him to call her "*du*". After he had gone she waited eagerly for his first letter, but when it came it was sadly realistic, recalling happy times that could be no more.[4] Leopold had been at it again.

Word was now sent to Albert that he could move off. He left Coburg in company with his brother Ernest and his beloved greyhound, Eos, and in a bad temper. He had been informed by his uncle of the Queen's message that she could make no final promise that year and that, "at the very earliest, any such event could not take place till two or three years hence".[5] He travelled to England with the firm intent of telling the Queen that the proposed marriage was off. In his own words:

I went therefore with the quiet but firm resolution to declare, on my part, that I also, tired of the delay, withdrew entirely from the affair.[6]

His behaviour *en route* pointed to the bitterness in his mind. Word having permeated through the countryside that the sons of the reigning Duke were bound for London and that one was to claim the hand of the Queen, little groups gathered along the roadside to watch the carriages go by and wish God speed. These well-wishers were therefore both dismayed and disappointed when they saw at the window of the ducal carriage, not the smiling face of a princely suitor, but the long nose and startled eyes of a greyhound. Ernest and Albert were out of sight upon the floor, rocking with laughter.[7] This piece of unkindness and thoughtlessness was regarded by nineteenth-century biographers as most humorous.

More bad news was awaiting Albert at Brussels. He was met with the information that his departure for Windsor was to be further delayed. At this stage in the game such a move could easily have led to the match being abandoned, undue importance being attached to a decision which, in the event, was simple of explanation. Arrangements had been made for the Princes to arrive at the Castle on 30th September, but, as Melbourne pointed out to the Queen, there was a Council that day and the Ministers attending might conclude that matters were settled if they saw Albert.[8] Victoria agreed and wrote to King Leopold explaining the position and postponing the arrival date until 3rd October. Her closing sentence was scarcely tactful but was indicative of her attitude:

I think indeed a day or two at Brussels will do these young gentlemen good, and they can be properly fitted out for their visit.[9]

Albert now took matters into his own hands. He wrote to her saying that he did not think it would be possible for him to set out before the 6th and gave no date of arrival.[10]

On the evening of Wednesday, 9th October, Victoria and Melbourne sat chatting as usual after dinner and both were very sleepy. She complained that she had walked too far. "You'll be better tomorrow," he said, "after a deep sleep." She certainly slept long and perhaps this was fortunate as the 10th was to be an exciting day.

Got up at ½p. 10 and saw to my astonishment that a stone, or rather 2 stones, had been thrown at my dressing-room window and 2 glasses broken; the stone was found under the window; in the little blue room next to the audience room another window broken and the stone found in the room; in the new strong room another window broken, and in one of the lodging rooms next to this, another broken and the stone found in the middle of the room. This is a very strange thing . . .[11]

Albert, on the other hand, was not allowed to sleep through the perils of the night. Out of Antwerp and tossing in an October gale, "he was terribly sick".[12] On landing at Dover a messenger was sent ahead, while the Princes followed in more leisurely fashion, resting for a while at Canterbury so that their distressed organs might return to normal.

At half past seven the carriages came up the hill to the Castle. Queen Victoria took up her position at the head of the stairs.

Of all the fascinating "ifs" of the nineteenth century, maybe the most fascinating to consider is the question of what would have happened if Victoria had remained proof against the charms of Albert of Coburg—as indeed she thought that she would be. Individual tragedies would have been avoided, such as those that came to the granddaughters— "Alicky" gunned down in the cellar at Ekaterinburg, "Ella" thrown into the dark mine at Alapaevsk, "Ena" crying her heart out at El Escorial—but on a wider field there would have been differing relations with Prussia, no Emperor William II, and, maybe, no grey memorials of war in all the churchyards.

But Victoria did like him—she knew at a glance. "It was with some emotion that I beheld Albert, who is *beautiful*."[13]

She had made no effort to see him for three and a half years, but she had a picture of him at the back of her mind—the picture of an over fat boy of sixteen, suffering from the after effects of seasickness, often being excused for bilious reasons, falling over on the dance floor, nodding his head with sleep by nine.

Instead there rose up the treads towards her, making his great entrance, a star from the opera. The lamplight shone on his dark auburn hair. His skin was olive, ripened by the Italian sun. He was tall and broad[14]—the mists of emotion allowed the figure to gain a perfection which no Coburg ever reached. But it was the eyes, those upturned, magnetic blue eyes which held her—and were never to lose her.

Greetings over, a minor crisis was revealed. The dress clothes of the Princes had gone astray. The cause may well have been connected with the stormy passage, but two other possibilities present themselves. Albert may have been getting his revenge for the Queen's hint about getting "properly fitted out" at Brussels, or he may have considered that his stomach was not yet ready to receive the full treatment of a Castle repast. Anyway the Queen decided that they could not come in improperly dressed, a decision with which Lord Melbourne did not agree.[15] So the rules were relaxed and they "*débutéd* after dinner in their négligé".[16]

Albert fitted exactly into the requirements of Victoria, causing her to execute a *volte-face* on the subject of marriage. He had all the necessary assets; he was handsome and he was tall, yet not tall enough to make a violent contrast with her inadequate inches, as had been the case with the eldest son of Louis Philippe; under Stockmar's promptings he had become an accomplished dancer; he loved music, and this was a most important point with her; he was, apparently, tactful; he would not, she felt sure, "meddle" in political affairs[17]—an assessment which was to prove wide of the mark; he was not a flirt—she was on target here; and last, but not least, Albert allowed her to consolidate her position and gain confidence. There was no longer the frustration of knowing that a romantic attachment born on the dance floor or out riding must not be allowed to blossom into love, as the fulfilment of marriage was prohibited for dynastic or political reasons. There was no longer the fear that, of the few young men who held the suitable qualifications to marry her, she would find none who appealed to her—or even that she might not appeal to any of them. No longer, now, could Augusta of Cambridge poach upon her boy-friends, and fiddle-sticks to cousin George hiding away from her on the Mediterranean shores!

Many pints of sugared ink have been expended in describing the dawn of Victoria's love and the moment when she sent for Albert and asked him to marry her. The following is a sample:

It took less than a week for the chivalrous young knight to win his bride. He was graceful and devoted in his attentions to her; he never willingly absented himself from her; and in a dozen ways conveyed to her the fact of his attachment. As to the Queen, she soon confessed to herself that the love of such a man was more than the homage of courtiers or the applause of a world; and that life without him would fail to bring content. All her unwillingness had melted away, and all her heart went out to him, as they rode or talked together in those never-to-be-forgotten autumnal days.

But the difficulty was how to let him know this; for in the case of these lovers it was the lady and not the gentleman who must speak first. He was almost portionless; and how could he venture to pay his addresses to the greatest Queen in Europe? But then she was an English maiden, and how could she so far deviate from the traditions of her race as to show her preference unasked?

What a dilemma they were in! But they contrived to come out of it in some way or other; though exactly how it was managed will perhaps never be known.

There was a story afloat at the time, which said that at one of the Palace balls, the Queen, at the conclusion of a dance, presented the Prince with a flower. The significance of this act was not by any means lost upon him. He wore a close-fitting uniform, buttoned up to the throat; but he wished to wear the Queen's gift upon his heart, so it is said that with a penknife he cut a slit in his coat, and placed the precious flower in it.

Again, the Prince was on one occasion thanking her Majesty for the gracious reception she had given him, and expressing the delight his visit was producing, when the Queen replied, "If indeed your highness is so much pleased with this country, perhaps you would not object to remaining in it, and making it your home?"

This hint would be more than enough for any man; and if the story be true, there is no doubt that it filled the heart of the young German with great joy . . .

What followed can be better imagined than described; for there were no witnesses of the sacred love-revealing scene, which was given to these as to millions of other young folk who make their choice for better for worse . . .[18]

But Coburgs never allowed the results of great occasions, involving power and money, to rest on so chance a twist of fate as the sudden blooming of pure love in two hearts as one. In later years Queen Victoria—who was half a Coburg— showed clearly, when arranging the marriages of her children and her grandchildren, her belief that if two eligible young people were pushed into a double bedroom, love would be sure to follow. In her own case certain precautions had to be taken. Firstly, if Albert's suit was to prove negative, his visit must not be allowed to exceed that of the Coburg cousins who had preceded him in September. A prolonged stay would point to an obvious conclusion. Secondly, she must not be exposed to ridicule by offering her hand and having it refused. Nor must it be able to be said that she had tried out Albert and found him wanting.

There were therefore two isolated camps, the Victoria camp and the Albert camp and, if neither was to lose face, it was necessary that there should be some secret understanding before the two protagonists came out to parley in the open. And so it happened.

The Queen's emissary was an obvious choice—Baroness Lehzen, her governess through childhood days and now her Lady Attendant, a woman who knew every thought in her mistress's head and her doings through every minute of the day. Another advantage was that she was a German. In the other camp contact was made with Baron Alvensleben, Master of the Horse to the Duke of Coburg, who was in attendance on the Prince.[19] So it was that Baroness Lehzen, unnoticed, padded along the back corridors, tapped on a door and whispered her confidences.

By the second day of his visit Albert had learned that he had made a favourable impression. Back came Lehzen with the information that the Prince, for his part, was ready and willing. On the fourth day the information was passed that the Prince should stand ready for a summons to a proposal meeting on the fifth.[20] Thus he had a clear night to rub up his reply and concoct some roseate lines.

The summons was sent at half past twelve on the morning of 15th October. He came alone to the Closet. After a few minutes of light verbal prelude, she blurted out that it would make her so happy if he would consent to what she wished. Whereat he embraced her, which was, in all probability, her first experience of such male propinquity. He said he would be very happy "*das Leben mit dir zu zubringen*". She said that it was the happiest, brightest moment in her life, adding that he was making a great sacrifice, a statement which indicates that by this time her feet were on the ceiling. Ernest, who was standing handy, was called in and, for good reason, was highly delighted. Lord Melbourne was told an hour later.[21] Thus two people, plus the emissaries, were in the secret.

In the afternoon the Queen wrote to give her news to King

Leopold, entrusting him to pass on messages to Duke Ernest and Baron Stockmar. Queen Louise could be told, but none of her family. All were to maintain strict secrecy and no one, repeat no one, else was to be informed.

In his reply Leopold referred to the departure prayer of old Simeon in Luke II,* although in fact he had no intention whatsoever of departing, as those who have spent long in sowing like to sample some of the harvest. He ended by confirming that, until further orders, he would say nothing to the Duchess of Kent.[22]

The extraordinary situation had therefore arisen that the mother, who was also at Windsor, was being kept in ignorance of the engagement of her daughter, a pointer to the strained relations that existed between the two. While descriptions have been given of the happy couple running hand in hand to tell wet-eyed "Mama", in fact four full weeks passed before the Duchess was told. The Queen herself admitted it. When she was reading through the manuscript of Agnes Strickland's suppressed biography, she wrote against a paragraph which stated that the Duchess sanctioned the engagement: "*Never. The Dss of Kent never* knew anything of it until the Queen told it to her a few days before the Prince left."[23] Albert left on the 14th November. There must indeed have been an iron curtain between the two establishments, for Victoria made her feelings plain for all in sight to see. Her eyes never left his face, and she was forever planting kisses on the top of his head and running down the corridor to get one more kiss when the time came for them to separate.[24] But Victoria was a feuder and she had not forgotten the schemings of her mother and Conroy during the last days at Kensington.

In his correspondence during his engagement period Albert displayed both the dexterity of his pen and the transfiguration of his emotions. He wrote to Germany:

(To his stepmother, 5th November)
With the exception of my relations towards her, my future position will have its dark sides, and the sky will not always be blue and unclouded. But life has its thorns in every position, and the consciousness of having used one's powers and endeavours for

* Lord, now lettest thou thy servant depart in peace, according to thy word; For mine eyes have seen thy salvation. Which thou hast prepared before the face of all people; A light to lighten the Gentiles, and the glory of thy people Israel.

an object so great as that of promoting the good of so many, will surely be sufficient to support me!

(To the Duchess of Gotha, 28th November)
To live and sacrifice myself for the benefit of my new country, does not prevent my doing good to that country from which I have received so many benefits. While I shall be untiring in my efforts and labours for the country to which I shall in future belong, and where I am called to so high a position, I shall never cease to be a true *German*, a true *Coburg* and *Gotha* man.

(To Prince William of Löwenstein, 6th December)
My future lot is high and brilliant, but also plentifully strewed with thorns. Struggles will not be wanting, and the month of March already appears to have storms in store. The separation from my native country—from dear Coburg—from so many friends, is very painful to me! When shall I see you again, dear Löwenstein?[25]

He wrote to the Queen:

(15th October)
Dearest, greatly beloved Victoria—How is it that I have deserved so much love, so much affection? I cannot get used to the reality of all that I see and hear, and have to believe that Heaven has sent me an angel whose brightness shall illumine my life ... In body and soul ever your slave, your loyal, ALBERT.

(Calais, 15th November)
... I need not tell you that since we left, all my thoughts have been with you at Windsor, and your image fills my whole soul. Even in my dreams I never imagined that I should find so much love on earth. How that moment shines for me when I was close to you, with your hand in mine!

(Brussels, 17th November)
... Farewell, dearest Victoria, I kiss you a thousand times. Leave a little room in your heart for your faithful ALBERT.

(Wiesbaden, 21st November)
... Now I must say goodbye to you again. May heaven pour its best blessings on you, dearest Victoria. That is the prayer of your deeply loving ALBERT.

(Coburg, 30th November)
... Where love is, there is happiness. Love of you fills my

whole heart . . . I should have written in English, but German runs more easily with me, and as we always spoke in German together during that heavenly time together at Windsor, it does not sound right to me at all to address you in English. So a good, hearty goodbye in German!

(Coburg, 22nd December)
. . . Now farewell, dear, splendid Victoria; look after your health (one ought not to say that, but I dare do so) so that we may both be well when we meet, and may your dear heart be my dwelling place . . .[26]

On his way home Albert received a letter from the Duchess of Kent, to which he made reply:

What you say about my poor little bride sitting all alone in her room, silent and sad, has touched me to the heart. Oh, that I might fly to her side to cheer her![27]

Here the young man was well off course. The Queen records in her diary for an evening of the relevant period that she and the Lords Duncannon and Melbourne were playing with Islay on the floor. The dog was sitting up and begging the Prime Minister to be allowed to play with his spectacles and Lord M. was telling him that he was a real Campbell. Melbourne had many scenes yet to play.

During the stay at Windsor Prince Ernest had become ill and it was announced that he had jaundice. Albert informed the Queen that the journey back to Coburg was being made in easy stages in view of his brother's health. It is interesting therefore to look forward and read a letter which Albert wrote to Ernest from England a year later:

. . . I am deeply distressed and grieved by the news of your severe illness . . . I have to infer that it is a new outbreak of the same disease which you had here. If I should be wrong I shall thank God; but should I be right, I must advise you as a loving brother to give up all ideas of marriage for the next two years and to work earnestly for the restoration and consolidation of your health . . . to marry would be as immoral as dangerous . . . for you. If the worst should happen, you would deprive your wife of her health and honour, and should you have a family, you would give your children a life full of suffering . . . and your country a sick heir. At best your wife could not respect you and her love would thus not have any value for you; should you not have the strength to make her contented in married life . . . this would lead to domestic discord and unhappiness . . .[28]

It is therefore apparent that Ernest had contracted a disease of a more serious nature than jaundice.

CHAPTER TWELVE

The Spoils of Love

*A*FTER THE PASSING of a suitable period devoted to endearments and expressions of love, there came to be considered the basic question of preferment. Both Albert and the board behind him—King Leopold, Duke Ernest and Stockmar—had very definite ideas on this and demands were quick to arrive on the Windsor table. Some of the requirements did not please Queen Victoria and she declined to grant them. As a result by the end of the year certain of the letters reaching her from Coburg might well have begun, "Dear Madam, Unless . . ." For a period of ten days Albert ceased to correspond with his fiancée.

The points to be settled included the Prince's rank, precedence, arms, orders, household and income. Arguments, emanating from one quarter or another, waged around all these points but one—the bestowing of the Most Noble Order of the Garter. Here the decision lay solely in the hands of the Queen. On 7th December Albert wrote to her:

It gives me great pleasure that you intend soon to send me the Garter. I should like to have the uniform also, as I think it very essential to try it on and have it fitted here, so that when I come to England I am not made ridiculous by a badly fitting uniform, as I was the last time owing to having the wrong kind of hat.[1]

On the question of whether Albert should be given a peerage the Queen came into strong conflict with the King of the Belgians. Although she had been able to convince Albert that it would not be a wise step, and the whole Cabinet was against it,[2] Leopold was insistent. He avowed that his only reason was the wish that the Prince's "foreignership should disappear as much as possible", but he had other grounds. In 1816 he had been offered the Dukedom of Kendal and declined it. Ever since he had regretted his decision[3]—a point which he had made clear when he bestowed the courtesy title of Countess on his mistress, Caroline Bauer. Leopold, through his experience of the years, had come to realise a truth that was not yet clear to the young people— that the aristocracy was the bastion of England, that in that bastion dwelt the ruling club whose power it was to promote or to blackball. When he saw that he could not get his way the King of the Belgians sent a most "ungracious" letter to his niece and Victoria wrote thus to Albert:

> He appears to be nettled because I no longer ask for his advice, but dear Uncle is given to believe that he must rule the roost everywhere. However, that is not a necessity.[4]

As events were to prove, they would have been wise to listen to the advice, but at the time the Queen had other plans for her future husband. Unimpressed by the dukes and lords who passed through the daily scene at Buckingham Palace and Windsor, even declining to consider one of them as her mate, she had a loftier title in mind for Albert. She wanted him to be King.

She tackled Lord Melbourne about it during one of their evening chats by the fireside, saying that Queen Mary's Philip had been Titular King, that Princess Charlotte had always intended to give Leopold the title and that King William III had insisted on the status.[5] She came back to the subject a fortnight later, pleading that her husband "ought to be King", only to be told that an Act of Parliament would be necessary.[6] At length Melbourne came near to losing his temper. "For God's sake, Ma'am," he exploded, "let's have no more of it. If you get the English people into the way of making Kings, you will get them into the way of unmaking them."[7]

So poor Albert got nothing.

The discussions on his precedence ended with the same negative result. The Queen, quite naturally, wished that her husband should rank next to herself. Here she ran into opposition both with the royal Dukes and the Tories.

The surviving sons of George III—King Ernest of Hanover and the Dukes of Sussex and Cambridge—did not relish the idea of a penurious princeling from Coburg walking before them. Ernest announced, most forcibly, that he would not give way to any "paper Highness" and tried to persuade his brothers to do the same. Cambridge gave in under pressure from the Palace. Since the engagement the disagreement between the Queen and the Duke and Duchess of Cambridge had almost amounted to a scandal. They made this concession as a gesture of peace, but when the Queen received it, ungenerously, as a matter of course, the Duchess boiled over with rage and waited her chance to get even.[8]

At first Sussex refused, on the grounds of "the rights and interests of the family".[9] Melbourne received the letter as the Queen was dressing for church. He told her later: "I did not show the Duke of Sussex's letter to Your Majesty before you went to church; I thought it would discompose you for devotion."[10] But Sussex was playing canny and had his price. His morganatic wife, Lady Augusta Murray, had died in 1830 and thereafter he had married his mistress, Lady Cecilia Buggin. Not liking the label of Buggin, she adopted her mother's maiden name of Underwood. The marriage failed to satisfy the provisions of the Royal Marriage Act and legally was invalid. Sussex wanted his marriage to be recognised and a title given to his wife. He gave in on the point of precedence and in return the Queen accepted Lady Cecilia and created her Duchess of Inverness.[11] But Ernest of Hanover would not give way and his niece called him "an old wretch".

Out in the country the Tories, still smarting from the happenings of the previous May, were saying hard things about Queen Victoria, and even harder things about Prince Albert. The Duke of Wellington and Sir Robert Peel were strongly against the suggested precedence of the Prince, as was Lord Brougham. When the Bill which it was hoped would establish this came before the House of Lords, Brougham objected to giving the Prince precedence

. . . not only of the Dukes of the Blood Royal, but of the Prince of Wales. Suppose (which God forbid!) that the Queen had paid the debt of nature before any issue of the approaching marriage was born, we should have a King and a Prince of Wales, while Prince Albert would be placed in the anomalous position of a foreign naturalized Prince, the husband of a deceased Queen, with a higher rank than the Prince of Wales.[12]

The discussion became acrimonious and undignified and Melbourne withdrew the point of precedence from the Naturalisation Bill, it having been discovered that the Queen could bestow what rank she chose by Royal Prerogative. But she was furious and raging. She threatened that she would not ask the Duke of Wellington to her wedding. Sir Robert Peel she called "a low hypocrite" and the Bishop of Exeter "a fiend". Of those "infernal scoundrels", the Tories, she hissed, "Revenge, revenge!"[13] Her mood was scarcely suitable for a young lady about to enter holy matrimony.

Although in March she established her husband's position, her ruling only applied while he was in Britain. This led to difficulties when they travelled together abroad, as the Queen explained in a memorandum written in 1856:

When I first married, we had much difficulty on this subject, much bad feeling was shown, several members of the Royal Family showed bad grace in giving precedence to the Prince, and the late King of Hanover positively resisted doing so . . . When the Queen was abroad, the Prince's position was always a subject of negotiation and vexation; the position accorded to him the Queen always had to acknowledge as a grace and favour bestowed on her by the Sovereigns whom she visited . . . On the Rhine, in 1845, the King of Prussia would not give the place to the Queen's husband, which common civility required, because of the presence of an Archduke, the third son of an uncle of the reigning Emperor of Austria, who would not give the *pas*, and whom the King would not offend. The only legal position in Europe, according to international law, which the husband of the Queen of England enjoyed, was that of a younger brother of the Duke of Saxe-Coburg . . .[14]

On one point Albert gained an outright win. An attempt was made to deprive him of the right of quartering his arms with those of the Queen. Garter King of Arms was consulted and gave as his opinion that there was no precedent to allow of such action. He was quite emphatic about it. Albert, who had been carefully coached, asked whether Prince Leopold had not united the arms of Coburg and Brunswick when he married Princess Charlotte. Of course, he had.[15]

The issue on which Albert and Victoria came into direct conflict concerned the composition of his Household. Albert had imagined that this lay in his province and that he would be free to set up an advanced headquarters of Coburgers in London. He had decided on an able fellow called Schenk to be his Treasurer and general factotum. But Victoria was playing the rôle of mother-figure. She was ready to defend her new plaything, and even to attack those who interfered or criticised, but she was not prepared to allow him to make up his own mind on any point which bore in any way on her queenship. Lord Melbourne and herself were fully capable of attending to such matters. Albert's rôle was to give her a measure of social independence, to free her from the yoke of "Ma", to play with her in her idle hours, to stand beside her when she worked, ever ready to blot her signature in return for a smile, and, in due season (say two years) to sire a family. Obviously he must not be allowed to meddle in politics in any way and, owing to his lack of experience, he would need someone to look after his financial affairs. After discussing it with Lord Melbourne, it was decided that George Anson, the Prime Minister's secretary, was just the man for the job of guiding the young husband. Victoria had not realised, and probably never did, the inborn yearning for money which was strong in all the Coburgs. It was the *raison d'être* behind all the English marriages. When Albert learned that he was not to be allowed a free hand with finances he was furious. Thus the battle raged:

Victoria to Albert, 8th December, 1839,

As to your wish about your gentlemen, my dear Albert, I must tell you quite honestly that it will not do. You may entirely rely upon me that the people who will be about you will be absolutely pleasant people, of high standing and good character . . .[16]

Albert to Victoria, 18th December,

I am very sorry that you have not been able to grant my first request, the one about the gentlemen of my Household, for I know it was not an unfair one, for you yourself say, "Your people are appointed by you and not by me," and I was justified in hoping you might do me a favour in the matter which touches me so nearly . . . Think of my position, dear Victoria. I am leaving home with all its old associations, all my bosom friends, and going to a country in which everything is new and strange to me—men, language, customs, modes of life, position. Except yourself, I have no one to confide in. And is it not even to be conceded to me that the two or three persons, who are to have charge of my private affairs, shall be persons who already command my confidence?[17]

Victoria to Albert, 23rd December,

It is, as you rightly suppose, my greatest, my most anxious wish to do everything most agreeable to you, but I must differ with you respecting Mr. Anson . . . I am distressed to tell you what I fear you do not like, but it is necessary, my dearest, most excellent Albert.[18]

Victoria to Albert, 26th December,
Now, my dearest, to be about what is not so pleasant or amusing. I mean, now for business. I always think it safer to write that in English, as I can explain myself better, and I hope you can read my English, as I try to be very legible. I am much grieved that you feel disappointed about my wish respecting your gentlemen, but very glad that you consent to it, and that you feel confidence in my choice. Respecting the Treasurer, my dearest Albert, I have already written at great length in my last letter, so I will not say much more about it today, but I will just observe that . . . it is absolutely necessary that an Englishman should be at the head of your affairs . . .[19]

Albert to Victoria, 6th January 1840,
Your remark at the end of your letter about "a new proposition concerning the management of my money affairs" rather worries me. The accounts are so simple that I could manage them myself, if I had the time and inclination . . . As the Queen's husband, I shall be in a dependent position, more dependent than any other husband, in my domestic circumstances. My private fortune is all that remains to me to dispose of. I am therefore not unfair in requesting that that which has belonged to me since I came of age a year ago shall be left under my control.*[20]

Albert to Victoria, 13th January,
One remark I venture to make, namely this: you should not confuse personal matters with business, but keep them strictly separate, so that if I, following my duty and conscience, say what I think about business matters, you may not take it as a failure of my love towards yourself, which nothing can shake.[21]

Albert to Victoria, 20th January,
Repeating a former argument is no answer, when someone has produced reasons in opposition to it. I stick to what I said.[22]

The young man had effectively showed that he was well advanced in financial acumen for his age. But he was due for a secondary monetary shock. He had assumed that the income granted to him would be in line with precedent. When the news reached him that this was not to be so, he had passed the point of no return. He was well on the way to London.

On 14th January Lord Torrington, Colonel Grey† and

---

* The amount bequeathed to him by his mother—about £2,400 per annum.
On his marriage, the Prince transferred the estate to his brother.
† Lieutenant-General Hon. Charles Grey (1804–70).

Frank Seymour left Buckingham Palace, with three of the Queen's carriages, to fetch Albert. They reached Gotha in six days. There they invested the Prince with the Garter, met a multitude of his German relations, ate some heavy German dinners and shot a great number of animals. The return journey began on the morning of the 28th.

The travelling vehicles had been sent ahead along the road to a small inn not inaptly called "The Last Shilling". Albert's procession through the town consisted of twenty carriages, every notability wishing to take part in the historic occasion. The people of Gotha town packed the streets, filled every window and climbed on to the roofs. It was the greatest gilt-and-gingerbread day since Duke Ernest had come to claim his girl-bride, Louise, a quarter of a century before. The emotional titbit of the departure came when the Duke and Albert stopped their carriage outside the house of the Dowager Duchess to say goodbye. She was generally referred to as Albert's grandmother, but in fact was his mother's step-mother. She raised a fearful scene. As the carriage drove away, she came to the window and shouted "Albert, Albert", "in tones that went to everyone's heart". Half-fainting, she was carried away.[23] As the railways were expanding rapidly and Albert was free to run over to Coburg when he wished, the cause of her grief seems rather remote.

At "The Last Shilling" the party changed vehicles and set off westward. Duke Ernest's travelling chariot was at the head, followed by Queen Victoria's three carriages, two britzkas and two fourgons loaded with trunks. The unkind comment was made in England that the trunks were empty as Albert had nothing to put in them.

In the early afternoon of the fourth day the procession stopped at an hotel at Aix-la-Chapelle for dinner. In the dining-room Albert spotted a newspaper and picked it up. He then experienced one of the most unpleasant shocks of his life, and one which he never forgot or forgave. He read that the British Parliament had refused to grant him the expected annual allowance.[24] The wives of the last four British Kings, even Caroline, whom George IV had kept away from his Coronation, had received £50,000 per year. Leopold had been granted it, for life, on his marriage to Princess Charlotte. Now the husband of the Queen was to have his apanage trimmed by almost half.

The feeling was strong among the Tories and Radicals—
and certain Whigs joined them—that the weak state of the
national economy should be a primary consideration in the
determining of the Prince's income. Precedent alone was not
sufficient reason for once again allotting £50,000—obviously
he would not require so large a sum for his outgoing expenses.

The Times, which had previously demanded proof that
Albert was not a Papist, took up the cry:

> The young Prince is not to purchase at his own expense so
> much as one basin of soup, a bottle of wine from January to
> December in any given year.
> The chair he sits upon, the fire that warms him, the chandelier
> that lights him, are ready for him—all as if they had dropped
> from the skies.
> The horse he rides is from the royal stables, the book he reads is
> from the library of the Palace, every accommodation, every
> luxury of human life starts up for this fortunate and, we are willing
> to hope, this accomplished and estimable youth, without cost or
> trouble, without stint or censure.
> The demand therefore for Prince Albert of £50,000 is among the
> most indecorous proposals that could be made to Parliament.

When the matter came before Parliament Lord John
Russell proposed the sum of £50,000. Begging the Government to consider "the danger of placing a young man in
London with so much money in his pocket", Mr. Hume, the
economist, moved to reduce the sum to £21,000. This was
negatived by 305 votes to 38. Then up rose Colonel Sibthorp,
eccentric, blunt and the only man in the House with a beard.
He moved that the amount be reduced to £30,000. This was
supported by the Opposition, including Sir Robert Peel, and
was carried by 262 votes to 158.

This, then, was the story that Albert read over his dinner
at the hotel at Aix. He scribbled off a note to Victoria:
"You can imagine how annoyed I am at the news of the really
most indecent vote in the Commons . . ." His troubles were
not over. That night, at Liège, a brass band played under his
window until midnight. Merrymakers took their place and
sang and danced until two. One can only hope that the
experiences did not spoil for him the memorable event of the
morrow. He went in a train. A "special", laid on by King
Leopold, was waiting at nearby Ans and rushed the party to
Brussels in four hours.[25]

Leopold was now in an invidious position. As King of the Belgians he would be receiving from Britain a gross figure (subject to the amount which he chose to rebate) considerably greater than that allowed to the husband of the British Queen. He sent a long and indignant protest to his niece, but it was too late to alter matters now. So many parts of his master plan had gone adrift in recent weeks that he was worried about the effect on Albert. Having greeted him, Leopold reported to Victoria that her fiancé was "much irritated". Perhaps fortunately, there could be no serious discussion that evening as Albert's eyes were closing with the sleep that his body ever demanded—or, as Leopold put it, "inclined to surrender himself to Morpheus".[26]

In the next few days many serious conversations took place and Leopold managed to smooth out some of Albert's problems and complaints. Yet it was a somewhat depressing despatch that he mailed off to Victoria. Albert, he wrote, was exasperated and "pretty full of grievances". Though not inclined to be sulky (the introduction of the word pointed to the fact that he was), he was subject to fits of depression if he considered himself to have been unfairly treated.[27]

On the 5th the Coburg party set off on the last stage of the journey to London, travelling by train to Ostend and then by carriage to Calais. Next came the twenty-odd miles which Albert dreaded. On his two previous crossings the Channel had treated him roughly. Would the third time be lucky?

The morning of the 6th came in bright and sunny, with a light breeze from the north-west. Lord Clarence Paget, who had come over in *Firebrand* to fetch the Prince, was optimistic, but could not sail until a little before noon as the tide was too low. In the interval the worst happened. The wind swung round to the south-east and half a gale blew up. By half past eleven there was still not enough water for *Firebrand*, so it was decided to switch the party to the packet, *Ariel*, as it was essential to catch the tide at Dover.

Within minutes of clearing Calais the deck of *Ariel* was a scene of universal misery. There were many passengers and nearly all of them were sick. The wily Duke Ernest secured a berth, but it did not avail him much. Ernest and Albert were less fortunate and lay, helpless and suffering, on either side of the cabin staircase. For five and a half hours the little steamer fought her way westwards, the gale reaching its climax as the cliffs of Kent came into view. She had but five minutes to spare as she passed the Dover piers, and even then she grazed the bottom.[28] Albert reported to Victoria: "When we landed our faces were more the colour of wax candles than human visages."[29]

Yet Albert was to find consolation in the warm welcome extended to him upon his arrival in England. Having spent the night at the York Hotel, he was given a rousing send off, and a loyal address, as he departed for Canterbury. There he created a good impression by attending divine service. On the 8th he started on the last stage to London and cheering and curious crowds were out in every town and village, though it must be added that part of the attraction was his escort of the 11th Regiment, the pride and joy of Lord Cardigan. Prince Albert was now made their Colonel-in-Chief and the name of the regiment was changed from the 11th Light Dragoons to the 11th, Prince Albert's Own, Hussars.[30] *The Times* wrote of them: "The brevity of their jackets, the irrationality of their headgear, the incredible tightness of their cherry coloured pants, altogether defy description."*

Undoubtedly Albert suffered from the handicap that photography was not yet sufficiently advanced to allow of his likeness being widely distributed, for his good looks would have gained him many supporters among the womenfolk. There were no pictures of him whatsoever. But there was plenty of space in the newspapers and magazines for the cartoonists, versifiers and the satirists.

In strong royal support was Elizabeth Barrett, later to become Mrs. Browning:

> And since, Prince Albert, men have called thy spirit high and rare,
> And true to truth, and brave for truth, as some at Augsburg were.
> We charge thee by thy lofty thoughts, and by thy poet-mind,
> Which not by glory and degree takes measures of mankind,
> Esteem that wedded hand less dear for sceptre than for ring,
> And hold her uncrowned womanhood to be the royal thing.

Charles Dickens contributed:

> My heart is at Windsor,
> My heart isn't here;
> My heart is at Windsor
> A-following my dear.[31]

* In 1842 Prince Albert retired from the Colonelcy of the 11th Hussars and became Colonel of the Guards.

THE SPOILS OF LOVE

The satirists concentrated on the financial liability of Albert:

> *Quoth Hudibras of old, "a thing*
> *Is worth as much as it will bring."*
> *How comes it then that Albert clear*
> *Has thirty thousand pounds a year?*
>
> *He comes the bridegroom of Victoria's choice,*
> *The nominee of Lehzen's vulgar voice;*
> *He comes to take "for better or for worse"*
> *England's fat Queen and England's fatter purse.*

There seemed to be little doubt in their mind as to who was going to wear the breeches:

> *She says when we are wed,*
> *I must not dare to tease her,*
> *But strive both day and night,*
> *All e'er I can to please her;*
> *I told her I would do*
> *For her all I was able,*
> *And when she had a son,*
> *I would sit and rock the cradle.*
>
> *She's all my Lehzen painted her,*
> *She's lovely, she is rich,*
> *But they tell me when I marry her*
> *That she will wear the* britsch.

Albert's aims were laid out in a version of the National Anthem published as a broadside:

> *God save sweet Vic, mine Queen,*
> *Long live mine little Queen,*
> *   God save de Queen.*
> *Albert is victorious;*
> *De Coburgs now are glorious,*
> *All so notorious,*
> *   God save the Queen.*
>
> *Ah, Melbourne, soon arise*
> *To get me de supplies—*
> *   My means are small.*
> *Confound Peel's politics,*
> *Frustrate de Tory tricks,*
> *At dem now go like bricks,*
> *   God d—n dem all.*

155

The greatest gifts in store,
On me be pleased to pour,
And let me reign;
Mine Vic has vowed to-day
To honour and obey,
And I will have de sway—
Albert de King.

In Scotland there was a revival of Jacobite songs. These verses came from a favourite, *The wee, wee, German Lairdie*:

Wha the Diel hae we gotten for a King,
But a wee, wee German Lairdie?
And when they gaed to bring him hame
He was delvin' in his little kail-yardie . . .

He's pu'ed the rose o' English blooms,
He's broken the harp of Irish clowns,
But Scotia's thistle will jag his thoombs,
The wee, wee German lairdie.[32]

Victoria prepared herself. As a gesture of her purity she sent fifty pounds, and a kind letter for Mrs. Elizabeth Fry, to the Manor Hall Refuge for Destitute Females.[33] Always practical about sex, she dismissed as ridiculous "Ma's" theory that it was indecent for Albert to spend the night before the wedding under the same roof. After dinner she sat between Albert and Lord Melbourne. They played at guessing words and discovered that all but four of those in the Lord's Prayer were of Saxon origin. She admitted of feeling odd on the last day of her maidhood, confiding to her diary that it was the last night that she would sleep alone.[34]

On the morning of the 10th February she sent Albert a note enquiring if he had slept well and informing him that she felt rested and comfortable. "What weather!" she added. "I believe, however, the rain will cease. Send one word when you, my most dearly beloved bridegroom, will be ready."[35] Albert was writing to his "Grandmama":

In less than three hours I shall stand before the altar with my dear bride! In these solemn moments I must once more ask your blessing, which I am well assured I shall receive, and which will be my safeguard and my future joy! I must end. God help me![36]

CHAPTER THIRTEEN

A Wedding at St. James's

*On Monday, 10 February 1840, in the Chapel Royal at St. James's,
Victoria, of the United Kingdom of Great Britain and Ireland, Queen,
Defender of the Faith, Sovereign of the Orders of the Garter, Thistle,
Bath, St. Patrick, St. Michael and St. George, married to His Royal
Highness Francis-Albert-Augustus-Charles-Emmanuel, Duke of Saxe,
Prince of Coburg and Gotha, K.G.*

DESPITE THE ice-cold showers, by eight in the morning
sightseers had begun to collect along the route between
the Palaces of Buckingham and St. James's and up Constitution Hill. Cockneys came from all parts of London and there
was a fair smattering of Irish. It was a crowd enjoying a
crowd—joking, laughing, arguing, and ready to fight in
order to gain a point of vantage. With those who arrived too
late to find a place in the front ranks, the touts did a brisk
trade in the hiring of benches and boxes, casks and tables,
prices for a view ranging from 1/6 to 5/–. The young and the
agile took to the trees, oblivious of the risk. When over-
burdened branches snapped, they fell, like apples, on the folk
beneath. Horse Guards struggled to keep the carriage-way
open and police good-naturedly chased away those who
perched where they were not allowed to perch. Martial music
came from the Palace courtyard and a "marrow-bone and
cleaver" band struck up in opposition, receiving strong
support. The wedding of the Queen was to provide Londoners
with their most memorable day since the victorious Allied
Sovereigns paraded in 1814.[1]

The procession was a prototype of the many which were to
move up and down the Mall in the century ahead. For the
first time there was some thought, at least, for the public.
For the first time the Metropolitan Police were able to play a
part in controlling the crowds. The celebration of the marriage
at noon instead of at a late hour in the evening was a change

in custom. This obviated the embarrassment of the presence of a concourse of festive guests milling round at bedtime, making unseemly remarks and peeping into the connubial chamber, as had happened to "poor Fred" and Augusta of Gotha. That would not have suited Albert at all.

It was also the last procession restricted to Londoners. A decade later, at the time of the Great International Exhibition, trains made journeys from most parts of the country comparatively easy. And it was the last procession to lack the backing of a national Press campaign. The withdrawal of taxes, the reduction in postage charges and the swift distribution allowed by the railways, coupled with new printing processes, brought into being a flood of new illustrated magazines aimed at the middle-class market, and royal occasions were among the most important features of these periodicals.

The Queen chose the Chapel Royal rather than Westminster Abbey because, she said, she did not wish her wedding to be classed with her coronation. There was another reason. As space was strictly limited at St. James's she had an excuse for not asking "those dreadful Tories". She made an exception in the case of Lord Liverpool, of whom she was very fond, and the Duke of Wellington.

The processions (Albert's first) passed through Queen Anne's Drawing-room, the Guard or Armoury-room, down the Grand Staircase and along the Colonnade. Seats and galleries had been provided for the guests. These, the man from *The Times* considered, were not a very distinguished lot. While the outfits of the ladies, each besporting a "favour", received his approbation, he noted disapprovingly that few of the men had furnished themselves with a distinguishing emblem for the occasion. "Some gentlemen there were, also, who did not even pay the respect to their Sovereign of providing court dresses." There was a considerable amount of tittering, and this broke into loud laughter when the Rev. Augustus FitzClarence—the rollicking Rector of Mapledurham who had once cast a covetous eye upon his cousin Victoria—hauled a small choirboy from his seat and publicly upbraided him for his unseemly attire.[2] The only wedding guests to receive acclaim were the Duke of Wellington and pretty little Mary of Cambridge.*

Inside the Chapel, packed tight as sardines on their seats

*Mother of Queen Mary.

of crimson, gold fringed, sat some five hundred peers and peeresses, Cabinet ministers and their ladies, ambassadors and members of the Royal Household.

At 12.25 a flourish of trumpets gave notice of the approach of the bridegroom's procession. A few seconds later the band struck up "See the conquering hero comes"[3]—surely one of the silliest musical selections in English ceremonial history. Albert wore the uniform of a Field Marshal, the star and ribbon of the Garter and bridal favours on his shoulders. He was impressive.

> *Shaped in proportion fair,*
> *Hazel was his eagle eye,*
> *And auburn of the darkest dye*
> *His short moustache and hair.*[4]

The ladies loved not only Albert, but also his brother and Duke Ernest, in their picturesque Coburg uniforms. But while Albert remained "pale and pensive" and apparently oblivious of their adulation, the effect on Prince Ernest was very different. He beamed with delight and bowed constantly towards his admirers. He never could resist them. Fortunately they did not know that he had syphilis.

Ten minutes later the bride's procession was on the move. After the customary collection of gentlemen who head such affairs, under the watchful eye of the Earl Marshal, came the members of the Royal Family. Outstanding among them was the Duke of Sussex, who was to give away the bride. He wore a black skull cap as he insisted that it was the only way to keep his head warm.

There was a measure of pathos about two figures who walked immediately before the Queen. There were obvious traces of tears about the eyes of the Duchess of Kent and *The Times* described her as looking "disconsolate and distressed". She, poor woman, realised that her days of influence were over and that, within a matter of weeks, she must leave the shelter of the Palace and set up an establishment of her own. For her there was the bitterness of knowing that, on this day of all days, the relationship between her daughter and herself was far from harmonious—a point made obvious to all when, after the service, the Queen kissed Queen Adelaide but only shook hands with her mother.[5]

Lord Melbourne carried the Sword of State. For him it was

the end of the bright September day which the Lord had granted him. And it had been a truly bright and rewarding day, dawning with the moment when he had kissed the hand of the girl-Queen at Kensington Palace. The two had been mentally as close as man and woman can be: the intimacy could never be as true again. He had been very brave about it, ordering a new coat which, he told her, was causing as much trouble and work as the building of a 74-gun ship.[6] "I expect it will be the thing most observed," he added.[7] But in the Chapel Royal Melbourne and his coat were scarcely noted, for all eyes were on the bride.

Her dress was of white satin trimmed with blossoms of orange-flower. There was a chaplet of orange blossoms on her head and, above, a veil of Honiton lace, so arranged as not to hide her face. She wore the Collar of the Garter and a diamond necklace and earrings. The twelve bridesmaids were in white, with roses.[8]

Together, the Queen and Prince Albert advanced to the communion table and the Archbishop of Canterbury began the service. She promised to obey. When Albert came to the words, "With all my worldly goods I thee endow", tears welled from her eyes. At the same point in the wedding of Princess Charlotte and Prince Leopold in 1817, the bride had roared with laughter.[9]

Throughout she kept her eyes fixed on Albert's face as if hypnotised and some present considered that this unreserved staring was slightly indecorous. Owing to her lack of inches her head was necessarily thrown back, giving her the attitude of a votaress, but a reporter from Paris thought that this was her hour of beauty—the beauty of expression on a face that was most often devoid of it.[10] The *Morning Chronicle* agreed, thus commenting on the moment when the guns in the park announced that she was a wife:

Her Majesty, who, on her approaching the Chapel, had appeared rather pale, was now flushed, and looked, if possible, more lovely than before; while on the face of Prince Albert we did not perceive that any change had taken place.[11]

This was how a bridesmaid, Lady Wilhelmina Stanhope,* remembered the day:

* Afterwards Duchess of Cleveland (1819–1901).

I arrived about eleven with my *pendant*, Elizabeth West. Our orders were to go and lock ourselves up in the Queen's dressing-room till she arrived; and accordingly Lord Erroll, whom we found at the foot of the staircase, gave us in charge to a Mr. Dobel, who, to our horror, marshalled us through the State Rooms, filled with people waiting to see the procession—some, as I am told, having been sitting there since half-past eight!

The dressing-room, where the twelve young ladies in tulle and white roses were immured for one hour and a half, fortunately commanded a view of the park, and we spent our time in watching the lines of Foot Guards forming under our windows, the evolutions of the Blues, who looked a good deal rusted by the rain, the people in the park, etc.

At about half-past twelve the Queen arrived, looking as white as a sheet, but not apparently nervous. She was dressed in white satin and Honiton lace, with the collars of her Orders, which are very splendid, round her neck, and on her head a very high wreath of orange flowers, a very few diamonds studded into her hair behind, in which was fastened her veil, also, I believe, of Honiton lace, and very handsome.

Her train was of white satin, trimmed with orange flowers, but rather too short for the number of young ladies who carried it. We were all huddled together, and scrambled rather than walked along, kicking each other's heels, and treading on each other's gowns.

The Queen was perfectly composed and quiet, but unusually pale. She walked very slowly, giving ample time for all the spectators to gratify their curiosity, and certainly she was never before more earnestly scrutinised.

I thought she trembled a little as she entered the chapel, where Prince Albert, the Queen Dowager, and all the Royal Family were waiting for her. She took her place on the left side of the altar, and knelt down in prayer for a few minutes, and Prince Albert followed her example. He wore a field-marshal's uniform, and two large white satin rosettes on his shoulders, with the Garter, etc. Perhaps he appeared awkward from embarrassment, but he was certainly a good deal perplexed and agitated in delivering his responses.

Her Majesty was quite calm and composed. When Prince Albert was asked whether he would take this woman for his wife, she turned full round and looked into his face as he replied, "*I will.*" Her own responses were given in the same clear, musical tone of voice with which she read her speeches in the House of Lords, and in much the same manner.

The Duke of Sussex was greatly affected, and Lord Fitzwilliam was heard to sob responsively from the gallery, but no one else seemed in the least disturbed. The Duke of Sussex has a story that no one cried but one of the singing boys; however, I can vouch for *his* tears. The Queen's two tears, mentioned in the *Morning Post,* I did not see.

The old Duke of Cambridge was decidedly gay, making very audible remarks from time to time. The Queen Dowager looked quite the *beau idéal* of a Queen Dowager—grave, dignified, and very becomingly dressed in purple velvet and ermine, and a purple velvet *coiffure* with a magnificent diamond branch.

After it was over we all filed out of the chapel in the same order, the Duke of Cambridge very gallantly handing the princesses down the steps with many audible civilities. The Queen gave her hand to her husband, who led her back through the rooms (where her reception was enthusiastic) to the Throne Room, where the Royal Family, the Coburgs, etc., signed their names in the Registry Book.

The Queen then presented each of her bridesmaids with a brooch, an eagle (Prince Albert's crest) of turquoise and pearls. After this she took her departure down the back stairs, at the foot of which I consigned the train to Prince Albert's care, who seemed a little nervous about getting into the carriage with a lady with a tail six yards long and voluminous in proportion![12]

As the procession moved back to the Palace and the guests filed away, they left behind them a cloud of annoyance and disillusionment in St. James's. Back through the years it had been the custom, on occasions such as this, that the gentlemen of the Chapel Royal should be rewarded for their services. On this day there had been universal approval of the way that the service had been organised and carried out, and yet at its close they had been left empty-handed. They were not even presented with a pair of gloves, a rosette or a favour as a memento of the marriage of the Queen.[13]

The wedding breakfast was a family affair. The cake was nine feet in circumference, weighed three hundred pounds and cost one hundred guineas. Britannia stood in the middle and Cupids disported themselves on the white apron around her feet.[14] The bride and groom were due to leave for Windsor at four o'clock. The Queen had one last appointment to keep—alone.

At 20m. to 4 Lord Melbourne came to me and stayed with me till 10m. to 4. I shook hands with him and he kissed my hand. Talked of how well everything went off. "Nothing could have gone off better," he said . . . I begged him not to go to the party; he was a little tired; I would let him know when we arrived; I pressed his hand once more, and he said, "God bless you, Ma'am," most kindly, and with such a kind look . . .[15]

Albert and Victoria travelled alone, three carriages containing the members of their suite following, and the sun was shining as they drove up Constitution Hill. Two and a half hours later they reached Eton, to be greeted by 5,000 lights, 550 noisy boys and a sky full of rockets. Windsor was packed and festive, for that night there was to be a series of celebration dinners and a free repast with beer for two thousand poor, to which the Queen had contributed twenty pounds.[16]

The magic of the moment overcame even Albert and for the first time that day his face was lit with happiness as he waved to the crowds. At the grand entrance to the Castle he handed his wife from the carriage and arm in arm they entered. Then came the fun of exploring the new apartment that they would share. If there was a shadow for Albert that night it was the discovery that Baroness Lehzen's bedroom opened directly out of the Queen's dressing-room. Melbourne saying goodbye at Buckingham Palace . . . Lehzen greeting them at Windsor . . . the writing was on the wall, for Coburgs never shared.

There was a quiet dinner party with their ladies and gentlemen—Lady Sandwich, the Misses Cocks and Cavendish, Lord Torrington, Major Keppel and Mr. Frank Seymour. But Victoria had a headache, ate little and afterwards relaxed upon a sofa.

In London more splendid occasions were being staged. Queen Adelaide gave a banquet at Marlborough House. When the health of Prince Albert was proposed the Duchess of Cambridge remained seated.[17] It was a deliberate insult and tantamount to a declaration of war.

Part Two

CHAPTER FOURTEEN

The First Nine Months

*A*LBERT AND VICTORIA began their married life under a handicap. Both were lacking in knowledge of sex. She hated the thought of having babies[1] and planned to have at least a year free of the problems of pregnancy— problems exaggerated in the case of a Queen owing to her many duties—so that she could get to know her husband, who was little more than a stranger to her, and enjoy herself. Yet she was, as she termed it, "caught" within a matter of weeks—"and furious I was".[2]

The unsettled conditions of their childhood days lay at the root of their ignorance. Victoria had quarrelled with the Duchess of Kent when she was sixteen and the rift between the two had grown wider with the years. As the Duchess had not been told of the engagement for some weeks, quite clearly the relationship between mother and daughter precluded the passing on of intimate information. The woman who possessed all of Victoria's confidence—Baroness Lehzen—was a spinster and a very obvious one. Feodora, her half-sister, was a mother, but they saw little of one another. Lord Melbourne was in a position to guide on general principles, but not on detail.

Albert's life since the sad day when his mother was torn away from him, had been one long struggle to resist the attentions of women. The plan that the lovelies of Italy should baptise him had failed. Duke Ernest, whose own sexual life was suspect, had attempted to fulfil his duties by insisting that Albert accompany him on a visit to Carlsbad, but it is doubtful if this achieved the desired result. Doubtless the Prince studied all available and suitable printed matter on the subject, as he did when he approached any subject from drainage to art, but more than paper knowledge was needed. Brother Ernest, who was experienced, was available, and his unfortunate fate necessitated conversation between the two, but the information which Albert obtained from this source was hardly likely to enamour him with sex. His view then, and always, was that, while there was no sin in natural urges which led to the procreation of children in matrimony, all other temptations should be vigorously suppressed.

Victoria enjoyed physical love and made no secret of it. She considered that to have a husband whom one worshipped was a foretaste of Heaven.[3] Her feelings were plain to those who watched her early in the morning of her first day of married life, trotting beside Albert, her face flushed with happiness, as they made their way to a Windsor farm. News of the walk caused Greville to comment, in his crusty way, that this "was not the way to provide us with a Prince of Wales",[4] while the Duchess of Bedford concluded that Albert was "not being happy".[5]

Victoria was certainly in love and that morning "the happiest, happiest Being that ever existed" rushed off a note to her Uncle Leopold:

Really, I do not think it *possible* for anyone in the world to be *happier*, or AS happy as I am. He is an Angel, and his kindness and affection for me is really touching. To look in those dear eyes, and that dear sunny face, is enough to make me adore him . . .[6]

Born in the reign of George III, spending her formative years in the reigns of George IV and William IV, she was a Hanoverian by extract and environment and was no prude about sex, although her knowledge was limited. The family was not shy about such matters—there still exists a memorandum from the Duke of Clarence to the Prince Regent: "Last night I fucked two whores. I hope I do not catch a dose." The age of priggish and narrow morality, headed by the poor clergy, the "cantonment" officer and the middle-class business man, certain of whom produced prodigious families and yet never saw their wives naked, was still in the years ahead. This was no part of Victoria who, although she abhorred immorality, was always good for a laugh on the phallic theme.[7] In the late 1850s a Christmas present to her husband was "a life size statue of a male nude", which could have presented either a reminiscence or a reminder.[8] She herself wore a robe of natural silk after bathing, the garment leaving little to the imagination in a damp state.[9]

So it was that the young Queen on her honeymoon, without trace of shyness and in raptures with love, committed to her diary some very potent comments about the delight experienced during her initiation to marital relationship. For over sixty years the pages lay at Windsor, unread except by the lonely widow who turned to her Journal for comfort after her husband's death. When she herself died, the task of sorting out her papers was undertaken by Princess Beatrice, her youngest daughter. This very shy Princess experienced some considerable shocks. Among the pages committed to the flames were her mother's frank comments about her honeymoon.[10]

Characteristically, Prince Albert's reaction was very different. He confined himself to generalisations and informed his old tutor, Florschütz, in Coburg, a few days after the wedding: "I could wish for no happier family life than has been granted me . . . the change in my life is very great, but I am beginning to adapt myself."[11]

One of the changes was that, while in the German Duchies the Palace knew all about the activities of the people and the people knew little about what went on in the Palace, in England the people demanded to know all the details about life in the Palace, but the inmates of the Palace, and Albert in particular, knew little about the people. The gossip writers were ready to fulfil the demand and had their spies at Windsor. Hence the relevant paragraphs were appearing in the papers even before the honeymooners returned to London on 14th February. The general conclusion seemed to be that Albert had won himself "the grey mare" for a wife, and the Tories criticised "the severity of her domination".[12] This was justified, for the Queen, in their early days together, treated her husband as a tennis star might a ball-boy. She would send for him at any moment of the day and expect him to pop up, regardless of his occupation at the time. She did not mean to be like that—it was simply that for three years she had been telling statesmen when to stand up and sit down and making "Ma" knock at the door before she came in. Albert early decided that he would alter the attitude of both his wife and the Press. He succeeded better in the case of the former than the latter. It took him nearly all the remaining years of his life to realise that a "good Press" is an essential to gentlemen who marry into the British Royal Family.

At the time of the arrival of Prince Albert there existed at Buckingham Palace and Windsor two very different levels of moral propriety. The Queen walked in a walled garden of purity—Lord Melbourne saw to that. He was very strict. His factotum, Lady Lyttelton, reported:

> The maids of honour are very coaxy and wheedly with me, and nice creatures both of them. "Lady L., *mayn't* I walk *just for once* by myself on the slopes? I know it's against the rules, but what harm *can* it do? We *used* to be allowed, but now Lord Melbourne won't let us. I'm sure we *never* have met anybody there, except once only Mr. Van de Meyer, and what could that signify? *Pray* let me." (Says Lady L.: "No, no.") . . . My *business* is properly to look after these maids . . .[13]

The Queen was kept in ignorance of the happenings in the wider garden beyond her walls. There the older members of her staff still pursued the ways and customs of the days of George IV and William IV. For example, both the Lord Chamberlain and the Lord Steward had bestowed Palace posts on their mistresses. Nocturnal wanderings were commonplace and aroused little interest. It was with these adherents to past customs that Albert clashed, and in doing so revealed his horror of promiscuity.

Lord Melbourne took no action to clean out the Georgian stable, for several reasons. Firstly, he was too easy going and too much occupied. Secondly, he was in no position to preach as it was well known that his footsteps had strayed in the past. Thirdly, Lord Palmerston was in the van of corridor creepers until his marriage to Melbourne's sister, Lady Cowper, on 16th December 1839. He was fifty-five and she was fifty-two, and there had long been an understanding between them.

The announcement of the engagement of the Foreign Secretary brought smug comment from the other engaged couple, secure in the flush of youth. In giving the news to Albert, Victoria wrote: "I feel sure it will make you smile."[14] He replied:

> Your news of the marriage between Lord Palmerston and Lady Cowper amuses me; she must be an old flame. By your reckoning they together make up a century; but they are quite right, and I am delighted when ever I hear of marriage, for I always imagine the people must be as happy as I am.[15]

This patronising approach to sex in the fifties was to be rudely shattered. It had been the custom of Lord Palmerston, when on visits to Windsor, to repair to the bedroom of a certain lady after her young Majesty had wished her guests goodnight and retired.

On a visit earlier in the year he had followed the procedure but received a surprise. There had been a sudden switch in accommodation arrangements and, instead of being welcomed from the pillows by the smile of his regular bedmate, he encountered the alarmed and angry countenance of Mrs. Brand,* one of the Queen's Ladies of the Bedchamber. Now the Foreign Secretary was an imperturbable man and he entered the room, closing the door behind him. He had made previous note of the good looks of Mrs. Brand and had taken a fancy to her.[16] He may well have considered that he had done enough wandering for one night and might as well take his pleasure where he found it. But Mrs. Brand thought otherwise and her most audible distress signals brought neighbours into the passage. "Palmerston, caught red-handed, passed it off with a nonchalant air,"[17] and padded off to his own room.

The news of this brief encounter was kept from the Queen, but in the end she found out about it, as she found out about everything. She was furious and passed the story on to Albert. He was revolted but used the aberration to serve his own purpose. He tried to get Palmerston out of office. He miscalculated on the British character but in his written account of the affair, based on second-hand evidence, he made clear his abhorrence of promiscuity:

> How could the Queen consent to take a man as her chief adviser and confidential counsellor . . . who, as her Secretary of State and while under her roof at Windsor, had committed a brutal attack upon one of her ladies? Had at night, by stealth, introduced himself into her apartment, barricaded the door and would have consummated his fiendish scheme by violence had not the miraculous efforts of his victim and such assistance attracted by her screams, saved her.[18]

He had no sympathy for the sinner, in this contrasting with his wife. He once wrote to his brother: "There is only one truth, as in mathematics . . . for a man of honour there is only the bird's-eye view, standing firmly above the low actions of the world, supported by noble principles."[19] But before he attacked the man who became a great Prime Minister of

---

* Afterwards Lady Dacre.

Britain, he might have recalled the misdemeanours of his brother, of King Leopold and of Duke Ernest.

Such expressions of opinion came after he had consolidated his position. In February 1840 he was like a new boy at boarding school and not far away from tears. They flooded out on 28th February when Duke Ernest returned to Coburg, and again when his brother left. Twenty years later the Queen commented on the strange tendency of the family to weep and admitted that she had been prone to it when young. She considered that it was a sign of a warm heart but should be kept within bounds.[20] Her eldest son did not cry, which annoyed her,[21] and nor did the weakness appear in his descendants. But Albert was prone to tears all his life, emitting a downpour at Coburg in 1860. The British public thought this very strange, while his secretary, George Anson, was shocked and horrified. The cause was probably a physical defect, other weaknesses becoming apparent as the years passed.

Although the Queen repeated again and again in those early days that everything about her husband was perfection, there was one point on which she decided to make amendment. This was Albert's seat—it just was not good enough. He rode with the meticulous correctness of a German student, but it was not English and quickly led to criticism, particularly from army officers smarting from the Queen's somewhat injudicious act of promoting the Prince to be a Field Marshal over the heads of men with long experience and service.[22] An incident, which might well have led to serious result, hastened her actions.

There was to be a stag hunt on Ascot Heath. Albert was to ride and his wife and Prince Ernest to follow in a phaeton. Whether Albert had upset someone in the royal stables or there was a general dislike there of Germans and their riding methods can only be hazarded, but the point remains that a most unsuitable mount was provided. By name of "Tom Bowling", he was a real handful. After treating the spectators to two circles of equine aerobatics, Tom Bowling found himself the master and set off across the Home Park at full gallop. Such was the position as the frenzied Queen watched the two pass out of sight. Shortly afterwards Tom Bowling elected to pass under a tree from which protruded a low branch, a manœuvre which emptied the saddle. Albert escaped with a skinned arm and a bruised hip.[23]

Victoria was most particular about riding and herself very accomplished. Albert disliked riding for riding's sake. He said: "*Es ennuyirt mich so.*" (It bores me so.)[24] But he agreed with his wife that when in England, one must do as the English do. Thus each afternoon the two would go together to the royal riding school. Certain biographies have given a picture of her sitting there, her face glowing with delight and admiration, as Albert sailed round waving as he passed. That was somewhat far away from the truth. Victoria was acting as instructress, and she did it very expertly. When he rode with the Belvoir in 1843 he acquitted himself so well that he did more to boost his popularity in one morning than he had achieved in the previous three years.

The Queen's daily routine changed little after marriage. The time that she spent with Lord Melbourne remained as before and Baroness Lehzen handled her personal affairs as if she was still seventeen and the husband did not exist. So apart from the two hours in the afternoon when the Queen rode or went for a drive, and in the evenings, Albert was much on his own. Not that he was any less tired at nights for this, as the Queen indulged in an orgy of dancing. Now that she was married, she could, with propriety, valse, and Albert valsed very well, and she loved it. He wrote to Coburg: "The late hours are what I find most difficult to bear."

General Grey gave the following description of how the Prince passed his early days in London:

From the moment of his establishment in the English Palace as the husband of the Queen, his first object was to maintain, and, if possible, even raise the character of the court. With this view he knew that it was not enough that his own conduct should be, in truth, free from reproach; no shadow of a shade of suspicion should, by possibility, attach to it. He knew that, in his position, every action would be scanned—not always, possibly, in a friendly spirit; that his goings out and his comings in would be watched, and that in every society, however little disposed to be censorious, there would always be found some prone, where an opening afforded, to exaggerate, and even invent stories against him, and to put an uncharitable construction on the most innocent acts.

He, therefore, from the first, laid down strict, not to say severe, rules for his own guidance. He imposed a degree of restraint and self-denial upon his own movements, which could not but have been irksome, had he not been sustained by a sense of the advantage which the throne would derive from it. He denied himself the pleasure—which, to one so fond as he was of personally watching and inspecting every improvement that was in progress, would have been very great—of walking at will about the town. Wherever he went, whether in a carriage or on horseback, he was accompanied by his equerry. He paid no visits in general society. His visits were to the studio of the artists, to museums of art or science, to institutions for good and benevolent purposes. Wherever a visit from him, or his presence could tend to advance the real good of the people, there his horses might be seen waiting; never at the door of mere fashion. Scandal itself could take no liberty with his name.[25]

Albert preferred Windsor to London and found much to occupy himself at the Castle. As he wandered through its many rooms he walked through the story of the centuries. Pausing in the library he thumbed through an untidy folio of drawings by Holbein and Leonardo da Vinci. Opening a cupboard he found bundle after bundle of letters and documents relating to the affairs of Kings and Queens who had passed that way before him.[26] Both artistic and scholastic, and possessing a tidy and orderly mind, he was ideally suited to tackle the task of reorganisation. He set in train a system of recording and documentation which was unique in its efficiency. Unfortunately, after his death, there was no one who could take his place.

In the grounds he found interest in building and landscape gardening, and with each passing year the interest, and his skill, increased. He designed new stables and procured a stud for the Arab horses which had been presented to the Queen. He laid out new gardens on the park land below the Terrace. In so doing he deprived the townsfolk of certain walks which they liked to follow and haunts which they liked to frequent, and robbed them of the close approaches to royalty which heretofore had been their custom and pleasure. On complaint being made, amazement was shown that the advantages of the new order were not immediately apparent. How much better was the Home Park with the symmetrical beds of plants than the untidiness of the old order:

> . . . the public road winding round it under a high brick wall that divided it from Frogmore—with its fashionable "Frying Pan" walk, and the low public-houses opposite—the footpath leading across the Park close to Adelaide Cottage, and totally destructive of all privacy, to the old Datchet bridge—and the slopes so overgrown with trees, dark, gloomy, and damp . . .[27]

Nevertheless there remained those who hankered for the footpaths and the old trees. Albert managed to secure his privacy but the price that he paid for it was unpopularity. On the other hand much credit was due to him for saving from demolition the Fishing Temple at Virginia Water and George IV's Cottage, where the King had spent much time in his last years.

One might well have thought that a young man of twenty, coming from a small Duchy and accustomed to living on a very restricted income, would, upon marrying the Queen of a great land, have been prepared to "play himself in" for a few years, until such time as he had completely mastered the language, have acquainted himself with the geography of the realm and have learned something of the minds and characteristics of the indigenous population, both those who governed and were governed. But not Albert. The initial excitement of exploring two great palaces passed within weeks. To fill his time he turned to etching, portrait painting and the study of British legal history. In May he made his famous comment to his "dear" friend, Löwenstein: "I am only the husband, not the master in the house!" His restless mind reached out for power, influence, achievement, knowledge, and though he moved in youth when it is customary to feel that life is for ever, he rushed through the days, never wasting an hour, as if he feared that he would be gathered in before he had fulfilled the programme that he had set himself to complete. Already by the spring he had established himself on the way to making his mark.

Two events influenced this. Firstly, Albert called upon Baron Stockmar to help and back him. The alliance had obvious advantages in the power game as it opened to the Prince a ready source of information on matters diplomatic and political throughout the field of Europe. The German doctor's experience was wide, his balance excellent, his reasoning unrivalled, and he was well thought of by senior statesmen, Melbourne included. The drawback was that Stockmar did not understand the English mind, or, for that reason, did not care to fathom it. Thus Albert gained a talking encyclopaedia and an hypnotic father-figure to whom he could turn to boost the battery of his morale and strength. He lost two assets—his own identity and a true link with the British people, many of whom were suspect of the German doctor hidden away in a back room at Windsor. In the long run the disadvantages outweighed the advantages.

The Queen, backed by Lehzen, did not wish her husband to play any part in politics. Not only did she consider that the people would object to a foreigner meddling in affairs but she also wished to forget about work when the day's routine was over, fearing that political discussion might lead to domestic acrimony. Deep inside of herself, she did not want to share her job with anyone, as she showed clearly in later years in her treatment of the Prince of Wales.

Stockmar took an exactly opposite view. He saw the husband as the natural adviser of the wife, assisting her in an equivalent rôle to Private Secretary.[28] With this King Leopold agreed. There was bound to be a clash.

Stockmar worked in devious ways. He went to see George Anson and told him that the Prince felt "shut out" and isolated. "The Queen has not started upon a right principle," he said. Anson listened and then had a chat with Lord Melbourne. Melbourne talked with the Queen and reported:

> I have spoken to the Queen, who says the Prince complains of a want of confidence on trivial matters, and on all matters connected with the politics of this country. She said it proceeded entirely from indolence; she knew it was wrong, but when she was with the Prince she preferred talking upon other subjects. I told Her Majesty that she should try and alter this, and that there was no objection to her conversing with the Prince upon any subject she pleased. My impression is that the chief obstacle in Her Majesty's mind is the fear of difference of opinion, and that she thinks that domestic harmony is more likely to follow from avoiding subjects likely to create difference.[29]

Melbourne did not think that Lehzen was to blame, adding that the Queen never mentioned the Baroness's name to him. Both Stockmar and Albert thought otherwise. But the first step had been successfully taken up the stairway that was to lead to Albert being King in all but title.

The second event was Victoria's pregnancy. This transformed Albert from being a decorative boy drawing £30,000 a year into a man who was the prospective father of Britain's next Sovereign. The build up began. On 1st June he made his first public speech when he presided at a meeting for the abolition of slavery, the audience numbering five thousand. He was terrified, learned the words by heart and rehearsed before his wife, but he was a success. Caroline Fox, the Quaker, reported:

The acclamations attending his entrance were perfectly deafening, and he bore them all with calm, modest dignity, repeatedly bowing with considerable grace. He certainly is a very beautiful young man—a thorough German, and a fine poetic specimen of the race.[30]

A few days later the Queen and he drove over from Claremont to Epsom for the Derby the Grandstand Association spending two hundred pounds on redecoration to celebrate the occasion. Although Albert included racing in his long list of boring occupations, he was much impressed by the high spirits of the vast crowd.

At six o'clock on the evening of 10th June the pair drove out from Buckingham Palace to visit the Duchess of Kent, by this time installed at Ingestre House. In Constitution Hill a deranged youth of eighteen named Edward Oxford, who had until recently been employed as a barman in a public house in Oxford Street, fired two shots at the carriage. He fired from the park side, the bullets embedding themselves in the wall of the Palace garden. Victoria, who did not see what had happened, laughed. Albert, who was between her and the assailant, saw it all and next day told Prince Ernest that he had very nearly lost both his brother and sister-in-law. The crowds surged round Oxford, shouting "Kill him! Kill him!" The police saved him from this fate and he spent the next twenty-seven years in a lunatic asylum.

There can be no more certain way of escalating the royal popularity rating than a mean attack upon a pregnant member of the Family.

For many days after the dastardly affair there was an exhibition of almost unbounded loyalty. The journals of the day report that thousands of people continued to assemble before the Palace, and hundreds of noblemen, members of the Government, and private ladies and gentlemen, called to congratulate or inquire, and to present their grateful addresses on such a happy and providential deliverance.[31]

The rumour spread that Oxford's attempt was part of a wide conspiracy to dispose of Victoria and Albert and thus it was that each time the royal carriage emerged from the Palace it was surrounded by a posse of mounted citizens,

177

forming a most efficient bodyguard. The master mind behind the conspiracy was said to be none other than the dreaded King Ernest of Hanover, the obvious point being made that if the Queen was shot and killed before her child was born, her uncle would take over the Throne of Britain. At the time all evil was attributed to Ernest, not without reason, but in this case the suspicions were groundless. As a result of this attempt at assassination a step was taken to protect the Queen against any such further attacks—she was provided with a green parasol lined with chain mail.[32]

The Oxford affair also brought into prominence the necessity for the appointment of a Regent should the Queen be assassinated, or die in childbirth or from illness, before her eldest child was eighteen. It was the task of Lord Melbourne to tell the girl whom he loved, the girl who would be a mother before the year was out, that the passing of a Regency Bill was of great emergency. It was made the harder for him as the rumour was strong in London that the Queen was convinced that she would die in giving birth to her child, thus repeating the tragedy of Princess Charlotte, and that was why she and Prince Albert had visited Claremont and Charlotte's mausoleum there.

The Bill was an ideal opportunity for Stockmar to show his skill and, following his creed of *Coburg, Coburg über Alles*, he got to work. He did very well, as Albert showed in a letter to Duke Ernest of 24th July:

An affair of the greatest importance to me will be settled in a few days. I mean the Regency Bill, which will to-day be read for the third time in the House of Lords, after which it will be brought before the House of Commons. There has been much trouble to carry the matter through, for all sorts of intrigues were at work, and had not Stockmar induced the Opposition to support the Government, it might well have ended as did the £50,000. There was not a word of opposition in the House of Lords, except from the Duke of Sussex . . .[33]

To his brother Albert was jubilant: "I am to be Regent—*alone*—Regent, without a Council."[34] The point seemed to have escaped him that, to reach the pinnacle, it was necessary first for his wife to lie dead in the vaults of Windsor. But he did add, "Victoria is most satisfied with the arrangement."

One more step up the stairway. And in August there came

another. Victoria discovered that Queen Anne had taken her husband in her carriage to Parliament and that he had sat beside her at the Prorogation. There was considerable opposition in the Palace to Albert following in the footsteps of George of Denmark, Baroness Lehzen and the Master of the Horse being particularly obstructive.[35] During the rumpus Albert developed a fit of sulks and announced that he did not care if he went or not. But he did go, driving with her and sitting "on a throne especially built for me",[36] and Victoria found him a great comfort and considered that she read her speech the better because he was there.

Up one more step in September. Albert's writing-table was placed beside the Queen's. From there he despatched lengthy memoranda to the Prime Minister on foreign affairs, but seldom received any answer.[37] On the 11th he was made a Member of the Privy Council and commented to Stockmar: "The thing in itself is an empty form, but from a distance it sounds very grand."[38]

From now on the focus was all upon baby. Victoria hated being pregnant. She was shy and she hated always having to be "first", with nothing to screen her from the inquisitive eyes which sized up the increase in her girth and the state of her complexion. She objected to holding drawing-rooms and levées and being made to sit down. She was revolted by the constant precautions that she had to take and wearied by "the constant aches and sufferings, miseries and plagues". She was bitter at being robbed of her enjoyments, particularly dancing and riding. She felt pinned down, her wings clipped, and only half her real self. She referred to pregnancy as "the shadow side" of marriage and thought it unfair that men did not take a share of that shadow. A woman, she considered, was morally and physically the man's slave and that, she commented, "always sticks in my throat". "If these selfish men, the cause of all one's misery, only knew what their poor slaves go through." She thought of herself more in the rôle of cow than a blessed vehicle giving birth to an immortal soul.[39] The general attitude was not conducive to good temper.

The experience had an opposite effect on Albert. His behaviour was beyond reproach. He was always beside her. He sat beside her in a darkened room, reading aloud or writing her letters. His arm was always ready to lift her from bed to sofa. He wheeled her from room to room. His care, she later said, combined that of a mother and a judicious and kindly nurse.[40] Always that sweet smile on his face. The whole approach was in violent contrast with that of fashionable young men of the day who, under like circumstances, would find a convenient excuse for hunting in Ireland or joining some minor military adventure abroad.

Unfortunately Albert's sweet smile was insufficient to ensure an atmosphere of peace and relaxation about the Queen's bedroom.[41] One of the reasons was that the doctors had not yet discovered how to treat their imperious and tempestuous patient. The three—Sir James Clark, Dr. Locock* and Dr. Blagden—figured thus in the topical rhyme:

> Doctors Locock, Blagden, Clark,
> They made the great discovery,
> And having brought the goods to town
> Were paid upon delivery.

Their fee was one thousand guineas. A fourth medical man hovered in the background—Baron Stockmar. He sent a constant stream of instructions to Albert regarding his wife's treatment and doubtless, if anything had gone wrong, would have been wise after the event.

But the main cause of the upset was Baroness Lehzen. She meddled in everything. While the Queen was confined to her room she became virtually dictator of the Palace and, if the Prince had not been obstinate, she would have forbidden him entering his wife's presence.[42] By so doing Lehzen hastened her own end. The air of disquiet about her made Victoria restless and she could not sleep. Dr. Locock prescribed camphor lozenges and she found them very soothing. So reliant did she become upon them that in later years she would imagine that she would not go to sleep if the bottle was not by her bedside.[43]

Albert wanted their first child to be a boy. Victoria, contrary to general belief at the time, wanted a girl. She wanted a girl because the doctors had told her that boys caused so much more suffering and that it was better to buy experience with the first child.[44] Her wish was granted. A girl child was born three weeks prematurely at 1.40 p.m. on

* Afterwards Sir Charles Locock.

21st November, after a twelve hour labour. Albert remained in the room and witnessed the birth. He was "the greatest comfort and support".[45] Victoria emerged from the experience with little pain and a hearty appetite.

CHAPTER FIFTEEN

The Evening of an Englishman

QUEEN VICTORIA and Prince Albert were having tea. Those in attendance upon them noted that Her Majesty had the storm flags flying. There were red patches on her cheeks and her eyes were hard as glass. She raised her cup towards her lips. Then, quick as a flash, she hurled the contents into her husband's face.

He jumped up, dabbing his face with his handkerchief as the tea left brown stains on his cravat and coursed down his jacket. "Vot do you tink of dat?" he snapped and left the room.[1] Poor Albert. He was so very pernickety about his clothes as a young man.

Before her daughter, the Princess Royal, had been christened Victoria Adelaide Mary Louisa, the Queen had become pregnant again. The realisation flooded her with depression and anger and she made her feelings very clear to her husband. He, understating as was his habit, informed his brother: "Victoria is not very happy about it."[2]

Albert, of course, was most satisfied. He wished for nothing more than to sire a Coburg King who would rule Great Britain and her territories beyond the seas. While his wife was enceinte, he had more say in affairs. On the side of his personal comfort, it meant that he could spend more time in the fresh air of Windsor, avoid those boring long rides and go to bed early. He knew full well that if Victoria got half a chance she would be back on the dance floor, prancing round with young rakes like the Pagets until the early hours of the morning.

And she would have been. She was only twenty-one and she had not had enough fun in her life. Also she still clung to the old order, "Victoria, Melbourne and Lehzen—the old firm bound together by no articles of partnership except that of perfect understanding."[3] When Albert was out of the way she still liked to settle down with Lehzen and gossip and giggle about the latest Society doings and scandals.[4] She still preferred Melbourne's erudite and amusing chatter to Albert's double-chess or adolescent views on European politics. She was still a little bit in love with Melbourne—he just as much as ever with her. One evening Lehzen asked him why he was staring at the Queen so intently. He answered:

I am always watching her for fear she should say or do the wrong thing; but it is quite unnecessary, as she has never yet done so, and I feel sure she never will. If she did, I should rise from my grave to tell her.[5]

There was another reason why he gazed. It was so that he could engrave the image of her upon his mind with such detail that he would be able to recall her before his eyes when the end came. He knew that his time as Prime Minister was drawing to its close. She knew it too—that was why she wished the year of 1841 to be clear of the sickness and handicaps of pregnancy.

Queen Victoria did not like babies in their early months. She did not feed her children—in the case of the Princess Royal the wet-nurse being the wife* of a professional man who, very fittingly, hailed from Cowes.[6] She might well have understood them better if she had. Her views were therefore in conflict with those of a twentieth-century royal mother— Princess Grace of Monaco—who said:

It would seem to me that the closeness to the child resulting from breast-feeding is somehow an extension and affirmation of that very love that has resulted in its being there . . .[7]

The Queen, who thought of babies as mere plants, considered that a Lady, and still more a Princess, was neither fit for her husband nor her position if she indulged in a passion for nursery matters.[8] When, in due season, her daughters adopted the practice of breast feeding, she referred to them as "cows". The fact that the Princess Royal, as Crown Princess of Prussia, did not feed her elder children was perhaps a cause of the rift and lack of understanding between them— especially so in the case of Emperor William. She adored her younger children, whom she did feed. An incident which was

* She was paid £1,000, besides various emoluments and a pension of £300 per year.

183

kept from Queen Victoria was that the Princess Royal had on occasion acted as wet-nurse to a child of her sister Alice.[9]

To Victoria, an ugly baby was "a very nasty object" and even the prettiest was frightful in the nude until at least four months old. She recoiled from the sight of the big torso and the little limbs, while "that terrible frog-like action" was altogether too much for her.[10]

An unfortunate experience which the Queen had to face after the birth of the Princess Royal was the spate of rumours that spread from London to the Continent that the child was blind. These were embellished until she was deformed as well.[11]* A magazine suggested that the baby should be put on show in a glass case so that the public could see for itself. Certain it was that when at last visitors were allowed to visit the royal nursery considerable surprise was shown that eyes, limbs, let alone mouth, were all in fine form. In fact the Princess Royal, nicknamed "Pussy", was a particularly healthy and forward child. Her mother treated her as if she was a toy. As a doll, she was dressed and undressed. Each evening Nurse Pegley took the child to the dressing-room as the Queen changed for dinner. Up and down went the nurse's knee in an attempt to produce smiles and gurgles. The result was that "Pussy" became so lively and upset that she would not go to sleep.[12] She was fed on asses' milk, arrowroot and chicken broth.[13]

The relationship between Albert and Victoria—Joseph and Eliza as society called them—was made difficult by the jealousy existing in both of them. The jealousy in her was partly tied up with sex and partly with her inability to share her possessions, a characteristic which showed all through her life. As a child she had told a girl visitor: "You must not touch that doll. It is mine." She was intensely possessive with Lord Melbourne and, in later years, with both John Brown and Princess Beatrice. But her fears that Albert would flirt with the pretty ladies at Court proved groundless. Both Melbourne and George Anson had teased her by saying that the position would change with the passing years.[14] Maybe she would have welcomed such signs, touching the vanity and the streak of masochism in her, whatever indignation she might have shown. Anyhow she was forever on her guard and

---

*These and other untruths prompted Prince Albert to persuade the Queen to publish an official Court Circular daily, a practice which has continued.

there was no shortage of lovelies for her to watch, at their head the stately Marchioness of Douro. Miss Pitt came under suspicion for a time, as did Miss Spring-Rice, although her charm consisted in nothing more dangerous than the asset of being able to converse with the Prince in fluent German.[15] The one who really got into trouble was Olivia,* daughter of the second Marquess of Headfort. She was packed off home to Ireland when it was noticed that her Irish eyes flashed too often and too brightly in the direction of Albert. But of her it was said that "she would start a flirtation with St. Paul under the eyes of the Deity".[16] Victoria was even jealous of men.

On the other hand Albert's jealousy was directed at those, of either sex, whom, he considered, exercised undue influence over his wife. He was utterly ruthless in his plans to curb them or dispose of them. At the head of the list came Baroness Lehzen and Lord Melbourne. He also resented the close ties between Victoria and her half-sister, Feodora, and her husband, although they lived in Germany and were very poor.[17] He declared war on the Pagets and managed to eject Lord Uxbridge, the Lord Chamberlain, from his private apartments at the Palace. He wrote to his brother: "I can boast of the master stroke of having driven the Lord Chamberlain from his rooms."[18] Even the man who had put Albert where he was—King Leopold of the Belgians—was a casualty. That master of anecdote and twister of the English language, Prince John of Glücksburg†—he once announced that Queen Victoria danced "like a pot" and that a certain lady-in-waiting who had been accidentally locked in her room had been "confined before dinner"[19]—avowed that the Prince had curtailed his wife's correspondence with her uncle.[20] Yet to those with whom Victoria was on unfriendly or strained terms—such as the Duchess of Kent and Sir Robert Peel—Albert was all affability.

His arch-enemy was Baroness Lehzen. Although during the engagement period he was tactful enough to include in his letters to Victoria a message of kind thoughts for "the dear Baroness", from the moment of his marriage he was determined that her head should fall. The trouble was that he had not the courage to do the job cleanly. The drive in him was mingled with timidity: "They were both strong characters,

* Afterwards Lady Fitzpatrick.
† Brother of King Christian of Denmark.

warm and generous, but whereas Queen Victoria had a secret vein of iron, Prince Albert's hidden streak was of wax."[21] It was clear to all the Queen's advisers that Lehzen's task was now over, although it was anything but clear to the Queen. Anson and Stockmar were vehement about it. Melbourne was of the opinion that it would be better if she left while he was still at the head of Government.[22] From Coburg Stockmar urged the Prince to stand up and fight, to conquer the weakness and vanity and "not to rest satisfied with mere *talk*, when *action* alone is appropriate".[23] There were unpleasant scenes between the two and after one such Albert summoned up the courage to tell Lehzen to leave the Palace. She blazed back at him that he had not the power to order her out of the Queen's house, and, at the time, she was right.[24]

Thus it was that Albert decided to bide his time. The fortress that he could not take by frontal assault he would infiltrate and disrupt by stealth. He called into support the "feminine qualities"[25] which had lain close to the surface since he was a boy. These gave to him an inner understanding of the adversary and, in the event, proved most effective although rather nasty. He delayed action until the third director of the old firm—Lord Melbourne—had retired from the board.

Albert had no reason to dislike Lord Melbourne—in fact he owed him a great debt. He may have heard Stockmar's criticism that the Prime Minister was weak and lazy. He could have blamed Melbourne for allowing Lehzen to gain inflated powers and for the lack of morality at Court. But these were minor faults. Melbourne's "crime" was that he had won the friendship, confidence and trust of Victoria to an extent which, for the present, far exceeded his own. He hid well his disgust and anger at the romantic union between a girl of twenty and a man of sixty, but in the years ahead the venom of his hidden thoughts was to pour out. His brother Ernest noted the strange contradiction that, while Albert, despite his contempt for mankind, had a great depth of feeling for humanity in the abstract, the feeling was noticeably lacking when dealing with an individual. "With unmerciful argument he pulled to pieces other people's opinions and actions . . ."[26] Ernest had reason to know, as only eighteen months after the two had bid one another a tearful farewell at Windsor, Albert wrote to his brother, who had been having treatment at Marienbad for persistent venereal disease and thereafter wished to visit London, that "nothing would be more disagreeable than your visit, or any visit, in general".[27] Even for anyone in the peculiar position of Lord Melbourne there was to be little sympathy.

The two men were antithetical and the difference in age widened the gap. The older man was intensely English, the younger a thorough German. They clashed on every facet of life. Melbourne was gregarious—Albert solitary. Melbourne adored food—Albert regarded eating as a waste of time. Melbourne liked to gossip and chat until the early hours— Albert liked to be in bed by ten. Melbourne was lost without the company of women—Albert never noticed them. Melbourne loved horses—to Albert they were a boring means of transport. To Melbourne sport was a recreation—to Albert it was an exercise. The point at which they came together was in the brilliance of their minds. If Albert, for his first eighteen months in England, had been solely a pupil of Melbourne's instead of being subjected constantly to the lectures and exhortations of Stockmar, he would have become a more popular figure in his adopted land. The following is a sample.

The Baron wrote from Coburg in the spring of 1841:

Let us but cleave devoutly but unceasingly to high thoughts and noble purposes, and Heaven's blessing will not fail to attend us! *Not outward show—but Truth and Reality be the aim.* Only through self-knowledge can way be made. It is, however, a laborious and arduous business, and one that will have its share of troubles. It requires a man not to spare his own flesh, but to cut into his own faults as well as other men's. And yet it is only in this way that moral excellence and a character to be revered can be reached, and without these Your Royal Highness may say good-by for ever to any real success.

When I recall to mind the manifold and serious difficulties, as they stood before us a year and a half ago, and the insignificant means at our command for overcoming them, I am bound to confess that we have cause to be thankful and contented. We have walked *warily*, and therefore *slowly*, but at the same time *surely*. Still the result hitherto ought not to make us *presumptuous* or *careless*, but only more intent on further successes both within and without. *I look upon it as a signal favour of Providence, to have it in my power in my mature years to influence a Prince of Your Royal Highness's natural gifts and high position.* That I am thus favoured imposes

187

duties upon me, which at all times I must have wished conscientiously to fulfil. Hence the earnestness of my efforts to labour without ceasing at the cultivation of your mind, at the ennobling of your sentiments; hence the impossibility for me of flattering you, as well as the duty of stimulating you to deal with yourself sternly, and with an iron hand. [28]

Such was the Stockmar pudding which Albert had to digest on a spring morning as he breakfasted with his adoring wife when they were twenty-one. If there were faults in Albert which needed correction, how much more kindly would Melbourne have dealt with the situation, restfully sitting on the sofa after dinner.

Melbourne did not like the Coburg family and said so. But the faults which he found in its members—obvious in the case of Duke Ernest—did not appear in Albert. Here priggishness was his complaint—after a particularly unctuous utterance the Prime Minister exploded: "This damned morality will ruin everything!" [29] But as the months passed he became increasingly impressed with Albert's appetite for work and his capacity for reasoning. His one remaining task was to prepare the young German to play the support rôle to Victoria, to act as her private secretary, the rôle which he himself had played with such pleasure since her accession. To him, only the happiness and success of Victoria counted and he did everything in his power to make smooth the path into the future.

Early in 1841 it became clear that the Whig Government was losing its hold on the House of Commons. Four recent by-elections had been lost. In April Albert showed his hand. He asked Lord Melbourne to come and see him, and told the Prime Minister that, when his Government resigned, Sir Robert Peel should be sent for "through me". He also asked Melbourne to make it clear to the Queen that from the moment of the demise of the Whigs, he was to be her sole adviser. Though this was a strong ultimatum to deliver to the man who had for long been at the head of British affairs, Melbourne did nothing. The Prince made angry comment: "The old man has probably fallen into his old lazy ways." [30]

The Queen was dead set against sending for Peel—a cold, hard man she thought him. Albert was equally determined that she should. In order to make certain that there would be no repetition of the Bedchamber crisis of two years previously, he approached Sir Robert through the medium of George Anson, and with the knowledge of Melbourne. It was agreed that three ladies should go. They were the Duchess of Sutherland, the Duchess of Bedford and Lady Normanby. The Duchess of Bedford did not like it at all.

In May the Government was defeated on the Budget and on 4th June Peel carried a vote of confidence, against the Whigs, by one vote. Melbourne was faced with the alternative of resignation or dissolution. After lengthy discussions, he decided on the latter, moved by the Queen's feelings and wishes. On the 29th Parliament was dissolved.

As election fever swept through the country the Queen decided to move further afield, having since her accession stayed close to Windsor and Buckingham Palace. In June she and Prince Albert stayed with Archbishop Harcourt at Nuneham and from there she wrote to King Leopold:

This is a most lovely place; pleasure grounds in the style of Claremont, only much larger, and with the Thames winding along beneath them, and Oxford in the distance . . . I followed Albert here, faithful to my word, and he is gone to Oxford* for the whole day, to my great grief. And here I am all alone in a strange house, with not even Lehzen as a companion . . .[31]

This was the first day since 1824 that Victoria had been separated from her governess. It had been suggested to her that Lehzen should stay behind to care for the baby. She was also left out of the royal round to Woburn Abbey, Panshanger, Brocket and Hatfield House in July. For her it was the beginning of the end.

The Queen was always a welcome guest at the stately homes of England, but this did not apply in every case to her husband. There was antipathy between the Prince and the aristocracy and he made no effort to bridge the gap. In fact, by his increasing coldness, he made it wider. Firstly, he was bored by the recreational programme laid on for a country visit—inspection of the stables, balls for the "county", etc. Secondly, he was envious of the wealth and possessions of the big landowners—once he had Osborne and Balmoral for himself he cocked a proverbial snook at them and stayed well away. Thirdly, there was a difference of opinion, deeply

* To receive an address at Commemoration.

ingrained on both sides, as to Albert's rank. As a younger son from a minor Duchy with a total revenue of £30,000 per year, the peers reckoned him to be equal to a mere knight. Albert thought of himself as the son of a Sovereign Ruler. He was not the only German to face this view—the duel continued throughout the century and even Kaiser William was cut down to size. The British view was set firm by centuries of history and nothing less than a world war could alter it. There was a code and it must be adhered to. When Lord Ashburnham was dying and it was considered that the time was ripe for the administrations of the Church, his lordship's last moments were enlivened by a blaze of fury that the vicar came to the front door. A side door had been provided for the likes of him, doctors and governesses.[32]

Yet Albert returned with one small asset—a good story. Jokes, he was sure, were an essential to the English. Thus he would recount the tale of the gamekeeper's daughter who was appointed under-housemaid in the Duke's house. Before commencing duty her mother instructed her that, if the Duke should speak to her, she must say "your Grace". On her first morning she met the Duke in the corridor and he addressed to her some acid remarks about shaving water. The girl clasped her hands before her and recited, "For what we have received, may the Lord make us truly thankful."[33]

An example of how he spent his evenings in the stately homes comes from a memorandum made by his secretary, George Anson, at Woburn, on the 27th July:

Arrived here last night with the Prince and the Queen; this is now the second expedition (Nuneham being the first) which Her Majesty has taken, and on neither occasion has the Baroness accompanied us.

The Prince went yesterday through a review of the many steps he had made to his present position—all within eighteen months from the marriage. Those who intended to keep him from being useful to the Queen, from the fear that he might ambitiously touch upon her prerogatives, have been completely foiled; they thought they had prevented Her Majesty from yielding anything of importance to him by creating distrust through imaginary alarm. The Queen's good sense, however, has seen that the Prince has no other object in all he seeks but a means to Her Majesty's good. The Court from highest to lowest is brought to a proper sense of the position of the Queen's husband. The country has marked its confidence in his character by passing the Regency Bill *nem. con.*

The Queen finds the value of an active right hand and able head to support her and to resort to for advice in time of need. Cabinet Ministers treat him with deference and respect. Arts and science look up to him as their especial patron, and they find this encouragement supported by a full knowledge of the details of every subject. The good and the wise look up to him with pride and gratitude as giving an example, so rarely shown in such a station, of leading a virtuous and religious life.

On her travels the Queen had listened to the crowds booing Whig ministers and she feared the worst, but the election result, a majority of seventy-six, was a greater Conservative triumph than the party had anticipated. The Government fell on 28th August.

On his last evening as Prime Minister Melbourne stood beside the Queen in the starlight on the terrace at Windsor.

She was crying. He tried hard to be cheerful, wishing for these last moments together to be a happy memory. He was generous in his praise for Albert. She would be safe with him, he told her. But, looking up at him through the tears, she whispered to him that this was the saddest evening through which she had lived. Then he told her that the four years that he had been with her had been the proudest and happiest in his life. They turned their backs on the shadowy vista of the English countryside and moved towards the lights.

Thus, with courtesy and grace and true sentiment, did a great gentleman say goodbye to his Queen.[34]

There then came to be considered the question of the Queen's future contact with Lord Melbourne. He was most diplomatic. Realising that it would be unconstitutional for the Leader of the Opposition to write to the Queen without the Prime Minister being aware of the content of the letters, he suggested that, should she wish to contact him, she should inform the Prince who would in turn tell George Anson who would pass on the information to Melbourne. Albert was delighted with this idea. The Queen was not—she was adamant that she must be allowed to communicate direct with her old friend as and when she wished. So the correspondence began.[35]

Stockmar returned from his summer vacation in Coburg to find a situation very different to that which he had expected. On his instructions Albert had, throughout the summer, been making himself pleasant to Sir Robert Peel and doing all in his power to win the statesman's confidence. He had sent little presents. Peel, a shy man from an industrial background, warmed to the advances and one of his first actions on becoming Prime Minister was to place Albert at the head of a Royal Commission on Fine Arts. While Albert's relations with Peel were cordial, the Queen's were not. Thus Stockmar anticipated finding Albert the channel through which the Government approached the Queen and she, severed from Melbourne, taking the advice of her husband. As Albert spoke with the voice of Stockmar, it would appear that King Leopold's dream had come true. Instead the Baron discovered that a regular correspondence continued between Melbourne and the Queen. He became very angry and decided to put an end to it.

It must now be considered by what right the Baron interfered in a matter which concerned solely the Sovereign, the Prime Minister and the Leader of the Opposition. He had no official position in England. He had been sent by King Leopold to aid his niece during the difficult period before her accession and the Queen was grateful to him for the manner in which he had dealt with the scheming Sir John Conroy. Since that time he had established niches for himself both at Buckingham Palace and Windsor and the familiar way in which he flaunted Court etiquette planted in those who saw him the impression of an *alma pater*. He allowed himself to become a resident Solomon, to whom were carried problems of health and childbirth, of domestic and political differences, of appointments and dismissals, of finance and law. By consulting this encyclopaedia research was obviated. The growth in British industry had brought about a violent change in the mental approach to the general way of life—as violent as was the contrast between the stage coach and the railway train. English politicians were not trained to think, nor did they care to do so. They acted from a fount of mixed tradition and patriotism. They marvelled at the German doctor who could produce fact and reason on any subject from the endless pages in his mind. Melbourne, when Prime Minister, said of him: "Stockmar is an excellent and most valuable man, with one of the soundest and coolest judgments . . ." Palmerston considered him "one of the best political heads he had ever met with". Melbourne was soon to have good

Baron von Stockmar. From the painting by F. Winterhalter.

The Duke of Wellington and Sir Robert Peel.
From the painting by F. Winterhalter.

The Princess Royal, 1858. After a sketch by F. Winterhalter.

Leopold I, King of the Belgians. From a portrait by F. Winterhalter, 1845.

The Prince of Wales, 1859.
After a sketch by
F. Winterhalter.

The Prince Consort,
1861. From the
photograph by Mayall,
engraved by W. Holl.

Queen Victoria and the Prince Consort, circa *1860.*

Interior of the Creamery, Frogmore. Designed by Prince Albert.

The Royal Dairy from the outside.

Above, *La Filatrice Addormentata by Julius Troschel. A gift from Albert to Victoria on her birthday, 1849.*

Centre, *Osborne House.*

Below, *Schloss Ehrenburg, Coburg.*

BRITANNIA'S GREAT PARTY.

Punch's *forecast that the Great Exhibition of 1851 would not be ready in time.*

The Great Exhibition of 1851.

THE INDUSTRIOUS BOY.

"Please to Remember the Exposition."

"Dooced Gratifying, ain't it, Charles, to see sa much
In-dastry?"

Frogmore House, Windsor Great Park.

Prince Albert as Colonel-in-Chief of the Rifle Brigade. A contemporary copy of the original at Buckingham Palace, by Winterhalter.

Prince Albert. A statue of commemoration in Coburg.

TE DEUM!

THE MOMENTOUS QUESTIO

"TELL ME, OH TELL ME, DEAREST ALBERT, HAVE YOU ANY RAILWAY SHARES?"

Above, with the purchase of Osborne and the overhaul of palace expenditure, the public realized Albert's financial acumen.

Left and below, two cartoons concerning Albert's role in the Crimean War. Albert's Te Deum *was sung by a choir of 300 in Westminster Abbey on the occasion of Victoria's Golden Jubilee.*

"DANGEROUS!"

The Duchess Louise with Ernest and Albert (circa *1824*).
From the original in the Schloss Ehrenburg.

A CASE OF REAL DISTRESS.

"Good People, pray take compassion upon us. It is now nearly seven years since we have either of us known the blessing of a Comfortable Residence. If you do not believe us, good people, come and see where we live, at Buckingham Palace, and you will be satisfied that there is no deception in our story. Such is our Distress, that we should be truly grateful for the blessing of a comfortable two-pair back, with commonly decent Sleeping Rooms for our Children and Domestics. With our slender means, and an increasing Family, we declare to you that we do not know what to do. The sum of One Hundred and Fifty Thousand Pounds will be all that will be required to make the needful alterations in our dwelling. Do, good people, bestow your Charity to this little amount, and may you never live to feel the want of so small a trifle."

reason to change his opinion and a few years later Palmerston was to rage against "the employment of German physicians in political functions about a Constitutional Court".[36] If the *raison d'être* for the Baron being at Court was to help the Queen, in this case he acted strangely, for he was in direct opposition to her wishes.

In his supposed crusade to maintain the detail of the British Constitution, the Baron had one big advantage—both Melbourne and Peel were uncertain of their ground. Peel remembered well the rough handling that he had received from the Queen on the Bedchamber disagreement, was suspicious of both her and Melbourne and therefore only too willing to listen to whispers which came from those apparently in confidence at Court. Out of power, Melbourne was a lost man. He asked but one thing of life in his waning years— to keep in touch with his Queen and to see her sometimes. This precluded him from the obvious choice of telling the German doctor, bluntly, to mind his own business, as any form of row might have brought him into disfavour with the Queen.

The Baron decided to keep Albert completely out of his campaign to stop the letters of Melbourne. "I think it would be wrong to call upon the Prince to give an opinion on the subject," he said, although Melbourne had already discussed it with the Prince.[37] Naturally Albert knew all about the progress of the affair as each evening after dinner he would hurry to his mentor's room to pour out his problems and seek advice. Instead Stockmar decided to work through George Anson, the Prince's Private Secretary who had formerly occupied a like position with Lord Melbourne and therefore knew his man well. Although Anson's rôle was projected as altruistic, in fact he may well have either come under the spell of Stockmar or more simply have been furthering the cause of George Anson. It was noted that he now often occupied the position at dinner formerly reserved exclusively for "Lord M.".

Stockmar was tilting at a danger which did not exist. The harmlessness of the correspondence can be judged by a study of the many letters between Melbourne and the queen which were published in Volumes I and II of "*Letters of Queen Victoria*", edited by Arthur Christopher Benson and Viscount Esher. There the Editors commented:

Baron Stockmar's remonstrance on the subject shows that he misunderstood the character of the correspondence, and over-estimated its momentousness. These letters dealt chiefly with social and personal matters, and although full of interest from the light which they throw on Lord Melbourne's relations with the Queen, they show him to have behaved with scrupulous honour and delicacy, and to have tried to augment, rather than undermine, Peel's growing influence with the Queen and Prince.[38]

Melbourne had done his very best to smooth the way for Peel and the Tories. He had taken the trouble to prime his successor on the best methods of approach to the Queen—such as not to appear dismal before her as there was nothing that H.M. disliked more than that which she described as "a Sunday face".[39]

Out of office Melbourne tried to pick up the threads of a life which he had given up on the death of William IV. He dined out often and was much at Holland House. He avowed that he was happy in his new-found idleness. He took up again with Caroline Norton, but she had grown querulous and impatient and was forever harping on the favours which had been bestowed upon "the Royal Girl". After a few weeks it became apparent to his friends that he was finding life empty and sour. His eyes would stray from the pages of the book that he was reading. His brilliant conversation would stop abruptly, to be succeeded by a moody silence. Sometimes he did not shave until five-thirty in the evening. As he drove out from South Street to dine and saw the lighted windows of the Palace, the pain of remembrance of what once had been choked his ailing body.[40]

It was while in this frame of mind that, early in October, he received a visit from George Anson. The Prince's Secretary bore with him one of Stockmar's celebrated Memoranda and, on instruction, he read it aloud. Melbourne listened to the lengthy diatribe concerning his sins and then blazed out: "God eternally damn it! Flesh and blood cannot stand this . . ."[41] But he did stand it. He ignored the incident and continued to write to the Queen as before.

Stockmar was apparently under the impression that he had only to issue a memorandum for that which he decreed to be carried out. After waiting three weeks for the desired result and seeing no signs of its fruition, he decided that this was obviously a task which could not be entrusted to an underling and that he must do it himself. So round he went to South Street to have the matter out face to face with Melbourne. Having put his case, he sat back to receive the explanation of the former Prime Minister. He wrote in his report of the interview:

I listened patiently, and replied in the end: All this might be mighty fine and quite calculated to lay a flattering unction on his own soul, or it might suffice to tranquilize the minds of the Prince and Anson, but that I was too old to find the slightest argument in what I had just now heard, nor could it in any way allay my apprehension. I then began to dissect all that he had produced for his excusation . . .[42]

He noted that Melbourne was "nervous, perplexed and distressed". Then, having issued his ultimatum that, once the Queen's confinement was safely over, the "dangerous" correspondence should cease completely, he returned to his niche in the Palace.

Lord Melbourne wrote five letters to the Queen in the next ten days. Stockmar was unaware of this. He was to receive a shock. While on a walk through the London streets in company with Dr. Praetorius, Prince Albert's Librarian and German Secretary, the Baron found himself outside the house of a friend and decided to call upon him. He discovered that a small party was in progress. One of the guests turned to him and said:

"So I find the Queen is in daily correspondence with Lord Melbourne."

Stockmar replied abruptly: "Who told you this?"

"Mrs. Norton; she told me the other evening. Don't you believe that Lord Melbourne has lost his influence over the Queen's mind; he daily writes to her, and receives as many answers, in which she communicates everything to him."

"I don't believe a word of it," snapped back the Baron. An awkward silence descended upon the room, the conversation was changed and shortly afterwards the two Germans left.[43]

So, although the Queen's confinement was by now safely over, Melbourne still continued! Stockmar composed a mighty Memorandum, in which he used the threat that Peel might well retire if he discovered that Melbourne was giving political advice to the Queen. The manuscript was sealed and sent by special messenger to South Street. Back came a three-line note from Melbourne, saying that he considered it unnecessary to detain the messenger and that he would reply in due course through Anson.[44]

No reply came. The correspondence continued. Melbourne was invited to the Palace by the Queen.

By 1842 Victoria had come to terms with Peel. They had learned to understand one another's ways. They trusted one another. Sir Robert no longer had any qualms about the letters which flowed back and forth from South Street and Brocket. In truth there was no reason. The following is a sample of the contents:

Brocket Hall,

Lord Melbourne presents his humble duty to your Majesty. He received yesterday morning your Majesty's letter of the 30th ult., for which he sincerely thanks your Majesty. Lord Melbourne is delighted to find that your Majesty was pleased with the bouquet. The daphnes are neither so numerous nor so fine as they were, but there are still enough left to make another bouquet, which Lord Melbourne will take care is sent up by his cart to-morrow, and left at Buckingham Palace. Lord Melbourne is very much touched and obliged by your Majesty's very kind advice, which he will try his utmost to follow, as he himself believes that his health entirely depends upon his keeping up his stomach in good order and free from derangement. He owns that he is very incredulous about the unwholesomeness of dry champagne, and he does not think that the united opinion of the whole College of Physicians and of Surgeons would persuade him upon these points—he cannot think that a "Hohenlohe" glass of dry champagne, i.e. half a *schoppen*, can be prejudicial. Lord and Lady Erroll and Lord Auckland and Miss Eden are coming in the course of the week, and they would be much surprised not to get a glass of champagne with their dinner ...[45]

Stockmar's case had fallen down and he did not like it. But he did not have to wait long for the desired result of his campaign. In November Lord Melbourne suffered a stroke and for some days it was thought that he would die. He struggled up from his bed but only to enter a twilight zone in which he was a shadow of his former self. To the Coburgs he did not matter any more.

Through the years the Queen continued to write to her old friend. Before he died in 1848, it was an envelope from her which brought a last caress of happiness to the darkened bedroom at Brocket Hall.

CHAPTER SIXTEEN

Albert and the Dragon

*C*ONTEMPORARY OPINION on Baroness Lehzen was sharply divided. Charles Greville described her as being "very intelligent" and "much beloved by the women and much esteemed and liked by all who frequent the Court".[1] Lady Lyttelton, who was appointed royal governess in 1842, thought her "very kind and helpful" and the only person about the Queen "that seems to feel what is going on *at all*".[2] The Pagets were very fond of her and she was their ally. In a communication to his Government the Austrian Minister in London paid glowing tribute to the work and qualities of the Baroness, pointing out that, although she was a German by birth, she had brought up Queen Victoria to be English.[3] The Queen's own description was: "My dearly beloved angelic Lehzen."[4]

Albert took an opposite view. He labelled her "the House dragon spitting fire",[5] "a crazy, common stupid intriguer",[6] "the Yellow Woman"—this last because the Baroness suffered from frequent attacks of jaundice.[7] He announced that she regarded herself as a demi-god and spat venom at those who questioned or disagreed with her views. He considered that his wife was infatuated by her—and that was the real crime.

The counterparts of Baroness Lehzen were to be found in many of the big houses of Britain throughout the nineteenth century. Having devoted the best years of their lives to the bringing up of one generation, they stayed around to assist with the early days of the next and spent their old age in two rooms at the end of the corridor next to the sewing-maid. Advisers, comforters, friends, ever ready when called upon and pillars of strength in emergencies, they were part unselfish and part selfish, the latter stemming from the living of an unnatural life.

Lehzen's case was exceptional because of the great

responsibility of bringing up an only child who would one day be Queen; because she had supplanted the mother in her charge's affections; and because she had been allowed to assume powers at Court which were beyond her training and capabilities. But, to her everlasting credit, she had been responsible for moulding Victoria for her job and had passed a ready pupil into the hands of Lord Melbourne.

Lehzen was broad-minded and fitted in with the outlook of the times. That which she did not want to see, she did not see—such as certain aberrations of the Pagets. Victoria, influenced both by her and Melbourne, was the same. In a strolling conversation the Duke of Wellington told Greville that it was "the Prince who insisted on spotless character (the Queen not caring a straw about it)" and whereas he was a stickler for morality, she was "rather the other way".[8]

Lehzen and Albert were set on a collision course from the start in February 1840. She, a middle-aged governess, regarded him as a mere boy, while he had assumed that he would, automatically and at once, become master of his house and the confidant of statesmen. She had become intensely English, while his heart remained in Coburg. She was devoted to the cause of the Whigs and had spent £15,000 of the Queen's money in supporting the cause of Melbourne,[9] while he was more inclined towards the policies of Peel. But the main difference came in basic character. She liked strong and jovial men. She liked the smell of tobacco. If he had been able to laugh and talk with her, and take her into his confidence, in all probability she would have handed over to him by degrees the tasks and powers that were his by right, staying on at Windsor in the rôle of "old friend", as it was the Queen's intention that she should. In after years the Baroness said of the royal wedding:

We all felt that our duckling had taken to the water, that our young bird had found her wings, and that all the old birds must retire . . .[10]

But the Prince's cold manner was not conducive to co-operation. He was too abrupt and final without the inherent strength to back his stand. So the cold war began. She complained that his attitude made it impossible for her to consult him and that he had slighted her.[11] Greville reported that Albert considered her "to be obnoxious". But Albert could do little about it as, if he made complaints or criticism to his wife, she immediately let forth in a fury. So he decided to defer action until the time when his forces were of such strength that victory was assured.

These forces were the same as those being employed contemporarily to put a stop to the correspondence between the Queen and Lord Melbourne, namely George Anson and Baron Stockmar. Anson was convinced that there would be no true domestic happiness for his master until Lehzen was out of the way, a disappearance which would also lead to a brighter future for George Anson. Stockmar was in a more difficult position as he had, since before the accession, been the ally of the governess and had made good use of her in bringing about the royal marriage, but doubtless he found some clear piece of logic to satisfy his conscience on this point. The forces of the Queen and Baroness Lehzen were at the same time weakened by the retirement of Melbourne and Lord Uxbridge, the Lord Chamberlain, who was replaced by a Tory on the change of Government.

The first shot was fired when Lehzen was left behind during the Queen's country visits in the summer of 1841. "The moon is on the wane," commented Albert.[12] The main attack began in October. From the standpoint of strategy, the timing was effective, but unfortunately it entailed mental suffering for the Queen. In her last weeks of pregnancy, feeling deeply the loss of Melbourne and Whig members of her Household, not yet at ease with the Tory Ministers, she could not have failed to be conscious of the enmity between Albert and Lehzen—the two people nearest and most dear to her. In after years she admitted that the period was "far from comfortable or convenient" owing to "disputes and squabbles".[13] Then an illness of the Princess Royal brought the squabbling to a crescendo. It was a minor complaint caused by her teething, but there was general disagreement about the treatment and Lady Lyttelton was of the opinion that the child was "over-watched and over-doctored".[14]

The Queen's eldest son was born at Buckingham Palace at twelve minutes to eleven on the morning of 9th November. Her sufferings were very severe. Albert excelled in the rôle of nurse but defied procedure by delaying progress reports. Greville wrote:

From some crotchet of Prince Albert's they put off sending intelligence of Her Majesty being in labour till so late that several Dignitaries, whose duty it was to assist at the birth, arrived after the event had occurred, particularly the Archbishop of Canterbury and the Lord President of the Council.[15]

As it was the intention of the parents that the baby should be moulded into a replica—mind, body and soul—of his father, Albert was his name. Edward was appended in memory of the Duke of Kent. For convenience and distinction Albert was contracted to "Bertie". His mother sometimes called him "Albert Junior".[16]

The Queen knew from the start that there was something wrong with "Bertie". She attributed this to the short space of time which had lapsed since the birth of her first child. She told the Princess Royal in 1858:

Bertie and I both suffered (and the former will ever suffer) from coming so soon after you.[17]

Yet there was nothing amiss with the physical state of the Queen. Three weeks before the birth Lady Lyttelton marvelled at her health and was of the opinion that "she could run round the Great Park".[18] What, then, was the cause of the boy's lateness in talking and slow physical development, his lack of the ability to concentrate, his violent tempers which ended in a state bordering on illness? At the time of the birth of the Queen's eldest grandchild,* the Princess Royal, then Princess Frederick William of Prussia, was under most severe mental strain, caused by conflicting loyalties and the enmity and jealousy of the Berlin Court. As a result the mother was near to losing her life and the child was born with a withered arm and other physical defects. The same mental weaknesses and exaggerations showed in both "Bertie" and his nephew. They remained parallel throughout their lives—the Marquess of Carisbrooke† was of the opinion that they were "interchangeable".[19] It is likely that the Prince of Wales‡ was more a victim of the upsets and changes, "the disputes and squabbles", which were the lot of the Queen during the last weeks of her pregnancy, than a sufferer from following too closely upon his sister.

* Afterwards Kaiser William II
† Last surviving grandson of Queen Victoria. Died 1960.
‡ So created on 4th December 1841.

Victoria suffered from severe post-natal depression. She told King Leopold:

I am very strong as to fatigue and exertion, but not quite right otherwise; I am growing thinner and there is a want of tone.

Her uncle was in one of his frequent moods of misery and she reprimanded him:

You *must* not despond so . . . I have likewise been suffering so from *lowness* that it made me quite miserable, and I know how difficult it is to fight against it.[20]

Anson noted that she was becoming less and less interested in politics and spending more time with the Princess Royal. The question of evening occupation was a problem. Since her marriage she had passed the after-dinner hours in chatting with "her old Prime Minister", while Albert was immersed in chess. Now the brilliant conversation of Lord Melbourne was replaced by card games, and proved a poor substitute. This meant that Albert had to neglect his board and join his wife round the card table in an effort to relieve her depressed spirits with some German jollity.[21] There was one bright spot. To the Queen's delight, and Stockmar's chagrin, Lord M. arrived at Windsor for a New Year's visit.

There were also troubles to be faced and the Queen was in no state to withstand them. These involved public opinion and family squabbles. The Press, backed by the Whigs, attacked Prince Albert for trying to convert the advent of the Prince of Wales into a German festival. "Adverse criticism was excited by the formal bestowal on the little Prince of his father's hereditary title of Duke of Saxony, and by the quartering of his father's hereditary arms of Saxony on his shield with those of England."[22] The next broadside concerned the number of German guests pouring into London for the christening. One of them, Prince Ferdinand of Coburg, while shooting at Windsor, wounded the royal greyhound, Eos, and Victoria made herself ill from worry.

There was also public displeasure and family disagreements over the choice of sponsors for the baby Prince at his christening. There were to be six in all, one of whom was to be named as chief. Of the five in support, England was allotted two, both children of George III. They were the Duke of Cambridge (who had spent much of his life in Hanover) and

Princess Sophia, a spinster. The other three came from Coburg and Gotha. The balance was upset still further by the choice of the chief sponsor, a selection which caused much ill-feeling. Very naturally, the Queen wished to have her uncle, King Leopold, as he had acted *in loco parentis* since her babyhood. When the news of this reached another uncle of the Queen, King Ernest of Hanover, he exploded with anger. If, he said, the Belgian sovereign was preferred to himself, he would make trouble, and everyone knew that when Ernest Augustus threatened trouble, he meant real trouble. So it was decided that Leopold should not make the journey from Brussels.[23] There was another obvious candidate, a man who waited eagerly for the invitation which would enable him to do the honours at the christening of his first grandson—none other than Duke Ernest of Coburg. But he waited in vain. For some reason Prince Albert passed over the claim of his father, or at least that of the man whom history has accredited as such. Duke Ernest was enraged and made no effort to hide his pique.

In the event Albert had made his choice some months before and had paved the way for its fulfilment by a series of diplomatic and friendly letters. His selection was Frederick William IV, who had ascended the throne of Prussia in 1840. The news of the visit of the King of Prussia caused surprise in diplomatic circles and there were mutterings of discontent from Vienna, Paris and St. Petersburg, but Albert and Stockmar cared not, for this was the foundation stone of the temple which was to house a united Germany in close concert with Great Britain. The Ministry of Sir Robert Peel did not share in Albert's belief and at Holland House Lord Palmerston and his Whig friends made caustic comments concerning the leanings towards Germany of the Court of Queen Victoria. Sir Sidney Lee pointed out that there was a touch of irony in the prominence of the Prussian King at the christening of an English prince who was to figure in many scenes of coming history as Prussia's critic or adversary.[24] Yet, as a spectacle, Frederick William and his retinue were a great success and the baby Prince was showered with German honours and decorations. The Prussian King was gifted with neither political insight nor strength of character, yet established most friendly relations with the Queen and Prince. The result was twofold. Firstly, there began a confidential correspondence between the two Sovereigns on political affairs which led to "somewhat embarrassing results". Secondly, the idea was conceived of uniting by marriage the royal houses of Britain and Prussia, an idea which reached fruition sixteen years later when the Princess Royal married Prince Frederick William of Prussia. By that time King Frederick William IV was insane.

Amid all the excitement of the christening of the first heir to be born to a reigning Sovereign for seventy-nine years, the domestic scene in Buckingham Palace moved towards its crisis. The birth of a second child had weakened still further the position of Baroness Lehzen, and Albert and Anson kept up the pressure on her. The principle adopted was that everything which went wrong was Lehzen's fault—every upset was attributed to her. A young officer on duty at the Castle fell passionately in love with Queen Victoria. Lehzen knew this, but did nothing about it, apparently not rating the romantic interlude as important. Anson and Albert took a differing view and there was a blazing row. Then the Baroness was accused of withholding letters from the Queen and squandering her money, the donation to the Whig cause still rankling. In her summing up of the struggle between the Prince and the Governess, Dormer Creston wrote that whether he was "a little too relentless" could only be a matter of speculation, but pointed out that he spoke resentfully of her "dreadful counter-intrigues, ignoring the fact that those who use counter-intrigues have, *ipso facto*, already been intrigued against".[25]

The spark which led to the final flare-up came from the nursery.

In the middle of January the Queen and Prince visited Claremont and on their return were greeted with the news that the Princess Royal was unwell. Again the cause was teething trouble,[26] but Albert had for some time been critical of the diet prescribed for "Pussy" and, in his ice-cold tone, he made a derogatory remark to the nurse. Worried, independent as are the members of her calling, the nurse answered back. Seething with rage, Albert put the blame for the indiscipline squarely upon the shoulders of Baroness Lehzen and hastened away to tell his wife. Victoria opened up with all the guns in the royal armoury, accusing him of wishing to "drive her out of the nursery while he as good as murdered their child".[27]

Coburg, pulverised, retreated, praying for patience. His prayers not being answered, and the forces of resentment piling up, he returned to fire a bitter verbal broadside. Untouched by the tears that he caused, he followed up with the despatch of a missile of which he was most adept at handling, namely *the note*. He wrote:

> Doctor Clark has mismanaged the child and poisoned her with calomel and you have starved her. I shall have nothing more to do with it and if she dies you will have it on your conscience.[28]

So deeply were the contestants committed, so tense were the feelings of anger and rivalry, that the intervention of an arbitrator was essential if normal relationship was to be resumed. And, as usual, an arbitrator was handy, ever ready to solve the problems of others, ever willing to pour out his infinite wisdom if power was at stake—none other than Baron Stockmar, the doctor from Coburg.

Victoria emptied her heart to him, begging him to help her in her "dreadful dream". She asked him to try to persuade Albert not to take trifles seriously and to speak out straight if he considered that something was going wrong. She added that she forgave him.[29]

Albert's interview with the Baron consisted of the former letting forth with a frenzied tirade of hate against Lehzen, ending with the hysterical announcement that he would die rather than see his marriage and his children's lives ruined by the person who had warped his wife's outlook.

The next day the Prince went to London to lay the foundation stone of the new Royal Exchange. He did not return to Windsor until midnight, an hour most unusual for him, but that he did return was an indication that he had no intention of letting matters go too far. Victoria commented: "It was very kind of him to come."[30]

After a cold January night Albert heard from Stockmar that his wife considered that he should be more frank and outright, and that he was forgiven. This set the young man off again. How, he asked, could he be frank and reasonable when Victoria's outpourings of rage forbade him the chance of putting his case, how could he remain calm whilst being accused of ambition, envy and lack of trust?

Stockmar came to the conclusion that mere tact and diplomacy would not cure the trouble between man and wife.

Some more drastic step was necessary and he took it upon himself to take that step. Despite the Queen's plea that he would spare her the bitterness of listening to the detail of Albert's complaint, the Baron told her everything. He sent his ultimatum in writing. The ultimatum was that, if Baroness Lehzen did not leave Court, he would.[31]

Stockmar then went to see Lehzen and told her that, while the people of Britain would always be grateful to her for the care that she had taken over the upbringing of the Queen, they would never forgive her if she came between husband and wife.

After reading the ultimatum, the Queen shifted her ground. It was essential to her to have an older man at hand to whom she could turn for advice. She had lost Melbourne—she dare not now risk losing Stockmar. She trusted him implicitly. In addition, there was the relationship with King Leopold to be considered. So she said that the question of her intimacy with her Lady in Attendance was being exaggerated—it was the Baron who was her confidant and not the Baroness. She strongly refuted her husband's allegation that she was infatuated by the older woman, and denied that she chatted and complained about him behind his back. What she did want to ensure was that her old governess was able to live in comfort in her old age. Thus it was that Stockmar won, and the Invisible Man took over the diminishing rôle of the Invisible Woman.

As for Lehzen, the light came to her also. She was fifty-seven and it was obvious that the forces ranged against her were such that she could no longer resist them. As with Lord Melbourne, the only wish remaining in life was to retain the love and affection of Victoria. If the squabbles continued there was the danger that the bond which had existed since schoolroom days might grow weak and trust turn to rancour—in the event she had already outstayed her usefulness. She had also to consider the point of a pension for her retirement.

An uneasy peace fell upon the trio, each conscious of the watchful eyes of Stockmar upon them and each aware of the change which was about to take place. But the Queen shut her eyes and it was Albert who, in July, interviewed Lehzen and put forward the suggestion that she should take a holiday of some six months for her health's sake. The suggestion was agreed. Both understood that in fact the holiday would have no end. A pension of £800 per year was offered and accepted.

At the end of August the Queen made her first journey to Scotland, Lehzen staying behind to care for the children and to pack up the possessions which had accumulated over twenty years. But for a short visit to Edinburgh by George IV in 1822, there had not been a like occasion north of the Border since the coronation of Charles I in 1633. The Scottish holiday proved a triumphant success and at its close the Queen sent this message of gratification:

The Queen cannot leave Scotland without a feeling of regret that her visit on the present occasion could not be further prolonged. Her Majesty fully expected to witness the loyalty and attachment of her Scottish subjects; but the devotion and enthusiasm evinced in every quarter, and by all ranks, have produced an impression on the mind of Her Majesty which can never be effaced.[32]

She had fallen in love with the hills and the heather and the lochs and, as a new vista opened to her, so did the mists close in upon the days of Kensington, Melbourne and Lehzen.

Victoria could not steel herself to watch, and wave, as her old governess drove off at the beginning of her journey to Hanover. She said her goodbyes on the previous day, throwing her arms round Lehzen's neck, telling her to come back soon and how much she would miss her. It was Prince Albert who, early on the morning of the 30th September, escorted the Baroness to her carriage, assuring her that, as a visitor, she would always be welcome at Windsor.[33]

The sound of the wheels and hooves on the cobble-stones died out. He turned and strode back into the Castle—Albert de King.

Shortly afterwards the Queen said to the royal governess:

It was very painful to me, Lady Lyttelton, waking this morning, and recollecting she was really quite away. I had been dreaming she had come back to say good-bye to me, and it felt very uncomfortable at first. I had heard it mentioned before—that odd feeling on waking—but I had no experience of it. It is very unpleasant.[34]

Baroness Lehzen lived on for twenty-eight years in a ghost world of memories of Kensington and Claremont, Windsor and Buckingham Palace. When she became an invalid the

Queen sent her a wheel-chair, which gave her infinite delight. She was nearly eight-six when she died and in the last minutes of her wanderings those by the bedside picked out the words: "Victoria . . . Victoria . . . Victoria . . ."[35]

CHAPTER SEVENTEEN

A Man of Property

*W*ALMER CASTLE, Deal, November 1842 . . .
From where Albert lay in the bed he could see the travelling clock without raising his head from the pillow. He had requested his host, the Duke of Wellington, that this little luxury should be attended to and accordingly the carpenter had come from the village and fixed a shelf to the wall.[1] Albert was a man who insisted on exactitude in time and place.

Victoria lay quiet beside him. She was three months pregnant and he had decided that a short holiday would be of benefit to her health and help her to forget the loss of Lehzen. For the first time the two children accompanied them on a visit, the hundred-mile journey from Windsor being accomplished in nine hours in the new nursery coach designed for the comfort of the young.

The Duke, Lord Warden of the Cinque Ports, had willingly given up his favourite home and moved into the Ship Hotel at Dover. He had personally supervised the arrangements for the convenience of his guests, partitioning off Pitt's room to make a dining-room and converting the laundry into a guard-room. Each day he rode over to see that all was well.[2]

It was indeed well. The marital bliss was a joy to behold and none welcomed the change more deeply than the members of the Household who had suffered considerably during the quarrels and upsets which had preceded the departure of the Baroness. It was as if a new era had begun. Lady Lyttelton was intrigued.

We have, I begin to notice, rather a raised tone of conversation of late—many bits of information, and naval matters, and scientific subjects come up, and are talked of very pleasantly at dinner. The Prince, of course, encourages such subjects, and no gossip has been stirring since we have been here, but many things are said daily which I am sorry to forget. The Prince and Queen are reading Hallam's "Constitutional History of England" together, most carefully, and for a light book "St. Simon's Memoirs". Very pleasant to find him reading aloud to her, while she was at cross-stitch, as I did the other evening before dressing-time. Oh! what a blessing it is that "Love rules the court" as he does! What a mine of blessings there is, all sent thro' those potent blue eyes! . . .[3]

Hand in hand Albert and Victoria walked along the shingly beach, swopping pleasantries with the fisherfolk. With their children they paraded in the sheltered garden, which was full of robins, particular friends of the Duke. Of an evening, well muffled, they would climb to the ramparts and watch the great clouds scudding across the moon and out to sea. This was their real honeymoon.

Albert was boss, Albert was supreme, Albert was happy. Hand in hand with happiness went the Freudian theory of power with sex. The royal governess had noted the new potency in his unfathomable eyes. Victoria looked up into them and purred.

She had been whipped and she was contrite. In the peace of the low, castellated house by the Kentish shore, she saw the light. Walmer became her confessional. In her new rôle of proselyte she was ready now to denounce the two friends who had fashioned her—Melbourne lying ill and weak at Brocket and Lehzen lonely in her exile in Hanover. This she did under the encouragement and prompting of Albert—it was not the custom of Queen Victoria to betray her friends. He continued until he had convinced his wife that "the beginning of his marriage had been a martyrdom borne like a saint".[4] Her love for Melbourne he dismissed as mere foolishness.

That autumn she read back through the pages of her diary, pausing at the entries for the spring of 1839 when she had made clear her deep feelings for Melbourne as she thought that she was about to lose him. She commented:

Reading this again, I cannot forbear remarking what an artificial sort of happiness *mine* was *then*, and what a blessing it is I have now in my beloved Husband *real* and solid happiness, which no Politics, no worldly reverses *can* change; it could not have lasted long, as it was then, for after all, kind and excellent as Lord M. is, and kind as he was to (me), it was but in Society that I had amusement, and I was only living on that superficial resource, which I then fancied was happiness! Thank God! for *me* and others, this is changed, and I *know what* REAL happiness is![5]

While but a few months earlier she had ranted at Albert that she regretted marrying him so young, now she turned right about and confessed that she was foolish not to have married him earlier. The only excuse that she could make, she later wrote, was that the sudden change from the seclusion of Kensington to Queenship quite drove thoughts of marriage out of her head[6]—a poor excuse indeed and positively untrue. Suddenly she saw unnamed dangers lurking in the years when she had sat, evening after evening, laughing and learning by the side of Melbourne. She damned them as "the least sensible and satisfactory time in her whole life" and added, "I can never be sufficiently thankful that I passed safely through those two years of my marriage".[7] The point arises as to whether the danger referred to was real or imaginary. Before her marriage the Queen had sent a contribution to a home for fallen women. Perhaps it was a sympathetic gesture—there, but for the Grace of God, go I.

As for Lehzen, the confession was complete:

I blame myself for my blindness . . . I shudder to think what my beloved Albert had to go through . . . it makes my blood boil to think of it.[8]

There were other reasons for Albert's new-found happiness and complacency. It was during her third pregnancy that the Queen, when communicating decisions to her ministers, converted the personal pronoun from the singular into the plural, and in substituting "we" for "I" merged her own judgment with that of her husband. The growth of his authority became even more abundantly clear when the Prince held levées on the Queen's behalf if reasons of health dictated her absence. This forward step was received with severe criticism both from Press and public.[9]

On the Coburg side the Prince was able, in 1842, to close the cupboard door on a family skeleton, temporarily at least hiding it from public view. Wicked brother Ernest was married to the Grand Duchess Alexandrina of Baden. Victoria, who had recently become alarmed by her brother-in-law's strange behaviour,[10] wrote with relief to her uncle Leopold:

Ernest's marriage is a *great, great delight* to us; thank God! I say, as I so ardently wished it, and Alexandrina is said to be really *so* perfect.[11]

It would appear that the real state of Ernest's health had been withheld from her. Already by this time Albert had assumed that his brother would have no children born in wedlock and had made plans for his own second son, as yet unborn, to succeed to the Coburg dukedom. His assumption proved correct. Alexandrina put up with her pompous dandy of a husband, called him *"Der Lieber, Gute Ernst"*,[12] and never acknowledged his wickednesses. His desires increased with the passing years and H.R.H. Princess Alice, Countess of Athlone, reported that he had "numerous mistresses and a legion of illegitimates".[13] His Duchess thought that the ladies whom he kept in a house in the park really were translators and secretaries.

As the lights went green for Albert, he was quickly along the road towards his primary aims, the consolidation of his private position by means of an increase in income and the amassing of capital, the improvement of State homes occupied by the royal family, and the acquisition of private properties together with the necessary treasures with which to embellish them. At the same time he made clear that this was no selfish task and that he toiled for others. The children's governess noted:

On the Queen fidgetting after some book, and saying, "Where *can* it be? Does it belong to me?"—"*Everything* belongs to you," was her husband's answer, with a most graceful bow of real chivalry. "No, no, no!" she replied, very red, and more than half really angry.[14]

In these early days the critical financial state of Britain was not appreciated by the Prince, nor by the Queen. As early as the summer of 1841 he had asked for £70,000 to renovate the royal stables, a request which was smartly turned down by Lord John Russell, and when Peel came into power he wished the question of his allowance to be reconsidered and the original figure of £50,000 per annum to be granted, a pitfall from which he was saved by the wisdom of George Anson. Greville thus summed up the national situation:

Poverty and vice and misery must always be found in a community like ours, but such frightful contrasts between the excess of luxury and these scenes of starvation and brutality ought not to be possible. I am afraid there is more vice, more misery, more penury in this country than in any other, and, at the same time, greater wealth.[15]

In the spring of 1842 Peel's Government was confronted by a large deficit in the budget and accordingly imposed an income tax of sevenpence in the pound on all incomes exceeding £150 per year, a step which produced wails of agony and forecasts of ruin. The royal reaction was to stage a Bal Masque at Buckingham Palace, the avowed object of which was to stimulate trade. Albert appeared as King Edward III and Victoria as Philippa, his queen. Her upper abdomen was covered by a stomacher valued at £60,000. Guests hired full suits of armour and the revelries, lit up by 530 gas jets, continued until three in the morning. There was some public bewilderment as to how this display would stimulate trade. When, a few days later, John Francis fired a pistol at the Queen and Prince on Constitution Hill and, on being apprehended, said, "Damn the Queen! Why should she be such an expense to the nation!"[16] there was some sympathy for his feelings.

But where the finances of the Coburg coterie were intimately concerned, a very differing view was taken. No one knew more about royal accounts, or had greater experience, than Stockmar—he had been concerned with King Leopold's income since 1817—and he had long seen the great savings which could accrue from a reorganisation of the administration of the palaces. In intelligent anticipation he had, in 1841, prepared a memorandum on the subject, a memorandum which was detailed and voluminous even for him. It was clearly unwise to produce this paper while Melbourne and Lehzen were active about the Court and he had therefore taken a holiday in Coburg. Now the way was clear and at Christmas 1842 Albert wrote to his mentor asking him to return immediately to assist in the matter:

My attention hitherto has been directed to a host of trifles. It always seems to me as if an infinitude of small trivialities hung about me like an ever-present weight; I mean by these the domestic and Court arrangements, and to these I have chiefly applied myself, feeling that we never shall be in a position to occupy ourselves with higher and graver things, so long as we have to do with these mere nothings . . .[17]

The Prince had already spoken to Sir Robert Peel on the subject, but had been rebuffed. The Prime Minister deprecated any change, shrinking from altering age-old custom and offending a great number of people, many of high rank. Albert, whose true attitude to the problem was revealed in his description—"an infinitude of trivialities . . . mere nothings" —replied in a very changed tone:

I agree that ancient institutions and prescriptive usages in the Court ought never to be touched . . . Much as I am inclined to treat the Household machine with a sort of reverence from its antiquity, I still remain convinced that it is clumsy in its original construction.[18]

Certainly the organisation of the palaces, in particular Windsor, was clumsy and inefficient. But it was *English*. Procedure had not changed since the days of the Georges and many small customs stemmed from the Middle Ages. One portion of the staff came under the authority of the Lord Chamberlain, another under the Master of the Horse and the remainder under the Lord Steward. "The Lord Steward", wrote Stockmar, "finds the fuel and lays the fire, and the Lord Chamberlain lights it . . . In the same manner the Lord Chamberlain provides all the lamps, and the Lord Steward must clean, trim and light them." While the Lord Chamberlain's department cleaned the inside of the windows, Woods and Forests cared for the outside. Owing to the lack of unified control, there were the direst forebodings as to what transpired in the servants' quarters at night.

The Prince and Stockmar made much play over the absurdity of the situation, but every change which they tried to introduce was met with resentment and non-cooperation. Windsor town considered that it lived, by right, on the Castle, and Albert became most unpopular. His first step to rectify the economy was to end waste. He looked towards the Castle kitchens, to which many of the poor of the town turned for a loaf of stale bread or, with luck, a hot meal. A visitor who penetrated "below stairs" reported:

The fire was more like Nebuchadnezzar's "burning fiery furnace" than anything else I can think of; and though there is now no company at Windsor, there were at least fifteen to twenty large joints of meat roasting. Charles Murray* told me that last year they fed at dinner 113,000 people.[19]

There was a great saving to be made here and from then on any surplus bread had to be accounted for and transmitted to a recognised charity.

Albert soon put an end to the candle scandal. Each day, by custom, new candles were provided for all the public rooms. Each midnight the staff were swift to collect the issue of the day, some half consumed but many unlit, and there was a ready trade in them. A system of rationing was therefore introduced and it was laid down that visitors were to be restricted to two candles in their bedrooms. Madame Tietgiens† was summoned to Windsor to sing before the Queen. Finding difficulty in preparing for her rôle in the dim light, she rang the bell and asked for more candles. The maid informed her that no more were allowed but that there was nothing to prevent her from cutting the two in half to make four.[20] Visitors also discovered that matches were not provided and that the lavatories were stocked with neat squares of newspaper.[21]

The princely microscope examined the consumption of brushes, brooms, mops, mats, housemaids' gloves, soap, starch and leathers. Laundry arrangements were revised, providing an annual saving of £400.[22] Then Albert made his big discovery. He came upon an item of weekly expenditure labelled "Red Room Wine", amounting to thirty-five shillings. On investigation he traced that, during the days of George III, a room at Windsor had been converted temporarily into a guardroom and an allowance of five shillings a day had been allowed to provide wine for the officers.[23] The order had never been rescinded. This was now done. Thus came to an end the cosy evenings when a few junior staff gathered together to chat over a glass of red wine, while their betters sipped a wider variety at the royal dinner table. While nineteenth-century biographers applauded the Prince's zeal and efficiency, there was nothing but bitterness in the hearts of the victims of his petty economies.[24] Servants were no longer provided with toilet soap, and tea, as an alternative to cocoa, was cut out.[25]

Real trouble awaited Albert when he began pruning the

* Master of the Household.
† Theresa Tietgiens (1831–77).

number of royal servants. By so doing he saved the Queen £25,000 per year, but an enquiry revealed that the pensions due to the redundant personnel were coming from the public purse. It also emerged that there were over sixty foreign servants occupying the upper places in the palaces, at a time when one third of the indigenous domestic labour force was out of work. The inevitable happened—an injured party talked to the Press. Henry Saunders, Inspector of the Palace, infuriated by the sackings and economies being carried out by the Prince and Stockmar, resigned, and thereafter told the reporters all the tibits that they were so anxious to learn.[26] Among the newspaper men to whom he talked was Jasper Tomsett Judge, Windsor correspondent of the *Morning Herald* and the *Dispatch*. Judge was an outspoken and obstinate man and had already crossed swords with the Prince. The use of a little diplomacy would have obviated trouble, but the young German either did not appreciate this or would not stoop. Stockmar had so deeply planted in him the belief that he was superior that he now really believed it. This attitude riled Judge. Albert, who would not tolerate any inquiry into his private life, tried to hound the newsman out of Windsor. In retaliation Judge printed parodies of the official, and dull, *Court Circular*. "Her Majesty, attended by Viscountess Jocelyn, went riding in the park on two ponies." "Her Majesty was most graciously pleased during her stay at Windsor to enjoy most excellent health and spirits." Based on the information which he obtained from Saunders, Judge compiled and put on sale booklets with suggestive titles such as *Court Jobbery*, *Sketches of Her Majesty's Household* and *The Court and the Press*. As each booklet appeared Albert sent out servants to buy them up. It was an undignified affair. In the end the Prince took Judge to court and, although he won his case, he did not improve his public image by so doing.[27] As for the reorganisation of the administration of the palaces, it was not until 1846 that regulations were introduced which satisfied the requirements of the Prince and Stockmar.[28]

The Queen attempted to bridge the gap between the amount which she had expected her husband's income to be, and that which Parliament decided that in fact it was to be, by handing out to him valuable sinecures. He was a Field Marshal, Colonel of the 11th Hussars, Governor of Windsor Castle, Warden of the Round Tower and Lord Warden of the

Stannaries, the Stannary Courts holding jurisdiction over the tin mines in Devon and Cornwall. Of the last post one newspaper commented that Albert was admirably fitted to fill it as he was so well able to look after the "tin", but another was more severe:

Here was a beardless young gentleman, hardly able to speak consecutive sentences in English, totally unacquainted with English jurisprudence, to say nothing of the complexity of our laws, solemnly sitting for six hours, as judge, hearing long legal arguments of abstruse character. What a farce![29]

Yet it was from the Duchies of Cornwall and Lancaster that the main flow of the wealth of Albert and Victoria stemmed. In the late 1830s they produced approximately £16,000 and £27,000 per year. Both revenues were enjoyed by the Queen until 1841 when Cornwall, being the legal appanage of the heir-apparent, passed to the Prince of Wales on his birth. In the skilful hands of Albert, the income from the Duchy of Lancaster was increased to £60,000, and that of Cornwall to £66,000.[30] The royal bank account, which for some years had been close to the red, soon showed an impressive credit, the figure being further swelled, it was rumoured, by Albert's dabbling in railways shares.

As their family increased, the royal parents decided that the public owed it to them to provide them with a better house in London. Duly prompted, the Queen wrote to Sir Robert Peel early in 1845 stating that the accommodation in Buckingham Palace was not "decent" and that generally the place was "a *disgrace*". Peel replied that, owing to a nationwide perturbation about Income Tax, it would be advisable to delay a test of public feeling for a while. As George IV had squandered upwards of a million pounds on the building, the public reaction was not difficult to forecast. Albert kept up the pressure. He obtained from Mr. Blore, the architect, a heart-rending document, revealing that the children were confined to a few rooms in the attics, intended for servants, that all day long the noise of hammering came from the Palace workshop below and that the smell of oil and glue was stifling. The following year Peel quoted this report to the Lords of the Treasury and, touched, they passed an estimate of £150,000 to put matters right.[31]

Punch was incensed. A cartoon appeared showing the

216

Prince, cap in hand and surrounded by his family, addressing the ragged folk of London:

Good People, pray take compassion on us. It is now nearly seven years since either of us have known the blessing of a comfortable residence. If you do not believe us, good people, come and see where we live, at Buckingham Palace, and you will be satisfied that there is no deception in our story. Such is our distress, that we should be truly grateful for the blessing of a comfortable two-pair back, with commonly decent sleeping rooms for our children and domestics. With our slender means, and our increasing family, we declare to you that we do not know what to do. The sum of one hundred and fifty thousand pounds will be all that will be required to make the needful alterations in our dwelling. Do, good people, bestow your charity to this little amount, and may you never live to feel the want of so small a trifle.

The Palace at this time surrounded only three sides of the quadrangle, the fourth, facing the Mall, being open, the Marble Arch standing as a detached gateway. The estimate included the building of a new front, alterations to the north and south wings, new kitchens and offices, overhaul of the drains, removal of the Marble Arch, the building of a new ballroom, and painting and decorating throughout. The figure of £150,000 was patently unrealistic. The removal of the Marble Arch alone cost £30,000 and by the time the ballroom was finished in 1856 the figure for it was near to £300,000.[32] Another addition to the amenities was a pavilion erected in the grounds in 1846. A most interesting structure, the tiled floors being among the first of their kind, it was an indication of the Prince's flair for design and an example of how his taste was to change fashion. It was demolished in the late 1920s.[33]

For seaside holidays the royal pair could go to the Pavilion at Brighton, but neither felt happy there. Albert found the extravaganza of George IV exceedingly strange. In addition, it was someone else's idea and he liked to do his own thinking. He complained of the growth of the town, the size of the bedrooms, the lack of gardens and the general want in respect of the holidaymakers. Frankly, he did not like Brighton and Brighton did not like him.*[34] What he wanted, and his wife also, was a place where he could live in seclusion,

* The Pavilion was sold to Brighton Corporation in 1850.

design and organise as he liked, and spend money without asking for permission. Victoria thought of the Isle of Wight, which she had known as a child. She wrote in the autumn of 1843:

> During our usual morning walk, Albert and I talked of buying a place of our own; perhaps Norris Castle would be something to think of.[35]

Sir Robert Peel, called in to advise, made enquiries, as a result of which Osborne was recommended as a more suitable proposition, having a gentleman's residence, a park, a wood and a secluded beach. The drawback was the price. The owner, Lady Isabella Blatchford, was asking £30,000, quoting the obvious development possibility. The farm belonged to Winchester College, being held on copyright tenure, and the scholars wanted £20,000 for the freehold. Peel and Anson held up their hands in horror and beseeched the Prince to withdraw. Instead he took a year's lease for £1,000, maybe working on the theory that possession was worth.more than nine-tenths of the law when H.M. the Queen was *in situ*. In 1845 the whole estate was purchased for £26,000, which proved that Albert was growing up fast.[36]

Old Osborne House, as shown in a water-colour by H. M. Sinclair of 1833, was Georgian, of three storeys and somewhat dull.[37] It was quickly pulled down and the first stone of the new mansion was laid on 23rd June of that year. Albert had his plans ready—a version of an Italian villa with campaniles and a first-floor balcony. For professional advice he turned to Thomas Cubitt, the architect and builder of much of Belgravia. Thus came into fashion a style which spread throughout the country before the century was over. Under Albert's tireless direction the builders sped about their work and the royal family were able to move in in September 1846, although the accommodation for the Household was not completed until five years later.[38] The total cost was around £200,000. Additional land was purchased, bringing the acreage up to two thousand and allowing Albert to indulge in his hobby of tree-planting. He loved trees and was an expert upon them. Victoria bathed for the first time in September 1847 and considered the waters of the Solent delightful until she put her head under—"when I thought I should be stifled".[39]

Albert was never happier than when planning the details

for estates and buildings and, once Osborne had become a reality, he looked for a further project to occupy his restless, brilliant mind and also one which would prove a good investment. Both the Queen and he had fallen in love with Scotland, whither they had journeyed in 1842, 1844 and 1847. On their last visit, to Ardverikie on the shore of Loch Laggan, the weather had been terrible, but this did not deter them and during that autumn at Windsor evening conversation centred round the purchase of a home in the Highlands.

In Scotland Albert looked for certain essentials to his well-being, both of mind and body. His youth was slipping away from him with a rapidity which can only be described as startling. By twenty-six he had endured "frightful torture" from rheumatism,[40] and his comment in a letter from Blair in 1844 that "the romantic, mountain life acts as a tonic to the nerves"[41] shows a degree of mental strain unusual in a man so young. Peace, solitude, bracing air, a dry climate and the chance to relax while out with his gun were necessary as an antidote to the ceaseless round of State duties which were his lot at Buckingham Palace and Windsor.

The Queen was also suffering from twinges of rheumatism and her doctor, Sir James Clark, suggested that Deeside, sheltered from the wild weather by the Cairngorm mass, would be a suitable area for the royal couple to look for a holiday home. The Prince went into action, researching into weather records and commissioning artists to make drawings of the countryside. He was quick to decide and in May of 1848 signed a lease with the Fife Trustees, "assigning over Balmoral to Prince Albert".[42] Once again he had used the vehicle of a lease to gain possession, but this time the lease was in his own name.

Albert had astonishing vision. He not only wished to purchase Balmoral as soon as the chance came but also wanted to include Abergeldie—the neighbouring estate to the east— and beyond that the 6,500 acres of Birkhall, at the head of Glen Muick. Birkhall was to be the Scottish seat of the Prince of Wales, and bought for him from the income of the Duchy of Cornwall, and Abergeldie was to be available for visiting members of the family, in particular the Duchess of Kent. He also planned to purchase the great forest of Ballochbuie and, to ensure privacy, to close the road which ran along the south bank of the Dee from Balmoral to Invercauld.

Although the Prince succeeded in purchasing Birkhall from the Gordons, they could not bear to part with Abergeldie, with which they had been associated for so long and from which they had taken their name. Instead a lease of forty years was offered, and accepted. Successive leases followed and the arrangement continues to this day. Albert's dream of possessing Ballochbuie eventually became a reality but not until seventeen years after he was dead. The road along the south bank was closed in 1857. As for the purchase of Balmoral, Albert found greater difficulty than he had experienced in the case of Osborne, and it was not until June 1852 that he became the owner of the 17,400 acre estate, paying 30,000 guineas.[43] Meantime the royal family had to content themselves with the cramped conditions of the old castle. Yet it was perhaps fortunate that the start of a new house was delayed as Albert had much work concerning building on his hands. He was occupied with the Great International Exhibition.

It was the Exhibition of 1851 which, above any other achievement in his life, merited the Prince the right to stand in his high place on the Albert Memorial. It was in the Crystal Palace in Hyde Park that, to the minds of millions, a transfiguration took place, switching an obscure German princeling into a national figure and a leader in the spheres of industry, art and science. It was not only in the public eye that the image changed. On that triumphant May day when the crowds flocked to see the wonders housed in Paxton's "Palace of Glass", Queen Victoria revelled in the realisation that she was married to a man of achievement, a man who had proved himself. She wrote to the then Prime Minister:

> The Queen, at the risk of not appearing modest (and yet why should a wife ever be modest about her husband's merits?), must say that she thinks Lord John Russell will admit now that the Prince is possessed of very extraordinary powers of mind and heart. She feels so proud of being his wife that she cannot refrain from herself paying a tribute to his noble character.[44]

It was the Prince's idea that the Exhibition should be international—the first of its kind ever held. It was the Prince who had to take the burden of the attack which raged over the desecration of Hyde Park and the invasion of foreigners. His health suffered as a result of the strain of work and worry. He wrote:

I am more dead than alive from over-work. The opponents of the Exhibition work with might and main to throw all the old women into panic, and to drive myself crazy. The strangers, they give out, are certain to commence a thorough revolution here, to murder Victoria and myself, and to proclaim the Red Republic in England; the plague is certain to ensue from the confluence of such vast multitudes, and to swallow up those whom the increased price of everything has not already swept away. For all this I am to be responsible, and against all this I have to make efficient provision.[45]

Albert confounded his critics. Over six million people wandered, starry-eyed, round his dream palace, and the overall profit was £186,000. To this figure we owe, amongst other educational and cultural assets in South Kensington, the Victoria and Albert Museum.

The Prince made a special contribution of his own to the Exhibition—his idea of "model houses for the working classes". Three hundred and fifty thousand people inspected them at a site at the Cavalry Barracks, Hyde Park. Built to house four labouring-class families, they each had a living-room, three bedrooms and a scullery. An unusual feature was the use of hollow bricks, it being claimed that these prevented damp, lessened fire risk and deadened noise. The price of a set of four homes was £458. 14. 7.* A genuine Albert touch was that, from where the parents sat in the living-room, they were able to keep a watchful eye on their young in the bedroom.[46]

No sooner was the Exhibition closed than Albert set about preparing drawings for his *Schloss* beside the Dee, his architect being William Smith of Aberdeen. He planned in Scottish baronial style and the following September a site, one hundred yards to the north-west of the old house, was settled upon. Building began in the spring of 1853 and presented many problems. The workmen had been recruited from a distance and were housed in wooden barracks. One night these barracks were gutted by fire, necessitating rebuilding and the recompense from the royal purse for possessions lost. Working conditions were hard and there were several strikes, the Prince commenting, that these were "now quite the fashion all over the country". Yet when the royal family arrived for their autumn holiday in 1855 they were able to

* In 1852 the houses were transferred to Kennington Park and thereafter occupied by park officials.

move into the new Balmoral and by the following year all traces of the old house had disappeared. By 1859 Prince Albert had completed his plans for the policies.[47]

In his last decade the Prince was concerned with many other building projects—the Royal Pavilion at Aldershot, a pinewood-walled dwelling erected for the Queen's visit to the camp in 1854, and the library there[48]—the church of St. Mildred at Whippingham in the Isle of Wight—Wellington College—schools for tenants at Windsor and on Deeside— to mention but a few. At the same time he was farming, most efficiently, at Windsor, Osborne and Balmoral and introducing up-to-date cottages and farm structures. It was in the sphere of agricultural building that his best work of design is to be found—the dairy and creamery at Frogmore, which was completed in 1858. Here, in the elaborate interior, "he was able to experiment and to show that his taste was abreast of the times".[49]

Albert's last, and largest, property deal was made in the summer of 1861. It was a home for his heir. Prompted by Stockmar, he had come to the conclusion that the only hope of salvation for the flighty Prince of Wales was to install him in an establishment of his own (a wife, to decorate it, had already been selected). As through the father's efficiency, parsimony and astuteness, a sum of £600,000 had been accumulated in the son's bank account, finance was no problem. Here was a chance for the princeling who had arrived from Coburg twenty years before with a paltry allowance of £2,400 per year to really show his flair. He worked alone, not rating his son capable of making a railway journey unattended, let alone have a say in the handling of a business deal. Just as Albert had listed the likely young ladies as candidates to marry "Bertie", finally selecting Princess Alexandra of Denmark, now he made a list of possible homes. By 1860 three had survived his minute examination— Houghton and Sandringham in Norfolk and Bramshill in Hampshire. He decided on Sandringham and put down £220,000 for a sizeable shooting lodge, some 8,000 acres and a rent roll of £7,000.[50] Within weeks his agents and his keepers were in action, rebuilding Appleton farm, planning game-shelters and waging war on the poachers. The independent country folk of Norfolk felt ill at east as the influx of officials changed the order of life which had survived the centuries. But Albert never realised his dream of leading mighty battues and of building a royal mansion on the hill above Dersingham. Before the next year was out he was dead.

CHAPTER EIGHTEEN

Papa Albert

*A*LBERT AND VICTORIA had nine children. The crises and squabbles, tantrums and depressions which accompanied the births of "Vicky", Princess Royal, and "Bertie", Prince of Wales, disappeared once Albert became master of the house, and only reappeared during the Queen's last two confinements when the combination of pregnancy and surrounding adolescents proved a strain on her mental stability. The following is a time-table of later arrivals, together with christian name and sobriquet:

1843	Alice (Fatima)
1844	Alfred (Affie)
1846	Helena (Lenchen)
1848	Louise (Loo-loo)
1850	Arthur
1853	Leopold
1857	Beatrice (Baby)

With the passing years the Queen became accustomed to the invasion of her bodily privacy and at length reached a stage of familiarity with the situation which enabled her to issue instructions as to the action to be taken at critical moments. The births of Alice, Alfred and Helena were routine and uneventful. Louise arrived in the midst of a European storm, waves of revolution sweeping through France, Germany and Italy. Louis Philippe and his Queen reached safety at Newhaven disguised as Mr. and Mrs. William Smith. The King had discarded his wig and was wearing a flat cap and goggles.[1] Albert and Victoria were in a frenzy of worry and excitement at the thought of jobless and penniless Coburgs wandering around Europe and, maybe as a result, the Queen had a very difficult time during the birth of her fourth daughter. She forecast that the child would grow into "something peculiar",[2] which she did. The situation was relatively peaceful by the time of the arrival of Arthur, a child who "from his earliest moments, displayed that serenity of temper and sweetness of disposition which are greatly promoted by a fine constitution".[3] He lasted ninety-two years. "That blessed Chloroform" was used for the first time at the birth of Leopold, a sufferer from haemophilia. Nervous upset accompanied the belated appearance of the last child, Beatrice, yet all was well. Albert wrote to Princess Augusta of Prussia:

> We had to wait a fortnight beyond the time for the princess, and she kept us waiting at the door for 13 hours before she would come in. You will gather how nicely all is arranged when I tell that the two nurses' names are Mrs. Lilly and Mrs. Innocente![4]

The sense of humour of the pamphleteers on the subject of the Queen's expensive fecundity was of a more bawdy character:

> *I must get all things I can*
> *A child's chair and a small brown pan,*
> *Nine hundred and forty gallons of rum,*
> *And a sponge to wash her little bum.*

Sir James Clark, the chief physician, had already warned the Prince Consort* that the Queen should have no more children.[5] It was the mental state, rather than the physical, that he feared, for the feeling was now growing upon Victoria, during her pregnancies, that she would die in childbirth, a haunting echo from the fate of her cousin, Princess Charlotte. Yet, after the birth of Beatrice, a wave of elation flooded through her and Clark spoke to her directly on the point, fearing that she would attempt to bring her brood up to ten. Queen Victoria described her doctor as "He to whom I could say almost anything, who was so wise, so discreet".[6] Expert opinion was divided on the point of his wisdom, bearing in mind his diagnosis of Lady Flora Hastings and his treatment of Prince Albert during his last illness. As for discretion, it has been passed down that he revealed, to members of his own profession, the Queen's reply to his advice that she should have no more children.[7] The reply was: "Oh, Sir James, can I have no more fun in bed?"

The remark, coming from Queen Victoria and bearing in mind the image into which she was created, may appear out

---

* The title conferred upon Prince Albert on 25th June 1857.

of character, yet it might have been made in like circumstances by any woman seeking to avoid more direct wording. In truth, sex was both fun and a necessity to her. When she wrote of a miserable night spent with Albert at Dalwhinnie in October 1861—"No pudding and no *fun*"[8]—she was not referring to the lack of a ten-pin alley. One has only to read the letters which passed between the Queen and her elder daughters during the period 1862-4 to realise the necessity. When visiting England in 1862 "Vicky", by this time Crown Princess Frederick William of Prussia, wrote to her husband that her mother "is always consumed with longing for her husband . . . Mama had so desperately longed for another child".[9]

What Vicky was delicately touching upon was the Queen's sexual solitude and loss. She realised that her mother was, on her own account, a woman of violent emotions. Her reference to the longing for another child was a veiled allusion to the physical presence by her side in bed which was denied to her at a difficult age, forty-two, in the life of a woman. The Queen wrote frankly that she was being "driven mad with desire and longing".[10]

However, the doctor's warning must have been noted by Albert, for there were no more natal alarms. It was widely rumoured in April 1858 that the Queen was (to use her own words) in an "unhappy condition", but she dismissed this as, "Odious . . . Really too bad."[11]

It is interesting to note how the personal relationship between Albert and Victoria during the pre-natal period showed its lasting effect on the children. The two eldest, conceived and born while Lord Melbourne and Baroness Lehzen still held sway over the Queen, and Albert was fighting to overthrow their influence, were in a class apart from the other seven. These two caused their parents more trouble and anxiety than all the others put together. Albert and Victoria never guessed why or realised that the root cause lay with themselves. The Queen told "Vicky" very plainly in 1858, after her marriage, of the problem that she had been in her younger days:

> . . . a more insubordinate and unequal tempered child and girl I think I never saw! . . . The trouble you gave us all—was indeed very great. Comparatively speaking, we have none whatever with the others. You and Bertie (in very different ways) were indeed great difficulties.[12]

But if "Vicky" did not find favour with Mama, she had the consolation of knowing that she was her father's pride and joy and she became the willing receptacle for his dreams and hopes. The real tragedy came with "Bertie", picked, even before he arrived, to be the big, bright star in the Coburg firmament. It was his bad fortune that he was born while the relationship between his parents was at its lowest ebb, while Stockmar was striving to break the link between the Queen and "Lord M." and Albert was hurling his imprecations and accusations at Lehzen. Both growth and speech were retarded —his governess reported in 1844: "He is not articulate like his sister . . . altogether backward in language . . . still very small in every way."[13]

Alice, Alfred and Helena were normal, healthy, high-spirited children. That Alice later suffered from nerves was because she had to take the major burden during her father's fatal illness and thereafter support a mother who was near to a complete mental breakdown. Louise, born in the tumult of fears of 1848, was an odd child and apart from the rest, and in after years the intimate touch between mother and daughter just disappeared. Arthur was conceived at a very happy time for the Queen and her husband—the first, triumphant visit to Ireland, followed by a holiday at Balmoral. No bothers with this boy. He became his mother's favourite and could say things to her which none of his brothers and sisters dared. The birth of her youngest son, Leopold, upset the Queen considerably, although he arrived cushioned in the mists of chloroform. There were a number of reasons: firstly, she found the stares of her elder children, who knew nothing of sex, disconcerting; secondly, she began to feel that she was getting old, mourning the loss of familiar figures such as Melbourne, Peel, Queen Adelaide, the Duke of Cambridge and Louis Philippe; thirdly, the boy was plainly delicate and there was little place for weaklings in overcrowded Victorian nurseries. So often little boxes went up the churchyard path and only an entry in a family Bible thereafter gave trace of an infant's passing. The Queen's initial answer to the problem was to change the wet nurse. She was apt to bully the boy as he grew older, with the unfeeling towards the unorthodox which was the pattern of the times. Haemophilia was a mystery but when such information as was known was explained to the Queen, she affirmed, and correctly, that the disease had not appeared in the House of Hanover.[14] Accordingly one must search in the tables of Coburg. It has been suggested that the conveyor was the Duchess of Kent, yet no sign of it appeared in her two children sired by the Prince of Leiningen. Infant deaths might provide a clue—in 1834 Louis, son of King Leopold of the Belgians, died aged one year. The health record of Albert's mother, the Duchess Louise, must be considered. She is known to have suffered two haemorrhages, the second ending her young life. Here, possibly, is a more likely source than the boisterous Duchess of Kent.

Yet, despite haemophilia, nerves, the curiosity of adolescents and her dislike of the physical experience, Queen Victoria produced again in 1857. The Queen experienced post-natal elation, strangely enough, and this appears to have communicated itself to the daughter. Beatrice was an *enfant terrible*. At the age of three she tied her mother to her chair by her apron strings. On being told by the Queen that a certain pudding was not good for her, she replied, "But she likes it, my dear," and helped herself.[15] Albert held no terrors for her. One breakfast time she announced: "I was very naughty last night. I would not speak to Papa, but it doesn't signify much!"[16]

One of the reasons why Victoria continued to bear children was her belief that, by doing so, she kept her grip on Albert. She demanded all of him, every piece of him, and was even jealous of her daughters. When she was pregnant he was always kind, thoughtful, attentive of her every wish. Here was a problem that he could understand, a train of events to which he could attend. But he knew nothing of the imponderable in women. He was completely inexperienced. He did not appreciate the unreasoned emotions which surged like a maelstrom in Victoria's brain. Albert's answer to all the problems of life was to exercise reason. Coached in the art by Stockmar, he could out-reason nearly everybody, as men who served him, such as Sir Charles Phipps, bore witness. (Exceptions were Lord Palmerston and the Prince of Wales.) Collecting together all the relevant information on paper, he would analyse possible causes, situations and intentions, and produce the answer as a magician produces a rabbit out of a hat. When Victoria began throwing things and screaming her accusations into his face, he would retire to write a paper on the cause of the outburst. She would then receive a letter beginning "Dear Child" and containing simple ingredients for an antidote to emotion. This did not help matters. Albert soon learned that any action that he took at such times was wrong. Answering back led to faster, louder vituperation. Remaining quiet was classified as insulting. Retiring behind a locked door eventually led to an attack upon its panels by royal fists. If Albert had taken a stiff whisky, armed himself with a stick and chased H.M. along the corridor and up the stairs, he would have discovered that tantrums would have been less frequent and accompanied by less bravado. Yet, in fairness to Albert, that course would have called for a strong man. Even Melbourne, a pastmaster at dealing with women, had on one occasion quavered and feared to sit down as the fire blazed in the eyes of the eighteen-year-old Queen. A Cabinet minister was known to fly from her presence, too frightened to follow the rule of withdrawal. Thus Albert looked forward to the periods of pregnancy—it gave emotion a reason.

He might have tackled his wife's emotional crises by a simpler method—by making her laugh. Laughter was an essential to her, the natural safety-valve. Melbourne knew it. People who knew her before her marriage commented that she was always laughing. They seldom saw her so after her marriage: Coburgs did not laugh. As Leopold said to Charlotte, "Less of the lightness, if you please, Madame." Either the ridiculous or the bawdy would set Victoria off.

Thus Albert suffered in his marriage from the lack of two basic elements—strength and a sense of humour. Victoria, although not unsympathetic, never understood weakness, either in mind or body. The only excuse for not being present at dinner was sudden death. She credited the lack of physical desire to a diminution of mental love and trust. Albert was an ill man from 1851 onwards. Instead of slowing down, he speeded up—racing now to accomplish the tasks set for him by Stockmar, to overcome those who had opposed him, to right so many English wrongs.

In some ways Albert and Victoria were well suited to one another. When things went right, they went very, very right. They both loved music, history, fresh air and the mountains. They had a common interest in the family relationship. She admired his mental powers, his appreciation of the arts, his capacity for work, his efficiency. Because he had few, if any, close friends and was a lonely man, she was as necessary to his domestic life as Stockmar was to the processes of his mind. They missed one another desperately when apart, being more demonstrative in their letters than with the spoken word. In the summer of 1851 he attended the meeting of the British Association for the Advancement of Science at Ipswich and wrote to her from Shrubland Hall:

I feel the want of only one person to give a world of life to everything around me. I hope to fall into the arms of this one person by 7.30 to-morrow evening . . .[17]

In 1857 Albert went alone to Brussels for the wedding of Princess Charlotte to the Archduke Ferdinand Maximilian. Victoria wrote to King Leopold:

You cannot think *combien cela me coûte* or how *déroutée* I am and *feel* when he is away, or how I count the hours till he returns. *All* the numerous children are as *nothing* to me when *he is away*; it seems as if the whole life of the house and home were gone, when he is away![18]

Yet she had already showed the same demand for a man, and her dependence on him, in the case of Lord Melbourne, and she was later to do it again when John Brown came upon the scene.

Albert and Victoria were fortunate in their marriage in that they were spared any tittle of suspicion regarding the faithfulness of the other. This connubial hazard, which has to be faced by so many couples. simply did not exist in their case. Yet the condition was exceptional, such purity, extending through both the married and unmarried state, being unrivalled in the story of the royal house. It is most doubtful if the marriage would have survived a slip by either party. Her mental state, and his physical, would not have withstood the strain.

As the Queen showed in her letter to King Leopold, quoted above, Albert meant more to her than all the children lumped together. This was not just a random expression caused by loneliness at her husband's absence. She made it quite clear on other occasions. In October 1856 she wrote to Princess Augusta of Prussia from Balmoral:

I find no especial pleasure or compensation in the company of the elder children. You will remember that I told you this at

Osborne . . . And only very exceptionally do I find the rather intimate intercourse with them either agreeable or easy. You will not understand this, but it is caused by various factors. Firstly, I only feel properly à mon aise and quite happy when Albert is with me; secondly, I am used to carrying on my many affairs quite alone; and then I have grown up all alone, accustomed to the society of adult (and never with younger) people . . .[19]

Albert was a much more frequent visitor to the nursery quarters than Victoria. Each night he would check the security arrangements and the main key was always in his possession.[20] At eight in the morning he would be back again to see that all was well and would carry off one of the younger children to see "Mama". Although he believed in the dogma of Stockmar that "education begins at birth" (the antithesis of the views of Lord Melbourne), he was both sympathetic and understanding with the babies and they would do anything for him. Often he calmed outbursts of temper which had defied the efforts of nurses and governesses. It was only when the children developed views of their own and the capability to answer back that he lost his magic touch. The British public showed great interest in Albert and his growing nursery, fully realising that in due season demand would be made for a healthy income for each of them. A cartoon showed nurse Lilly rocking the Prince of Wales to sleep to the tune of "Hey diddle diddle, the cat and the fiddle". Viewing the scene, the Prince remarks:

Vat you talk such nonsense to mine son for? Tell him he be Prince of Wales and de Duck of Cornwall, den he will understand you much better.[21]

It was only natural that Albert should concentrate his energies on the training and education of his two eldest children. The embryo of the plan to marry "Vicky" into the royal house of Prussia dated from the visit of Frederick William IV to England in 1842. She was to be the British link with the unified, liberal-minded Germany of which Stockmar and his pupil dreamed. The plan worked very well—up to the time of the marriage. "Vicky" was bright, receptive, arrogant. She absorbed everything which her father told her in his nightly lectures as gospel and held on to her beliefs throughout her life. She played her mother off against her father. Victoria was jealous of her influence over Albert and went so far as to say that she would not miss her when she went to Germany as a bride of seventeen. In fact, she missed her a great deal. Albert missed her even more and her absence was a contributory cause for the decline of his health between 1858 and 1861. As a substitute, he took his second daughter, Alice, under his wing. It was she, and not his wife, to whom he turned for comfort and understanding during his last illness.

It was "Vicky" and Alice who laid the wreath of perfection on Albert's brow. The others contributed little towards it. Some did not agree. After Percy Colson had written a cynical study of the Prince Consort, Princess Louise asked him to tea. She greeted him with the words: "You were very naughty, but it is all true."[22] But it was the Prince of Wales who had most cause for complaint.

Albert's treatment of his eldest son was the ultimate in egocentricity. He set a pattern for bullying that was so strong that it reappeared in the parental periods of both Edward VII and George V. Here there emerged streaks of nastiness which it is hard to comprehend. Himself a delicate child, against whom no stick was raised despite his indulgence in unpleasant pranks, one would have thought that he would have been in sympathy with his own boy. Yet "Bertie" was flogged and harried, kept prisoner and fed on hospital diet, worked until his brain scrambled and the screams came and the feet stamped. Victoria joined in. She wanted, and she said so, a replica of Albert. That was precisely the pattern which Albert himself had in mind. He wished to leave behind a talking statue of himself, wafting words of purity and wisdom over Europe and the British Empire. Instead he found himself saddled with an heir whom he described as "the most thorough and cunning lazybones" that he had ever met and was left grieving that such a son would be called upon "to take over the reins of government of a country upon which the sun never sets".[23]

There were few problems with "Bertie" while he remained under the care of the women in the nursery. Lady Lyttelton found him affectionate, gentle and thoughtful for others. The trouble began when he moved into the hands of a tutor at the age of seven. Stockmar had announced that the parents were too young to direct the training of the boy, fearing that they would be too lenient. In the event Albert "devised for his

232

eldest son an educational plan of unparalleled rigour which made no allowance for human weakness".[24] He was to be an exemplar, morally and intellectually perfect. For a decade and more he laboured from Monday to Saturday, the daily stint of study beginning at five hours and later reaching seven. The only holidays were feast days and family birthdays, so that at no time did the boy have respite for more than a few consecutive days. Albert, fearing the upsurge of sexual awareness, ordered the tutors to ensure that their pupil was tired out at the end of each day. Accordingly he was taken for long rides and drilled and taught gymnastics by a sergeant until at bedtime he swayed upon his feet. Meetings with boys of his own age were rare and accordingly there was little rapport. In any case the visitors were too frightened of Prince Albert to be able to play to order. Something in the child had to give, and it took the form of near mental collapse. The first signs were disobedience, impertinence and a revulsion against all discipline. Then it was noticed that he lost his temper when faced with a problem which he could not immediately understand or after a few minutes of exertion at a game. On some days he would refuse to answer any questions at all. "Severe punishment" was inflicted as a possible antidote, but only made matters worse. It may well have been responsible for a new tendency to wish to hurt and discomfort others. One day he went berserk among a flock of sheep, chasing them wildly in all directions. He saw a Palace housemaid's bridal dress laid out on her bed prior to her wedding, smeared it with red ink, and thereafter was whipped by his father.[25] One tutor reported:

He takes everything that is at hand and throws it with the greatest violence against the wall or window, without thinking the least of the consequences of what he is doing; or he stands in the corner stamping his legs and screaming in the most dreadful way.[26]

Three of the men responsible for educating the Prince of Wales reported to his father that the boy was being over-worked and overstressed. Neither of the parents appeared to comprehend. Their contribution of understanding consisted in having "Bertie's" head examined, phrenology being much in fashion at the time. Albert could not bring himself to accept that his heir did not possess the same mental capacity as himself. Victoria saw him as a cartoon of herself, instead of the replica of Albert which she had prayed for. She should have known better, as much the same had happened to her in her childhood when, for a time, she was over-pressed by Lehzen and her mother. She did, in fact, notice the symptoms which heralded the outbursts of temper, in the way in which "Bertie" hung his head and looked at his feet. Too late the truth dawned upon her. In 1870 she wrote to the Crown Princess of Prussia, who was having problems with her second son, Henry. "Believe me," she then said, "more harm than good is done by forcing delicate and backward children."[27]

A particular request of "Bertie's" tutors was that irony and mockery should not be used by the parents as a means of correction.[28] The plea failed. As he passed through his 'teens constant criticism was made of his small head and "enormous features", his large mouth and nose, the way he plastered down his hair and lounged about, his choice of reading material and clothes, and unfavourable comparisons were made between him and his younger brothers and sisters.

The young Prince of Wales was rescued, and rehabilitated, by his visit to Canada and America in 1860. He was a riotous success there and praise flowed back across the Atlantic. Albert wrote with irony to Stockmar: "Bertie is generally pronounced the most perfect product of Nature." On his return he was told that his success had only been due to the fact that he was a child of Victoria and Albert.[29] He was put back at his studies under close guard, but now he was a very changed young man. He had heard the Canadian and American crowds shouting for him alone, he had seen the girls fighting for the chance to dance with him, he had held his own at great occasions. He had proved himself. In the result he began to revolt. He ran away from Cambridge but, owing to the new-fangled telegraph, was caught when he reached London.[30] He made friends of his own age who introduced him to the delights of tobacco and alcohol. While he was in camp with the Guards at the Curragh in 1861 a more sensuous delight in the comely shape of Miss Nellie Clifden, actress, was smuggled into his bedroom. The revelation of this sexual baptism reached Albert as the fever was born inside him. The news was to him a nightmare of physical revulsion of which he could not speak. Victoria, who saw the effect upon him, rated the shock as the cause of his collapse. She refused to summon "Bertie" to attend his father's deathbed. It was Princess Alice who took the action and the Prince of Wales reached Windsor just in time.

CHAPTER NINETEEN

Albert and the Aristocats

*F*OREIGNERS WERE not popular in England when Prince Albert arrived to marry Queen Victoria. The Napoleonic wars had caused the upper classes to become isolationist and events in Europe since Waterloo had done nothing to change their views. Suspicion of those who crossed the Channel showed itself in the studied rudeness so often evinced by those whose policies were walled in with class and nationalism. A German, distinguished in his own country, was invited to stay at a stately home. Conversation was restricted. In an attempt to break the ice with a fellow guest on the terrace after breakfast, the German remarked: "It is bad weather." The reply was: "Yes, but it is better than none." A Frenchman who underwent a similar experience pronounced at its close: "I smile ver' moche, but one such fun was enoff."[1]

Albert was therefore faced with an in-built opposition both to his presence and his position, regardless of his character and approach. As neither his character nor approach fitted in with the accepted ideas, he was obviously in for a hard time. In the event he made very little impression upon the "fine folk" during his twenty years in Britain and it was only at the close that a handful of informed men and women came to admire him for his foresight, intelligence and hard work. Even they never knew him as a friend. The eulogies which the Queen caused to be written by Grey and Martin after his death did not erase the deep-rooted unpopularity, and Sidney Lee, in the first authorised life story of Queen Victoria, published in 1902, wrote:

> Outside the domestic circle the Prince was not liked. He was cold and distant in manner, and his bearing, both mental and physical, was held to be too characteristically German to render it acceptable to Englishmen. His temperament was out of harmony with the habitual ease and levity of the English aristocracy.[2]

The fault lay partly in Albert's upbringing and partly in the preachings of Stockmar. The stock-in-trade of petty German Courts was rank, 'and etiquette was a passion. Frequently suffering from a shortage both of acres and income, the reigning families depended upon their offspring finding favour with the Kings and the Emperors, and marrying well. Small capital towns such as Coburg and Darmstadt owed their continuance solely to the reigning Duke and his Court. The frontage of the streets was decoration, with little thought for the comfort and convenience of those who lived behind it, and, to impress important visitors, avenues led towards the Residence. Policy was directed by the sovereign ruler and no rowdy general elections disturbed the political scene. Criticism was quickly dealt with and Albert never became accustomed to the attacks which were made upon him in Britain.

In these German Courts, where only purple blood counted, the members of the British aristocracy were looked upon as being profligate and flippant and having a false idea of their own importance. It was implanted in Albert that one of his tasks was to reform them and bring them into line. It never entered his calculations that British peers, on their own ground, might consider themselves vastly superior to him. He was surprised when the Duke of Beaufort turned down the suggestion that his son should become a Lord-in-Waiting. Greville commented:

Had he [Albert] not been infatuated with his own dignity, he would never have contemplated the possibility of a young man resigning his office of *aide de camp* to the Duke to go and wait upon him at his trumpery and tiresome Court.[3]

One of the main complaints of the old-established families against Prince Albert was that he attached undue importance to etiquette in everything relating to *himself*.[4] This attitude led to an increase in the number of refusals to meet him at dinner.[5] The grievance showed itself when, in the spring of 1843, the Prince understudied the Queen, who was expecting a child, at the Levées. There were mutterings about an unwarrantable assumption of royal functions, and a number of people stayed away.[6] The Queen was furious and told Peel that she would not tolerate her husband being snubbed. A compromise was agreed, members of the aristocracy being excused kneeling and kissing the Prince's hand.[7]

237

In the chilly, Teutonic atmosphere exuded by Albert, Victoria's Court returned to the exclusiveness of the early Georges. There was no relaxing of the rules. While Englishmen were reluctant to sit in the presence of ladies, the Prince took it for granted that they should stand while he sat—even if they were *enceinte*. The sight of Ladies-in-Waiting standing, often droopingly, in the royal opera box while the Prince sat through a long performance brought forth some very caustic comments.[8]

"Scenes" of any kind were not tolerated. Persigny,* Napoleon III's Ambassador to London, gave a ball for the Queen and Prince at the French Embassy. His wife, determined to steal the show, ordered a very special dress from Paris. Victoria and Albert entered. In their train came a Scottish peeress, garbed in an exact copy of the dress of the hostess. Uttering *"Traîtresse"*, the Ambassadrice advanced and smacked the peeress across the face. Immediately Albert led his wife away towards the peace of Albert Gate. Poor Persigny was recalled to Paris to make his explanations.[9]

An example of the rigidity of Court rule came from a Drawing Room. It was the custom of the Queen to kiss the daughters of dukes, marquesses and earls on their first presentation. In a forgetful moment she made towards bestowing the intimate salute on the wife of a mere knight: A distressed Gentleman-in-Waiting whispered in her ear. "Don't kiss her, Your Majesty, she's not a real lady."[10]

Men took exception to Albert's refusal to dally over the port after dinner at Buckingham Palace and Windsor. He considered that five minutes was enough and extinguished the spark of amusement and story as with a wet cloth. From his personal point of view, this was understandable. He did not like port. He was not interested in anecdotes concerning sex, soldiering or the sea. As most of his guests came from families which were interrelated and knew one another well, much of the conversation was unintelligible to him. So he would rise and leave them—a relief to both sides. Having joined the ladies, he would sing duets with the Queen—she not caring to sing before the gentlemen.[11] It was a most convenient arrangement.

Albert made no attempt to adjust himself to the way of life and thought of those with whom it was his task to mix in his

* Duc de Persigny (1808–72).

adopted country. He criticised accepted rules—such as that which forbade the talking of "shop" in regimental messes.[12] Then there was cricket. He watched a match on the playing fields at Eton. He made special study of one boy, who fielded throughout the period of inspection. It was noted that for some three hours he only moved when a ball came in his direction and when he changed position at the end of an over. To Albert, this was a most terrible waste of time.[13] The boy could have obtained as much exercise by jumping up and down in the same place continuously for a few minutes. And goodness only knew what thoughts of aberration might stray into his empty mind as he lounged about unoccupied in the deep field.

Albert was much disliked by the boys at Eton. They said that he dare not take "headers" when swimming, and were much annoyed when he broke off a fine run with the harriers so that he might return to have *Mittagessen* at Windsor. There were sniggers of delight when the Prince ruined a new pair of lavender kid gloves while laying a foundation stone for new school buildings.[14] Doubtless it was the attitude of the Eton boys which influenced Albert when he laid down the rules for good conduct and behaviour to be observed at Wellington College, an educational project in which he took the greatest interest, attempting to inject the German method.

It was his adherence to, and preference for, Teutonic ways which escalated his unpopularity and one of them, his method of slaughtering game, led to a Press campaign against him of unparalleled ferocity. Albert was a battue man. So, in truth, were his eldest son, Edward VII, and his eldest grandson, Kaiser William II—on a grey granite rock in the forest of Rominten was inscribed, in letters of gold: "Here His Majesty William II brought down His Most High's fifty thousandth animal, a white cock-pheasant."[15] True sportsmanship returned to Britain with George V and George VI. But while King Edward and the Kaiser revelled in the titillation of their egos through adulation, the splendour of the covert scene, the leisurely lunch in the marquee with the ladies, the oral resurrection of personal achievement when well dined and wined in the evening, Albert the Consort regarded the killing operation as one to be conducted with the maximum of efficiency in the shortest possible time, without interference with his hot lunch. Missed shots infuriated him.

Calling out, "*Anson, di gonn*", he would seize his secretary's weapon before that unfortunate man had had the chance to fire.[16]

To ensure the scheduled bag, a multiplicity of victims was essential, and hares were purchased in lots of a hundred. Bird and beast were preserved with such care that they learned little of self-preservation until it was too late. A morning's sport in Windsor Park in 1845 was thus described:

> The Royal Party repaired to a battue of hares; fifty beaters went forward in such close order that their sticks rattled against one another. The hares rushed out in masses and in a few minutes the ground was strewn with dead and dying animals, while the wounded tried to limp away. Keepers were ordered to follow them and give them the *coup de grâce*. "It was curious," wrote *The Times* correspondent, "how reluctant the hares were to leave their cover." The pheasants also afforded fine opportunity for butchery, some of them being so tame that they had to be shot sitting.[17]

The English could not understand this at all and they heartily disapproved. They themselves shot as a pastime and for the pot. A few friends would go out for the day, with a beater and a couple of dogs, taking a cold lunch with them. Birds flew fast and hares and rabbits were as wild as they should be.

But it was over the unhappy fate of deer that home opinion boiled over. At the time of the purchase of Osborne there was a herd of fallow-deer in the park and Albert considered that they would play havoc with the gardens which he had planned. So he introduced an idea from Coburg known there as "a drive in the old style". In brief, this meant that animals were drive into a stockade and then shot down by marksmen, secure on a raised stage. The throats of the wounded were cut and soon the ground was thick with corpses. Albert either knew so little of the British or was so entirely impervious to their views that he invited the Queen to take a comfortable chair and enjoy the sport.[18] There were cries of "massacre". Albert had been warned. Yet, when on a visit to Coburg, he and the Queen attended an even more bloodthirsty drive, bands playing as the slaughter took place.* The Press, and in particular *Punch*, decided that the Queen must not be again opened to criticism by her presence at such cruel scenes. On

---

* A detailed description appears in this author's *Victoria Travels*.

future journeys abroad the Prince was carefully watched and, although he took part in no more deer drives, he was severely handled for his participation in a drive of wild boars in 1860.[19]

His sporting activities in Scotland landed him in a certain amount of trouble. Of the day when he shot nineteen deer, it was written:

> *Then from the scene that viewed his warlike toils*
> *The blood-stained victor hastens with his spoils,*
> *And laid them humbly at Victoria's feet—*
> *To such a Queen most intellectual treat.*
> *So on the grass plot—to a shambles changed—*
> *The gory things were scrupulously ranged,*
> *Before the windows of the Royal guest*
> *Famed for the woman-softness of her breast.*[20]

There was a report that deer were driven past the Prince at Balmoral, so that he might have some practice and show his skill, but there was no recurrence. He adjusted himself to the accepted way of life in Scotland to a degree which he found impossible at Windsor. Even then the desire to win at any price still showed.

On the wide, flat peat land at the foot of Lochnagar the deer gathered in the evenings, for the feeding was good. They were at peace, the nature of the ground making stalking difficult. Albert conceived the plan of digging a trench two miles long, with side trenches branching from it, so that he might creep up unobserved upon his prey. The ghillies were forthright in their criticism of a "German trick" and "furrin ways".[21]

Albert and Victoria were happier and more relaxed in Scotland than in England. On returning to Windsor in 1858, the Queen wrote: "The heartache I suffer each year, on leaving Balmoral and coming here, is most distressing."[22] He felt a new man in the clean mountain air. He was complete master, as he owned Balmoral, and, as he was solely responsible for the domestic and estate arrangements, he was freed from the multitude of restrictions and customs which complicated life in the state-owned palaces. He was happier because the scenery reminded him of Thuringia—a similarity which he increased by the importation of trees from Coburg. He was more at ease with the Celt as there was in common a misunderstanding of the Sassenach. Before the railways bridged it, the gap between North and South of the Border was wide indeed. (There was a tale about the first English tourists. A baboon in a travelling menagerie died and its body was left by a lonely Highland roadside. Two crofters found it and, perplexed as to its identity, hurried to the new hotel to enquire if one of the English strangers was missing.)²³

Except for the short and flamboyant visit of George IV to Edinburgh in 1822, during which he managed to indulge in his favourite pastime of involvement with a lady, no reigning monarch had visited Scotland since Charles I. During the eighteenth century the sole royal incursion was that of William Augustus, Duke of Cumberland, son of George II, who was nicknamed "Butcher" for his cruelty and ruthlessness at the battle of Culloden in 1746. With the nightmare of Drummossie Moor and the torture, persecution and ignominy which came in its wake still strong in the memories of the Scottish people, it was refreshing for them to meet a serious young couple with children who were enchanted with the scenery and people of the Highlands. Even if the husband spoke with a strong German accent, he was obviously a friendly foreigner. The deep seated hatred of the Stuart followers for the Hanovers remained well hid away, dwindling with successive generations. Except for the throwing of a leg of mutton at the royal carriage in the streets of Edinburgh, there was little sign. The missile from the butcher's shop hit the Queen's bonnet and an onlooker recorded that he never saw such fierce ire expressed in any face.²⁴

There was, quite naturally, a segment of opinion in the upper classes which poked fun at the new-found nationality of the royal couple. Balmoral was known as "Kailyard Castle", but it was not until seventy years after Albert's death that the term "Balmorality" was coined—"the deadening slime of Balmorality, a glutinous compound of hypocrisy, false senti-ment, industrialism, ugliness and clammy pseudo-Calvinism".²⁵ That was back-looking with a magnifying glass which distorts the truth. In life the Prince had no such hostile attack to face. It was said of him that he was "excessively padded and belted"²⁶ when appearing at the Braemar games and it was noted that there was a lack of "whipcord in his thews". Odd indeed he appeared, as he aged, in the red and green of the Royal Stuart, for the Saxon countenance, the high temples and the slouching gait were never intended to be companions of the kilt. Yet Albert was more welcome at the great houses of Scotland than of England, and Scone, Blair Atholl and Taymouth remember him well. The mountains and the lochs brought out all that was good in him.

There were sly digs at the fondness of the Queen and the Prince for the tartan—"tartanitis" it has been called. Certainly the sudden royal efflorescence of Scottish garb and decoration must have appeared strange to lairds who well remembered that only a long lifetime before King George had forbidden Highlanders to wear the kilt or play the pipes. The Queen had her own Victorian tartan and the black, red and lavender on grey of the Balmoral was designed by Albert. The new Castle was clothed in tartan from the doorway to the roof. Carpets, curtains and upholstery and sofa covers[27] proclaimed the love for Scotland, while figures of Highlanders held lamps aloft and posed upon the tables. Lady Augusta Bruce described it:

The carpets are Royal Stuart Tartan and green Hunting Stuart, the curtains, the former lined with red, the same dress Stuart and a few chintz with a thistle pattern, the chairs and sofas in the drawing room are "dress Stuart" poplin. All highly characteristic and appropriate, but not all equally *flatteux* to the eye.[28]

Generally, the Scots accepted the tendency to exaggerate as a compliment to their country and a welcome boost to local industry.

When Albert was in Scotland, "his nature expanded and became simplified, and the hauteur in which he so often shrouded himself was banished". Sir Charles Lyell noticed this,[29] as did Greville on his first visit to Balmoral:

On Thursday morning John Russell and I were sitting together after breakfast, when he came in and sat down with us, and we conversed for about three-quarters of an hour. I was greatly struck with him . . . He seemed very much at his ease, very gay, pleasant, and without the least stiffness or air of dignity.[30]

Yet it was as if Albert carried a mask in his travelling bag, for there was little resemblance between the relaxed and happy face which left on the overnight train from Scotland and the tight-lipped, serious countenance which emerged at Windsor. The preachings and the presence of Stockmar had something to do with the change, for the German doctor had allowed no time for relaxation and humanity in the curriculum which he had set. Yet in the main it was the under-beat of hostility from the élite of England which caused the transformation. Albert did not mind opposition—on occasions he even welcomed it—provided he was allowed to reason with his opponent, but one could not reason with an unwritten code of class behaviour which had been passed from father to son through the centuries. His wife was fully conscious of the rift—she had learned her lessons well from Lord Melbourne. It worried her. She watched closely and was delighted when a Duke went so far as to hand coffee to the Prince after dinner, for she knew that that Duke was "immensely proud".[31] Yet Albert's attitude of aloof non-cooperation grew more marked with the passing years and he restricted his conversations to those with men of the arts and sciences. Not even the Great International Exhibition earned him good marks. Lady Lyttelton wrote:

I believe it is quite universally sneered at by the *beau monde*, and will only increase the contempt for the Prince among all fine folk. But so would anything he does . . .[32]

Overwork and ill health caused an increase in his irritability and impatience. More and more did he treat the members of the Household as if they were recalcitrant schoolboys. When an engagement took him near to the famed gardens of Mr. Fulke Greville, Albert, as President of the Royal Horticultural Society,* decided that it was an excellent opportunity to inspect them. Accordingly an equerry was sent up to the house with the message that the Prince Consort would like to walk round the gardens incognito. The morning peace of Fulke Greville being shattered by the news that the husband of the Queen was within his boundaries, the detail of the message was not absorbed. The first duty, as he saw it, was to be a good host, and a message was hurried to the kitchen that a special luncheon should be prepared. Then, having gathered all available members of his family about him, Mr. Greville set off to greet the royal visitor. Albert was sighted in contemplation of a flower bed. The owner halted his party, delivered a short speech of welcome, stressed the honour of the occasion and extended an invitation to lunch.

The result was very different to that which he had anticipated. The Prince turned his back and in ice-cold tones

* 1857–61.

addressed the members of his suite: "Didn't I say I wished no notice taken of me?" Nonplussed, Greville stammered out an apology, but added that he still considered that he should honour the Consort of the Sovereign. Albert ignored him and once again addressed his silent suite: "Didn't I say I wished no notice taken of me?" This studied rudeness proved too much for Fulke Greville to bear, and he snapped out to those in attendance on the Prince: "Warn the Prince Consort off my grounds!" This producing no effect, the order was repeated, more loudly: "Warn the Prince Consort off my grounds." With the solemnity of a funeral procession, the royal party moved away in silence towards the gate.[33]

Soon afterwards Albert died and on many country estates was remembered, rather mistily, as "that German fellah" whom the Queen had married. As Victoria looked for the last time at his dead face she turned to the Duchess of Sutherland and said: *"Will they do him justice now?"*[34]

Some men, like Lord Palmerston and the Duke of Argyll,[35] paid full tribute. Others did not. The Earl of Orford exclaimed, "That at least is one foreigner safely out of the way,"[36] and Lady Dorothy Nevill's husband sported a pair of light check trousers which he had been keeping on one side for the occasion.[37] As Lord Lennox remarked to Sir Henry Cole in October 1862, "Truth to say, the 'Swells', as a class, did not much like the P . . ."[38]

CHAPTER TWENTY

A Dream Beyond Recalling

*A*LBERT THE Prince Consort died in a most peculiar way. Although infectious fever was responsible for a high percentage of deaths at the time, the degree of severity of the illness, coupled with the facilities available to the husband of the Queen, point to the conclusion that a normal body of forty-two years of age would have survived the ordeal. The truth was that he had no zest for living. He had told his wife shortly before:

I do not cling to life. You do; but I set no store by it. If I knew that those I love were well cared for, I should be quite ready to die tomorrow . . . I am sure, if I had a severe illness, I should give up at once.[1]

Afterwards Queen Victoria made direct comment. She said: "He *would* die", adding that the real cause was a lack "of what they call pluck."[2] But "pluck" was a hard word to use— "constitutional ardour" would be nearer the mark. The Victorians had a word, since fallen into disuse, which was generally used to describe a condition such as this: spunk.

Victoria could not bring herself to face the thought that the partnership might be dissolved in early middle-age—"I pray God never to let me survive him".[3] She could not see that which others saw plainly—the death wish in his eyes. Lady Lyttelton, who knew the Prince as well as any woman, gave up all hope from the very first.[4] So did Dr. Robertson, the Commissioner at Balmoral, who had noted with dismay the lack of strength and the early fatigue on the Great Expeditions which were a feature of the last Deeside holiday.[5] Mr. Anderson, the minister of Crathie, was convinced that he would never see the Prince Consort again.[6] Plain-spoken John Brown, when saying goodbye to the Queen, hoped that they would all remain well through the winter and return safe to Scotland, "and above all, that you may have no deaths in the family".[7]

Albert's presentiment that he would not survive an attack of fever stemmed from his childhood days when such minor attacks brought with them nightmares of terror. A weak stomach was the cause of the melancholia which spread like a miasma through his last years.

Such a state of deep mental depression had appeared in a Coburg before. In the 1820s Stockmar had become worried at a similar condition in the then Prince Leopold, when not even the presence of a lovely mistress could set a spark to conversation or ardour. Muffled in his overcoat, he would turn the handle of his drizzle box, hour after hour. In later years the Queen often urged her uncle to throw aside his misery and see the brighter side of life.

Albert referred to his stomach as a "shocking bore",[8] this being a fashionable expression with the bright young things of the day. It was also a handicap, particularly in the sphere of politics. If he had been content to follow the rôle of Prince George of Denmark, the husband of Queen Anne, all would have been well from the health angle. But here was an ambitious young man, with an inflated ego, who had been hypnotised by Stockmar into the likeness of a reforming and infallible messiah. Criticism, abuse, antagonism and strain are the lot of all reformers, and Albert was no exception. He had ample mental capability to cope with the problems which faced him, but he lacked the physical staying power. Bitter opposition really hurt. This was neither understood nor appreciated by British politicians who could hold forth in the House until the early hours and then, after partaking of chops and claret, refresh themselves with a few hours of undisturbed slumber.

Albert's halcyon days lasted from 1842 until 1846. Then came the fall of Peel's Government and the return to the Foreign Office of Lord Palmerston. Married to Melbourne's sister, he had begun his parliamentary career twelve years before the Prince was born. A mettlesome man, he was not open to advice or interference. During the next five years the two clashed continually over the policy to be adopted towards the majority of countries in Europe. Albert tried every trick in the Coburg book to rid himself of his adversary, even resorting to insinuations regarding his sexual escapades, and when at last the Foreign Secretary was dismissed for his unauthorised recognition of the régime of Napoleon III, the Prince labelled him as "the man who has embittered our whole life".[9] This could be interpreted as meaning that Palmerston would not do as he was bid.

During those five years Albert aged the equivalent of twenty. He was balding, over fat, unfit from lack of exercise and the victim of a series of minor illnesses. Purging with hot water did little good. The Queen, perplexed and worried, consulted her doctor. She wrote to Stockmar: "Clark admits that it is the mind. Diet has been of no avail."[10] Then, to add to the royal troubles, Palmerston returned to office the following year, this time as Home Secretary, and all set to get his revenge on those who had toppled him, the Prince being included in this number.

In the winter of 1853/4 there was staged one of the most bitter attacks ever directed at a member of the Royal Family. In another century he would have been beheaded, crowds gathering at the Tower of London to see Prince Albert brought in, there to suffer a traitor's fate. The cause of the trouble lay in far-off Crimea. The Russians, who had long cast covetous eyes on Constantinople, now pressed their claims to protect the Christians in the Turkish empire with such ferocity that in October Turkey declared war. The British public was solidly in favour of going to the rescue of the Turkish ally, but the Prime Minister, cautious Lord Aberdeen, held back, hoping that a way could be found to avoid hostilities. Palmerston, spoiling for a fight, made the theatrical gesture of resigning from the Home Office on a minor point of reform. The outcry was loud and threatening, and Aberdeen was forced to recall him to avoid the fall of the Government. A section of the Press, headed by the *Daily News*,[11] seized upon Prince Albert as being responsible for Palmerston's resignation and Britain's tardiness in entering the war. The campaign swept through the country as a fire races through dry gorse. Now all the pent-up suspicions of the ordinary folk for the foreigner, the jealousies and grievances of the army officers, the dislike and distrust of the aristocracy, the fears and objections of the politicians, swamped his tired body and uncomprehending mind. Albert was labelled a traitor and a spy—agent for Stockmar who operated an espionage net from Germany. He was in the employ of the hated Austro-Belgian Coburg-Orleans clique. The Queen was completely under his thumb. He was in direct contact with the Emperor of Russia.[12] In a newspaper article, signed *Diogenes*, questions were asked:

Did you, Albert . . . warn the Russian Ambassador of the contemplated movement of the combined fleets in the Black Sea? Is it true that you have a third key to the Queen's Despatch Box, that you open the box before the Queen sees it, and alter the despatches intended for foreign Ambassadors? that you receive important communications from Courts abroad relative to our foreign policy, which you do not show to Ministers? . . . that you interfere at the Horse Guards to an extent which has excited general surprise and condemnation? . . . that you dined off turkey on Christmas Day, drank the health of the Czar, and led the chorus, "For he's a jolly good fellow"?[13]

Albert's feelings were that England had, quite suddenly, turned into a madhouse. He told Stockmar:

The stupidest trash is babbled to the public, so stupid that (as they say in Coburg) you would not give it to the pigs to litter in.[14]

But he was hurt, miserable and confused. As usual at such times his health suffered and an attack of catarrh and insomnia kept him (perhaps conveniently) within the Palace walls. Stockmar, upon whom he relied strongly for moral support, was verbose, platitudinous but hardly helpful. Safe in Coburg, he was rather enjoying the excitement and notoriety. He told his protégé that the Tories were "degenerate bastards"[15] and how fortunate he was to be able at last to take part in some manly action, as since his marriage he had led "nothing but a peaceful, comfortable, pampering and enervating garrison life".[16] That message was the writing on the wall, but Albert could not read it so.

Fiercer and fiercer became the exhibition of malevolence and it was decided that a statement must be made in Parliament. At the end of January the leaders of both Houses strongly repudiated the calumnies and vindicated the Prince. The attacks lessened and when, two months later, Britain declared war, they faded away as mysteriously and quickly as they had begun.

The Crimean war marked the beginning of a new chapter in the lives of Victoria and Albert. From it stemmed her love and compassion for soldiers, a love which continued through the years, reaching its climax with the Boer war. However heavy was her programme, she would always find time to inspect them and visit them in hospital, to wave goodbye as they departed overseas and to greet them on their return. The interest brought her closer to Palmerston. When, a few years later, a company of perspiring volunteers doubled past her on a sultry summer's day, she could not resist putting her handkerchief to her nose. "Don't you think there is rather a —,' she remarked. "That", he replied, "is what we call *esprit de corps*."[17]

To Albert the war came as an opportunity to demonstrate his exceptional efficiency and organising powers, already proved in his conduct of the Great International Exhibition. Military affairs occupied his attention throughout every day. He became ultra-English, even angry with Prussia for not coming to England's aid. That his light shone so brightly during the next eighteen months was in part due to a comparison with the inefficiency of the military leaders. Wellington was not yet two years dead and while he lived the files in the War Office had lain unopened and dusty with the passing time from Waterloo. The creed of the Horse Guards was that a new war began where the old one ended and, throughout the campaign, the British commander, Lord Raglan, referred to the enemy as "the French", although the forces of Napoleon III were fighting by his side.

By the time that hostilities ended, Albert's military memoranda filled fifty large volumes. His eyes were everywhere. He plagued the so-called planners on points of information, intelligence, security, communications and training. If a camp was built without the necessary adjunct of a parade ground (as happened at Colchester),[18] he was the first to spot it. He was forever urging greater manpower and he knew the strengths of all the units to a man. He designed the "Albert cap", a much derided adornment which nevertheless had practical advantage in the cold of the Crimean winter. He harried commercial interests to part with ships in order that essential supplies could be sent to the theatre of war. He urged the conversion of sail to steam, and advocated the use of assault landing rafts and submarines.[19] The net result of his efficiency was that his stock rose in the eyes of the leading statesmen (including Palmerston, who became Prime Minister in 1855) and thereafter his advice was sought on a great variety of subjects. He could not bring himself to say "No" and became over-burdened.

During his last five years of life Albert complained of suffering from the following physical disabilities: rheumatism, catarrh, migraine, choleraic attacks, cramp, toothache, insomnia, inflamed gums, jumping nerves, upset liver and biliousness. Victoria considered him somewhat of a hypochondriac, commenting that he was "as usual desponding as men really only are when unwell—not inclined himself ever to admit he is better".[20] Yet, in truth, he was not in sufficient strength to withstand the loss of the company of two people most dear and comforting to him—Stockmar and his eldest daughter. After 1857 the old Baron came no more to England. In 1858 Vicky married and left for her husband's home in Germany.

The love of Albert for his first-born child was the sap which fed his tree of life. When she went away, the leaves began to wither and to die. The admixture of husband and wife produced two distinct and recognisable parts—the body of a Hanover and the brain of a Coburg. The health of the body was responsible for the high spirits and also lent the power to the brain to absorb knowledge without effort. Albert, tired from his struggle with Crimean problems and his weak stomach, would look at Vicky in much the same way that, ninety years later, his great-grandson, George VI, also warweary and with but a handful of years left to him, would regard Princess Margaret—as if to say, in wonderment, did I create this effervescent, entertaining girl?

Vicky's eyes were green as the sea on a summer's day. Her nose was small and turned up.[21] She matured fast. At the age of three, as she rode in Windsor Park, she announced: "*Voilà le tableau qui se deroule à mes pieds.*"[22] At seven her governess said of her that, if she could be heard and not seen, she might pass "for a young lady of seventeen in whichever of her three languages she chose to entertain the company".[23] She was Stockmar's favourite. He wrote of her: "I have always loved her . . . I hold her to be exceptionally gifted in many things . . ."[24] And it was Stockmar's idea that she should, by her marriage, become the keystone in the bridge linking Britain and Germany.

Albert and Victoria revelled in the marriage game. Intimately and secretly, behind their screen, they danced the puppets on their strings. Albert played three times; Victoria went on to become, as Bismarck described her, the biggest matchmaker in Europe, and it was not until when, in her seventies, she made two tragic mistakes, that she swore that she would match no more.[25] In the case of Vicky, they were taking two grave risks, but, believing in the infallibility of their own judgment, they did not fully consider them. When twenty-four-year-old Prince Frederick William of Prussia proposed to the Princess Royal at Balmoral in September 1855, she was only fourteen. By allowing the proposal the parents robbed their daughter of the chance of making her own choice once her feet were on the firm ground of maturity. By omitting prior consultation with their statesmen, they upset power politics in the international sphere. The proposed marriage was unpopular in Britain, Prussia, France and Russia. When the news leaked out, *The Times* did not mince words in pointing out the dangers, but Albert dismissed the attack as "scandalous and degrading".[26] He told Lord Clarendon, the Foreign Secretary: "What the world may say, we cannot help." He could have helped—by allowing Vicky to reach the age of eighteen before making up her mind. But he must forever race to get results as if death was at his heels—as, in fact, it was. In the event, when the Prussian Prince passed a sprig of white heather to the young Princess Victoria as they rode down Glen Girnoch[27] together, it was a portent, not only of his true love, but that the lights would go out in Europe one lifetime ahead.

During her engagement period Vicky went to her father's study every evening, there to discuss the lesson which he had set her the previous day—a compendium of Roman history, an essay on a poet or a musician, a criticism of art. It was a conversion course to Germanism, and it was German that they spoke. Teaching was Albert's *métier* and during these two years father and daughter came very close to one another—too close for the liking of Queen Victoria. He did not appreciate the deep loneliness to which he had condemned himself until he stood on the wharfside at Gravesend, watching the departing ship which carried the seventeen-year-old bride on the first stage of her journey to Berlin. It was the 2nd of February, 1858, and the snow was falling, turning into slush. She had buried her head in his wet coat, sobbing, whispering that she felt that the parting from him would kill her. She could not bear to wave from the deck and to see his image fade across the grey water. So he stood still and silent as his daughter, and his heart, went out on the midday tide. Next day he wrote to her:

You can hardly know how dear you have always been to me, and what a void you have left behind in my heart; yet not in my heart, for there assuredly you will abide henceforth, as till now you have done, but in my daily life, which is evermore reminding my heart of your absence.[28]

The tragedy of Vicky's adult life began. The members of the Berlin Court—and in particular her mother-in-law—were determined to wring the English out of her and fashion her into a subservient and silent Prussian wife. Her father continued to pour out, in writing, the love and liberality which he had previously spoken in the evening study sessions, in general advocating a policy which was far removed from that of the rising power-men of Prussia. Her mother aggravated matters still further by refusing to loose her grip on her married daughter, treating her as if she was a schoolgirl on a visit to some poor relations. In addition Vicky became pregnant after three months. The strain of the quartet of problems proved too much for her nerves. Stockmar, who was visiting Berlin at the end of 1858, saw the danger and spoke with Lord Clarendon, also there at the time. He told the Foreign Secretary that "the poor child" was being treated abominably by her mother, was being accused of "forgetting what is due to her own family and country" and bullied until she was worried and frightened to death. "Unless a stop is put to it, I know not what might be the consequences." The Baron said that he was tempted to send the Queen "a letter as she probably had never had in her life".[29]

When Lord Clarendon asked why Prince Albert allowed it, Stockmar replied that he was "completely cowed"[30] and that he refrained from exciting her for fear of upsetting her mental stability. The truth was that Albert was frightened of his wife in a temper. At such times she pitched into him with ferocity, as happened on the occasion in Windsor Park when her Skye terrier was involved in a fight with a collie and Albert was slow to intervene.[31] On his return to London, Clarendon spoke with the Prince, the Prince was persuaded to speak with the Queen, and the Queen then talked with Lord Clarendon. She proved sensible and receptive, but behind the mask she took reproof ill from any man. The improvement in her future behaviour stemmed from the birth of her first grandchild in January 1859, when the life of the mother was despaired of and the baby, miraculously saved, was born with a withered arm.

During these last years in the life of the Prince Consort Queen Victoria showed many signs of petulance, obstinacy, even of bitterness and cynicism. Of sex she said that women only existed for man's pleasure. She complained that Albert could seldom enter into her "very violent feelings". Of her job, she announced that she was sick of everything and wanted to go away for a rest. She was of the opinion that Albert never loved her as her mother had done. She moaned about Albert's duties ("Tomorrow Papa insists on our going to Town for no earthly reason but that tiresome horticultural garden—which I curse for more reasons than one . . .")[32]

A short while before Sir James Clark had expressed uneasiness about the Queen's mind, being of the opinion that there might be danger ahead if she was not kept quiet and amused. It all depended on the Prince. He ended his note:

If I could impress him [Albert] with what I consider necessary I should consider the Queen safe.[33]

But Albert was a greying, tired man, a strong contrast now with the potent lover who had tamed and quietened his high-spirited wife at Walmer Castle in 1842. Her health was perfect, robust, and she said how lucky it was that one of them was made that way.[34] She was a woman of "passionate uxoriousness",[35] "the passionate wooer of her consenting mate".[36] He was weakened, disillusioned, fast losing the will to live. The problem was beyond the understanding, and the knowledge, of the age. Although the Queen shared out the blame for her husband's death upon her eldest son, upon Stockmar and upon the politicians who overworked him, it was she who was in the main part responsible. The final straw which she put upon his back was her exaggerated and self-pitying behaviour after the death of her mother in March 1861. The Duchess of Kent was seventy-five and had been suffering from cancer for six years. Despite the long-lasting rift between the two, the Queen's grief now bordered on derangement. She sat alone and crying most of the day, emerging only to make pilgrimages to the room in which her mother had died at Frogmore. She could not tolerate her children near her and she complained that the distant voice of the Prince of Wales was driving her mad. In fact the rumour that she had gone mad spread round the Continent, was widely believed, and the Prince was hard pressed to contradict it. Not only had he much of his wife's work to do, but he was sole executor for the Duchess, and her affairs were a maze indeed.

By July the Queen had recovered, although she was still apt to burst into tears at the sound of a tune which Mama had loved, at the sight of a carriage in which she had travelled, at the touch of a toy which Grandmama had given to "Baby". But now it was holiday time and Queen Victoria was always happiest when on the move. The summer holiday of 1861— that was to be the dream beyond recalling.

After visiting Dublin, where the Prince of Wales was in camp with the Guards, they took train westwards to Killarney, staying with Lord and Lady Castlerosse. Princess Alice considered that it was the loveliest place that she had ever seen[37] and her father strode up and down the lakeside proclaiming, "This is superb! This is utterly superb!"

There followed for him another mountain scene. When, on their way to Scotland, the royal yacht docked at Holyhead, he left his wife and daughters on board and made a day-long excursion to Snowdonia, driving through the Vale of Llanberis to Beddgelert.[38]

Six weeks were spent at Balmoral. Peace reigned and romance was in the air. Alice had become engaged to Prince Louis of Hesse and by the Rhine, and he was a guest at the Castle. A fun-loving and not too German German, he proved an antidote to the sadness which had clouded the earlier months of the year.

Albert became fitter. The bracing air and the exercise brought the colour back to his cheeks. The melancholia faded away and he laughed again. There was excitement and exertion to chase the shadows from his mind, as on the day when they came from Blair Castle to Balmoral by pony, foot and carriage. The Duke of Atholl and his retainers led the way and the water was waist-deep as they crossed the flooded Poll Tarff. Speeches were made and whisky drunk at the "County March", where Perth meets Aberdeen, and darkness was falling as, with the pipes playing, they came to the Bainoch shiel.[39]

There was a night to remember. They had ridden through the lonely glens of Mark and Esk, putting up at the Ramsay Arms at Fettercairn. They supped in the commercial room, and nobody knew who they were. Then they went for a stroll in the moonlight. The square was deserted and they passed into the shadows of a lonely lane. For them it was a strange interlude of anonymity and isolation, and they stood still together to feel the silence. This was shattered by a drum and fifes. Startled, certain that their presence had been discovered, they hurried back towards the inn. On the way a six-man band marched by them as if they did not exist. Albert asked the young maid what was happening and she answered, "Och, it's just a band."

It was half past ten when they went to bed, but Victoria did not sleep. She stored each passing minute in her memory—the bark of a dog on a distant farm, the picture of the moonlit countryside framed by the window, every detail of the small, neat room. She knew not whether it was two or three o'clock when she dreamed away into sleep.[40]

After the dream soon followed the nightmare of Windsor. Within a fortnight of the return south worries and sadness had robbed Albert of the beneficial effects of the Scottish holiday. Early in November two Coburg cousins of the royal house of Portugal—King Pedro V and Prince Ferdinand—died of typhoid fever. "It has shaken me in an extraordinary way," wrote Albert.[41] This shock was closely followed by another. It came in a letter from Stockmar. The Baron announced that Europe was buzzing with rumours about the love affair of the Prince of Wales and Nellie Clifden. It was the memory of the look on her husband's face when he showed her this letter that later convinced the Queen that the news was in part responsible for his death.

For Albert there was not only the bitter truth to face that he had failed in the upbringing of his heir, but also the danger that the parents of Princess Alexandra of Denmark might now well cancel the planned engagement. The old ills returned—sleeplessness, neuralgia, coughing. He caught a cold after being drenched on a visit to Sandhurst, but, though the germ of typhoid was already within him, he insisted on making the journey to Cambridge to remonstrate with his son. He dragged his way through the days, to chapel, to meetings, walking with the Queen to please her. She shut her eyes to the danger, spurning the need for bed and warmth and nursing. The doctors dare not mention the word "fever" for fear that, if he heard it, he would cease to resist. So he frittered his life away, dressing and undressing, moving his room, changing his bed, restlessly crawling from chair to sofa. But, despite the doctors, Albert knew that there was no hope, and so told Princess Alice. He died at ten minutes to eleven on the night of 14th December.

Gladstone spoke his epitaph:

He was free from the temptations of other men . . . the standard is one that it is not fair to judge others by.[42]

Albert had told Victoria that he wished to lie in a garden. She built him a last home among the trees and the flowers of Frogmore.

Appendices

The House of
Saxe-Coburg and Gotha

1100-1900

CONRAD *the Great*, Count de Wettin, Margrave of Meissen, and Margrave of Lower Lusatia, son of Thimo, Margrave of Meissen, and grandson of Theodric II, Count de Wettin, representative of that distinguished line, joined the Crusade and died in 1156. He had three sons, Otto, *the Rich*; Dietrich, Margrave of Lusatia; and Henry, who married Sophia, daughter of Leopold IV of Austria. The eldest son,

OTTO *the Rich*, so named from the silvermine discovered at Freyburg, in 1170; married Hedwige, daughter of Albert, Margrave of Brandenburg; and died 1189, leaving two sons, Albert *the Proud* (who died 1195) and Theodric, Margrave of Meissen. The second son,

THEODRIC, Margrave of Meissen, married Jutta, daughter of Herman, Landgrave of Thuringia, and dying in 1222, was succeeded by his son,

HENRY *the Illustrious*, Margrave of Meissen and Thuringia, one of the most powerful princes of his time, descended, through his mother, from Louis *the Bearded*, son of Charles, Duke of Lorraine, and grandson of Louis IV of France. He married Constance, daughter of Leopold VI, Duke of Austria, died in 1288, and was succeeded by his son,

ALBERT *the Froward*, Landgrave of Thuringia, who died in 1314, leaving, by Margaret, his first wife, daughter of the Emperor Frederick II, and granddaughter of John, King of England, two sons, Frederick, Margrave of Meissen and Thuringia; and Diezman, a distinguished soldier, killed in 1307. The elder son,

FREDERICK, married Elizabeth, daughter of Otho von Arnshang; and died in 1324, leaving a son,

FREDERICK, *the Grave*, who aided John, King of France, in his war with Edward III of England. He married in 1329, Mechtild, daughter of the Emperor Louis VI, and was succeeded at his death, in 1349, by his son,

FREDERICK *the Severe*, who acquired Coburg by his marriage with Catherine, daughter of Count Henri de Henneberg. He died in 1380, and was succeeded by his son,

FREDERICK I, *the Warlike*, who purchased the town and castle of Saalfeld, and became possessed, by the gift of the Emperor

Sigismund in 1422, of the Duchy of Upper Saxony, and the dignity of Elector and Arch-Marshal of the Roman Empire. He married Catherine, daughter of Henry, Duke of Brunswick, and died in 1428, leaving Frederick, his heir, and William, Duke of Thuringia, who refused the Crown of Bohemia, and died without male issue, in 1483. The elder son,

FREDERICK II, *the Gentle*, Elector of Saxony, died in 1464, leaving two sons, Ernest and Albert. These princes, after governing their country conjointly, according to their father's will, for more than twenty years, finally determined on a partition of their dominions, by which Ernest obtained the greater part of Thuringia, with the Electoral dignity, and Albert, who was one of the most distinguished warriors of his time, acquired Meissen. In this partition originated the distinction of the Ernestine and Albertine lines. From Albert, the second son, descends the Royal House of Saxony; from the elder son, Ernest, the House of Saxe-Weimar and Saxe Coburg. This

ERNEST, Elector of Saxony, died 26th August 1486, leaving, by Elizabeth, his wife, daughter of Albert III, Duke of Munich, two sons, Frederick *the Wise*, Elector of Saxony, the patron of Luther, who had died in 1525; and John, *the Constant*, Elector of Saxony. At the decease of the Emperor Maximilian, in 1519, Charles, King of Spain, and Francis I, King of France, offered themselves as candidates for the Imperial diadem. The Electors, however, objecting to both as foreigners, wished to place the crown on the head of Frederick *the Wise*, but that Prince, then far advanced in years, declined the dignity, and gave his support to the King of Spain. The second son,

JOHN *the Constant*, Elector of Saxony, died in 1532. He married Sophia, daughter of Magnus, Duke of Mecklenburg, and was succeeded by his son,

JOHN-FREDERICK *the Magnanimous*, distinguished for his unbending integrity and many vicissitudes, who suffered much from the hostility of the Emperor Charles V, by whom he was taken prisoner at the Battle of Muhlberg, and deprived of the Electoral dignity and a great part of his dominions. These were conferred on his cousin, Duke Maurice of Meissen, who gave up Weimar, with some other towns and districts, to the children of the deposed Prince. John-Frederick *the Magnanimous* formed the plan of the celebrated Seminary, at Jena, which was afterwards completed by his son. He married Sybilla, daughter of John, Duke of Cleve, and sister of Anne of Cleve, Queen of Henry VIII, and had two sons, John-Frederick II, who died in 1595, leaving two sons, who died without issue; and John-William, who founded the House of Saxe Weimar and Saxe Coburg. The second son,

JOHN-WILLIAM, Duke of Saxe Weimar, married Dorothea-

Susanna, daughter of Frederick III, Elector Palatine, and died in 1573, leaving two sons, Frederick-William, Duke of Saxe Altenburg, whose male line became extinct, 1672; and

JOHN, Duke of Saxe Weimar and Gotha, who married Dorothea-Maria, daughter of Joachim Ernest, Prince of Anhalt, and had several sons, of whom

    I William, Duke of Saxe Weimar, died 1662, leaving John-Ernest, Duke of Saxe Weimar, ancestor of the reigning Duke of Saxe-Weimar.

    II Albert, of Eisenach, died without issue, 1644.

    III Bernard, a celebrated military commander, distinguished at Lützen, one of the heroes of the Thirty Years War, known in German history as "the brave Duke of Weimar" and "the successor of the great Gustavus Adolphus"; died in 1639.

    IV Ernest *the Pious*, ancestor of the House of Saxe Coburg Gotha.

The Duke of Saxe Weimar died in 1605, in his thirty-sixth year; his youngest son,

ERNEST *the Pious*, Duke of Saxe Gotha Coburg, partitioned his inheritance amongst his sons; to the eldest, Frederick, were assigned the Duchies of Saxe Gotha Altenburg, while the Duchy of Saxe Coburg Saalfeld was given to the youngest, John Ernest, the immediate ancestor of the Prince Consort. Ernest *the Pious* married Elizabeth-Sophia, only daughter of John-Philip, Duke of Saxe Altenburg, and had seven sons,

    I Frederick, Duke of Saxe Gotha Altenburg, died 1691, whose line became extinct in 1825.

    II Albert, died without issue in 1697.

    III Henry, died without issue in 1710.

    IV Bernard, Duke of Saxe Meiningen, ancestor of the reigning Duke of Saxe Meiningen, and of Adelaide, Queen Consort of William IV.

    V Christian, of Eisenberg, died in 1707.

    VI Ernest, ancestor of the Duke of Saxe Altenburg.

    VII John-Ernest, ancestor of the House of Saxe Coburg Gotha.

Ernest, Duke of Saxe Gotha Coburg, died in 1675. His youngest son,

JOHN-ERNEST, Duke of Saxe Saalfeld, had by Charlotte Jane, his second wife, daughter of Josias, Count of Waldeck, two sons, Christian-Ernest, Duke of Saxe Saalfeld, who died unmarried in 1757, and

FRANCIS-JOSIAS, Duke of Saxe Coburg Saalfeld, born in 1697, who married in 1723 Anne-Sophia, daughter of Lewis-Frederick, Prince of Schwartzbourg Polstadt, and had four sons and two daughters,

    I Ernest-Frederick, his successor.

II Christian.

III Adolphus, killed when young in the Seven Years War.

IV Francis-Josias, who commanded the allied armies in the Netherlands at the opening of the French Revolutionary War, and achieved the victory of Neerivinden; he had previously gained distinction in the Turkish campaign, where he defeated the Grand Vizier, and conquered the principalities of Moldavia and Wallachia; for this brilliant achievement he received the baton of Field Marshal and the Grand Cordon of Maria Theresa. This great soldier died in 1815.

I Sophia, married the Duke of Mecklenburg Schwerin.

II Amelia, married the Margrave of Brandenburg Anspach.

Francis-Josias, Duke of Saxe Coburg Saalfeld, died in 1764, and was succeeded by his eldest son,

ERNEST-FREDERICK, Duke of Saxe Coburg Saalfeld, born in 1724; married in 1749 Sophia-Antoinette, daughter of Ferdinand-Albert, Duke of Brunswick Wolfenbuttel, and died in 1800, leaving a son,

FREDERICK-FRANCIS-ANTHONY, Duke of Saxe Coburg Saalfeld, born on the 15th of July 1750; married first, 6th March 1776, Princess Frederica-Ernestine-Sophia (born 22nd February 1760), daughter of Ernest-Frederick-Charles, Duke of Saxe Hildburghausen, but by her (who died 28th October 1776) had no issue; and second, 13th June 1777, Augusta-Caroline-Sophia (born 19th January 1757), eldest daughter of Henry XXIX, Count of Reuss-Ebersdorff, and by her (who died 16th November 1832), His Serene Highness had issue,

I Ernest-Frederick-Anthony-Charles-Louis, Duke of Saxe Coburg and Gotha, his successor.

II Ferdinand-George-Augustus (Duke), born 28th March 1785; married on the 2nd of January 1816 Princess Maria-Antoinette-Gabriella, only child of Francis-Joseph, Prince of Kohary, and died 27th August 1851, leaving by her (who died 25th September 1862) issue:

1 Prince Ferdinand-Augustus-Francis-Anthony, Duke of Saxony, born 29th October 1816; married on the 9th of April 1836, Donna Maria da Gloria, Queen of Portugal, and by her (who died 15th November 1853) left, Don Pedro, King of Portugal (who died 11th November 1861); Louis, King of Portugal, and other issue.

2 Prince Augustus-Louis-Victor, Major-General in the Austrian Service, born 13th June 1818; married on the 20th of April 1843 Princess Clementine, third daughter of Louis-Philippe, King of the French, and died 26th July 1881, leaving issue.

3 Prince Leopold-Francis-Julius, Major-General (retired) Austrian Service, born 31st January 1824.

1 Princess Victoria-Augusta-Antoinetta, born 14th February 1822; married on the 27th of April 1840 Louis, Duc de Nemours; and died 10th November 1857, leaving issue.

III Leopold (prince) K.G., eventually King of the Belgians, born 16th December 1790; married first, on the 2nd of May 1816, H.R.H. the Princess Charlotte of Wales, who died without issue 6th November 1817; and second, on the 9th of August 1832, the Princess Louise of Orleans, eldest daughter of Louis-Philippe, King of the French, by whom (who died 11th October 1850) he left a son, Leopold II, King of the Belgians, and other issue.

I Princess Sophia-Frederica-Caroline-Louisa, born 19th August 1778; married, on the 22nd of February 1804, Emanuel de Pouilly, Count von Mensdorff (born 24th January 1777; died at Vienna, 28th June 1852), Field Marshal in the Austrian Army; G.C.B.; younger of the two sons of Albert Louis de Pouilly, Baron de Pouilly et du Chauffour, Count de Roussy, Seigneur de Pouru-Saint-Remy, &c., by his second wife, Maria-Antoinette-Phillipine de Custine de Guermange. Princess Sophia died 19th July 1835, leaving surviving issue, four sons,

1 Hugo Ferdinand, born 24th August 1806; died 1842.

2 Alphonse-Frederick, Count von Mensdorff-Pouilly; General of cavalry in the Austrian Service; born 25th January 1810; succeeded his father as Count, 28th June 1852, and died 10th December 1894, having married, first, on the 22nd of July 1843, Theresa-Rose-Frances, (born 31st August 1823; died 29th December 1856), third daughter of Count Xavier-Francis von Dietrichstein, of a colateral branch of the princely house of Dietrichstein, and had issue, two daughters,

1 Victoria-Theresa-Rose-Sophia, born 28th September 1844; married on the 4th of November 1865 Charles, Count von Oberndorff, who died 27th December 1889.

2 Sophia-Julia-Maria-Emanuela, born 30th July 1845; married on the 17th of May 1864 Frederick-Charles, Count Kinsky.

Count Mensdorff married second, on the 31st of May 1862, Marie-Charlotte, second daughter of Francis-Philip, Count von Lamberg, and by her (who died 1st February 1876) had issue, a son,

1 Alphonso-Vladimir-Francis-Emanuel-Rochus, the chief of the Counts von Mensdorff-Pouilly; born 16th August 1864; succeeded his father 10th December 1894.

3 Alexander-Constantine-Albert; General of Cavalry in the Austrian Service; K.C.B.; born 4th August 1813; married on the 28th April 1857 Alexandrina-Maria, second daughter of Joseph, Prince of Dietrichstein-Proskau-Leslie; born 28th February 1824. The Prince of Dietrichstein having no sons, Count Alexander von Mensdorff obtained, in right of his wife, the title of Prince of Dietrichstein-Nicolsburg, on the decease of his father-in-law, 10th July 1858. He died 14th February 1871, having had issue,

   1 Hugo - Alphonso - Edward - Emanuel - Joseph - John - Wenceslaus, Prince of Dietrichstein-Nicolsburg, through his mother; born 19th December 1858; married on the 27th of July 1892 Olga Alexandrovna (born 27th November 1873), daughter of Alexander Sergeiovitch, Prince Dalgorouky, and his wife, Olga Petrovna, *née* Chouvalow.

   2 Albert-Victor-Jules-Joseph-Michel, born 5th September 1861, Secretary to the Austrian Embassy at St. Petersburg.

   1 Marie-Gabrielle-Josephine-Sophie-Frances, born 29th January 1858; married on the 23rd of October 1887, Hugo, Count Kólnoky von Káröspatak, and died 17th July 1889.

   2 Clotilde-Wilhelmine-Josephine-Gabrielle-Marie, born 23rd December 1867.

4 Arthur-Augustus, General in the Austrian Army, born 19th August 1817; married on the 25th October 1853 Madamoiselle Magdalena Kremzow, who was born 13th November 1835.

II Princess Antoinette-Ernestina-Amelia, married on the 17th November 1798 Duke Alexander-Frederick-Charles of Würtemberg, and died 13th March 1824, leaving issue, Duke Alexander of Würtemberg, married to the Princess Mary of Orleans, second daughter of Louis Philippe, King of the French; and the Princess Antoinette-Frederica, married to Ernest, Duke of Saxe Coburg and Gotha, K.G.

III Princess Juliana-Henrietta-Ulrica (Anna Feodorowna), married on the 26th of February 1796 the Grand Duke Constantine of Russia; and died 15th August 1860.

IV Princess Victoria-Mary-Louisa, born 17th August 1786; married first, 21st December 1803, Emich-Charles, then reigning Prince of Leiningen, and by him (who died 4th July 1814) had issue,

   1 Charles-Frederick-William-Emich, Reigning Prince of Leiningen, K.G. (who died 13th November 1856), father

of the Reigning Prince, Ernest, Vice-Admiral in the Royal Navy of Great Britain, G.C.B.

1 Anne-Feodore-Augusta-Charlotte-Wilhelmina, born 7th December 1807; married on the 18th February 1828 Ernest-Christian-Charles, Prince of Holenlohe Langenburg, G.C.B., and died 23rd September 1872, leaving issue,

1 Prince Charles, who resigned his succession.

2 Prince Hermann, Reigning Prince of Holenlohe Langenburg.

3 Prince Victor, Count Gleichen, Vice-Admiral, R.N.

1 Princess Adelaide, married on 11th September 1856 to Frederic, Duke of Sleswig-Holstein-Sonderburg-Augustenburg.

2 Princess Feodore, married to George, Hereditary Prince of Saxe-Meiningen, and died 10th February 1872.

The Princess Victoria-Mary-Louisa married second, 11th July 1818, H.R.H. Prince Edward, Duke of Kent, K.G., K.P., Field Marshal, fourth son of King George III, and had by His Royal Highness (who died 23rd January 1820) an only child,

2 Alexandrina-Victoria, Queen of Great Britain and Ireland, and Empress of India.

The Duchess of Kent died 16th March 1861.

Francis-Frederick, Duke of Saxe Coburg and Saalfeld, died 9th December 1806, and was succeeded by his eldest son,

ERNEST I, Duke of Saxe Coburg and Gotha, K.G., born 2nd January 1784. To the inheritance he received from his father he added the Duchy of Gotha, by a family arrangement made in 1826, after the death of Frederick IV, the last male descendant of Frederick, Duke of Saxe Gotha Altenburg (eldest son of Ernest *the Pious*), and ratified, 1826. By the same arrangement, however, he had to surrender the Duchy of Saalfeld to the Duke of Meiningen, Saxe Altenburg being at the same time separated from the Duchy of Gotha and given to the Duke of Hildburghausen. His Serene Highness married first, on the 31st July 1817, Princess Louise, only child of Augustus, then Reigning Duke of Saxe Gotha Altenburg, by his second wife, Princess Caroline, of Hesse Cassel; and second, 23rd December 1832, Princess Antoinetta-Frederica, daughter of the Duke Alexander-Frederick-Charles, of Würtemberg, and left, by his first wife (who died 30th August 1831), two sons (who bore the names of the two sons of Frederick *the Gentle*, the founders of the Ernestine and Albertine lines of the Royal House of Saxony),

1 Ernest - Augustus - Charles - John - Leopold - Alexander - Edward, his successor.

II Albert, Prince Consort, K.G., K.P., Duke of Saxony, and Prince of Saxe Coburg and Gotha, Consort of Her Majesty Queen Victoria of Great Britain, born at the Rosenau, the summer palace near Coburg, 26th August 1819; died 14th December 1861.

Ernest I, Duke of Saxe Coburg and Gotha, died 9th September 1845, and was succeeded by his elder son,

ERNEST II, Duke of Saxe Coburg and Gotha, K.G., born at Ehrenburg, the ducal Palace of Coburg, 21st June 1818. His Serene Highness married on the 3rd May 1842 Princess Alexandrina-Louisa-Amelia-Frederica-Elizabeth-Sophia (born 6th December 1820), eldest daughter of Leopold, Grand Duke of Baden, and died without issue at the Castle of Rheinhardsbrunn, 22nd August 1893, when he was succeeded by his nephew,

ALFRED ERNEST ALBERT, Duke of Saxe Coburg and Gotha, Duke of Saxony, Duke of Edinburgh, &c., second son of Queen Victoria; died 30th July 1900.

(*Taken from* Burke's Peerage, *1897*.)

The Funeral of His Royal Highness the Prince Consort

(*from* The Daily Telegraph, *December 24th 1861*)

IT IS PART of the state of princes to be buried almost by the sides of their beds, and to look from their palace windows into the mouths of their sepulchres. The meaner sort can stave off the remembrance of the grim hour until its very imminence of chiming—they can be interred without that pomp and pageantry of death which is ofttimes more appalling than death itself. They find quiet graves in green country churchyards, where the moon shines with a soft and tender kindness on the stones above them, or where the village boys gambol in the sunshine on the turf. They can be borne in peace and tranquillity to some placid cemetery where their children can come year after year and tend the little flower garden that has blossomed over their ashes. No swelling organ, no sounding chants are needed to give impressiveness to their obsequies. A few weeping friends, the tranquil and decorous performance of the office for the dead, the gravedigger's sprinkling of dust, one last long look at the narrow black box that holds that which a few days since was sentient with life and love, and this mortal who has put on immortality can be left in quiet to be disturbed no more till all shall be summoned to move. But those of Royal lineage have, in their decease, no such immunity from parade. The very utmost privacy that can be preserved in their funerals is gorgeous. They must be buried in purple or in crimson. A shroud and a winding-sheet suffice for the obscure, but the monarch or he who stands on the steps of the throne must go through the splendid but ghastly toilet of the grave. That poor stiffened mass of impassible clay must be clad in gold and scarlet ere his face is covered and his coffin is soldered down. The anthem must ring out over his bier. The requiem must resound. Priests and bishops, canons and choristers, must have their part. There must be a procession to be marshalled; nobles to hold the insignia of his dignities; a herald to proclaim his style. Not for him are the quiet country churchyard— the verdant "God's acre," where the lambs browse and the wild flowers bloom—the Prince must pass but a few paces from the Chamber of Death to the House of Silence. In his daily work he looks on the vault of his predecessors. From the closet in his Royal

Chapel he can see the stone that marks the entrance to the tomb-house of his race. In the heyday of his youth, in the pride of his prosperity, in the meridian of his glory, he knows that he is waited for—that precedents for the interment of Princes so potent as he are laid up in Chamberlains' archives and undertakers' muniment rooms—that vergers, and ushers, and choir-boys have learned by heart the ceremonial to be observed at his death—that herald painters are ready to emblazon his achievement of arms, and sempstresses prepared to embroider the escutcheons which are to bedeck his pall. It may have been something of this conscious-ness of being expected—this prescience of being made a pageant and a show of after death, which in this country at least has induced a marked repugnance among the members of the Royal family towards the garish splendour formerly lavished on Royal funerals. A system of comparative privacy in these ceremonials has for several years prevailed. The vain and empty formality of lying in state has been dispensed with, and crowds of gaping sightseers are no longer wedged together in a room hung with black to stare at a velvet coffin, surrounded by tapers in sconces, and guarded by grenadiers with arms reversed. Of old, whenever a Royal person lay in state, there were sure to be half-a-dozen of the spectators crushed to death: just as, when Royal funerals at midnight were the rule, a certain number of accidents from the blazing torches, or from the hoofs of the Life Guards' horses, could always be calculated upon. And, again, although we wish to speak of this topic with reticence, we have every reason to believe that the senseless and useless practice of embalming has been virtually abandoned, and the relics of regal mortality are no longer stuffed with herbs and spices, which assist the progress of corruption instead of retarding it.

Although the funeral of his Royal Highness the Prince Consort, which took place in St. George's Chapel, Windsor, yesterday, between twelve and one o'clock was, from its commencement to its termination, a most sumptuous and majestic ceremony, it was entirely devoid of unnecessary display, and so far as the attendance of spectators and assistants was concerned, the rule of privacy was observed in a degree even more rigid than was the case at the interment of the Duchess of Kent. The list of invitations was scrupulously limited to the personal friends of the lamented Prince and the representatives of those foreign Powers with whom he had, through ties of kindred, a connection. The persons who figured in the procession were the officers of his household, his servants, and his medical attendants. When to these are added the clergy and the choir of the chapel, the undertaker's assistants, and those privi-leged representatives of the public in the columns of the press, part of whose functions it is to see everything without being seen, the entire assemblage who were permitted to witness the ceremony of yesterday have been classified. A few of the Royal pages occupied seats on one side of the organ loft; but beyond this not the remotest or the slightest concessions appear to have been made by the officials of the Lord Chamberlain's department towards the never-failing public greed of curiosity. We believe that no amount of backstairs influence or official intrigue would have been successful in gaining admission either to the nave or the choir. The gates were closely watched by the Chamberlain's *employés* as well as by the police. Not even a guard of honour lined the aisles of the sacred edifice. With the exception of two or three ladies in the deepest mourning, who sat shrouded in the recesses of the Royal closet over Cardinal Wolsey's gates, no female was present; and so strictly had the decree of exclusion been carried out, that the vast castleyard and the green, from the fourth door of the chapel to Henry VIII's gate, were swept clear by the police long before the procession started, and, on its arrival, the expanse tenanted only by the soldiers on duty, and by an insignificant sprinkling of Royal retainers.

At half-past ten o'clock yesterday morning St. George's Chapel, although well-nigh deserted, presented a most striking and solemn sight. The spectator, taking a central position, saw first, stretching away from him towards the great west door, the stately nave, with its magnificent roof and lofty aisles gleaming in their white and fretted stonework, the bosses in the groining picked out with heraldic emblazonments, the vista terminated by its gorgeous stained glass window. In sharp and sudden contrast to the whiteness of the stone came—almost blinding in its intense depth—the carpeting of black cloth, covering the whole of a raised dais or stage which extended from the west door to the entrance to the choir, which last was draped by heavy sable curtains. On either side of the dais were lines of benches covered with black, and with black rails before them, where ample accommodation could have been afforded for hundreds more than were actually allowed to be present. From the great south door, which was likewise shrouded with black curtains and vigilantly guarded with officials, rose an inclined plane, and this, together with the line of procession which stretched along the southern aisle, was also covered with black carpeting. The morning was bleak and cheerless. Save here and there in the scutcheons on the roof and in the painted window looming in the distance, there was an utter absence of prismatic colour. White and black, black and white, were all that the fatigued eye had to dwell upon. Stay—gazing down on the austere perspective, one other object met the vision—the Bier—a huge, black, quadrangular mass, a dreadful catafalque, unrelieved in its naked blackness save by the bands which crossed its surface. For more than half an hour this vast desert of sable was almost un-tenanted. Now and then some official in deep mourning, with fluttering scarf and drooping hatband, would hurry towards the choir or hold a whispered conference with one of his brethren. Then the locomotive capacity of the bier would be tested, and grave-looking undertakers' assistants put their shoulders to the cumbrous chariot, and roll it backwards and forwards a few steps. The silence was something awful. For minutes together it reigned supreme, so that a spectator might hear his own respirations, the ticking of the watch in his own pocket. Then sounds, trifling in themselves, but jarring to the senses, would come and break the monotony of immobility. The pace of the policemen outside crunching the gravel on the path could be plainly heard, although the footsteps of the few sable ministrants within, as they flitted about, were inaudible on the thickly-covered dais. Anon the sharp, rasping noise of the brooms with which the vergers were sweeping the last vestiges of workmen's litter from the carpeting echoed through the stillness. To this succeeded a subdued sound of whispering and rustling. It was very soft—very low; it was difficult at first to know whence it proceeded; but if a person stationed in the organ-loft turned his gaze downwards towards the south, he could see, directly beneath him, one of the minor chapels, which had been converted for the nonce into an undertaker's workshop. And there were the busy bees of Death, the under-taker's myrmidons—plump men in raven black, rosy girls in brand new sables—stitching and tacking and folding scarves, and tying bands and sewing on rosettes, until the very last moment. These industrious harbingers of mortuary vanities had partially veiled their proceedings, and some black drapery was hung over the lower portion of the chapel's arched tracery; but it was easy to see them in full conclave, cheerful, and nimble, and businesslike, working for the prince of illustrious descent as they would work for the commoner, ever ready to make Death elegant, and dress the grave up with millinery. Their active forms stood in dark relief against the uncoloured window of the chapel, through which could be seen the Castle-green, and the serried ranks of the Grenadiers, drawn up to receive the funeral procession. A stranger spectacle than this bustling work-room, full of people so intimately con-nected with the conduct of the pageant, yet so unknown to the chief actors therein, could be scarcely imagined. It must be always so, we presume. The most lugubrious drama must always have its by-play behind the scenes; and while the poor player is strutting and fretting his hour on the stage, the needlewomen are busy at the wings, hemming the edges of his pall, and 'broidering the cloaks for those who are to bear him to the tomb.

We turn once more, and look, not towards nave, or aisle, or

porch, or chapel, but far away to the east, and right into the choir of the noble chapel of St. George. Here a far different sight is manifest. A blaze of colour, the warmest, richest, and most glowing, comes into trenchant relief with the panoply of the grave. Below, all is blank. The pavement bears a continuation of the dais, laid from end to end with black cloth. The communion-table is a mass of the same gloomy hue. The communion rails are thickly draped in similar fashion. On the altar glances out against the gulf of blackness the massy plate of gold and parcel gilt, flanked by the gorgeous candelabra with their unlighted tapers. Black draperies hang in thick folds on either side; and above all looms the enormous window painted from the designs of Benjamin West, with its colossal forms, its uncouth and exaggerated composition, its now dun now lurid colour, harmonising but strangely with the exquisite Gothic decorations of the rest of the chapel. The desks of the canons and vicars-choral are laid with programmes of the ceremonial, which, in tiny white patches, somewhat relieve the mass of shadow which clings to the base of the edifice; parallel with the stalls run two white lines on the black carpet, serving as guides for those who wheel the bier. The black carpeting on the steps of the altar is likewise intersected with these white lines, which against the sea of blackened cloth has an inexpressibly weird and skeleton-like effect; and at the end of the guide lines, and in the centre of the space at the foot of the communion table, there is an awful parallelogram likewise bordered with white. That parallelogram is the entrance to the vault. Unfenced, unbarricaded, it yawns in the midst, open, yet but for its skeleton border so undistinguishable where all is black, that a verger, incautiously stepping backwards to survey the scene, is within an ace of falling headlong into it. This opening, however, is but an antechamber to the tomb; as the coffin of the Prince Consort is to remain on its bier, at the gates of the Royal tombhouse, until the completion of the mausoleum which her Majesty intends to build, exclusively for the members of her own family at Frogmore. A variety of reasons have been given for this step; and among them few have been so industriously repeated as the one which ascribes to our benignant and pure-minded Queen an invincible reluctance to permit the ashes of those she loves to rest near that huge, dingy coffin, wherein lies in gloomy unlamented state all that remains of him who was once George the Fourth, King of England.

Dark and awful as was the appearance of the lower part of the choir, the eye, when turned upwards, was dazzled with rich hues. There no mourning drapery, no funeral carpeting, no skeleton guide lines, found a place. The stalls of the Knights of the Garter, with the brazen plates telling of chivalrous celebrities dead centuries since, were untouched. All above and around was that magnificent display of oak carving, unequalled perhaps in Europe. High overhead towered the carved canopies, the helmets and coronets of the knights of the most noble order. Higher still hung, in a glittering file, blazing with heraldic devices and silver and gold, the banners of the knights. There were two of these banners which might well have struck a stranger with thoughts now suggestive and now melancholy. One was a radiant banner wherein was embroidered in silver the elaborate cognisance, in oriental characters, of Abdul Medjid, Sultan of Turkey—a strange visitor here, among *preux chevaliers* whose ancestors had fought against the Paynim hosts in Palestine; the other was a banner covered with many quarterings, indicating the ancient and illustrious descent of its possessor. But it was fringed with black, and its dexter quarter barred with black velvet. It was the banner of a knight whose sword is rust, and whose soul is with the saints—it was a banner which the heralds must speedily take down—the banner of Albert, Prince of Saxe Coburg and Consort of the Queen of England.

From about a quarter past eleven until nearly noon the stalls and benches of the choir became gradually tenanted by the invited guests, who were noiselessly conducted to their seats by the attendants. Sir George Grey was among the first of the arrivals. Afterwards came the Dukes of Wellington, Rutland, Newcastle, Somerset, Buccleuch; the Marquises of Exeter and Breadalbane; the Earls of Derby and Carlisle; Lord Portman, Lord Colville of Culross, Lords Clarendon, Bury, Talbot; the Speaker of the House of Commons; Sir Charles Wood, the Chancellor of the Exchequer, Sir G. C. Lewis, and Mr. Charles Villiers. The distinguished guests, in fact, succeeded each other thick and fast; but one of the most peculiar features of this solemn gathering was the chilling uniformity of costume which prevailed. Only here and there some nobleman or gentleman in scarlet uniform, with crape round his arm, and an ample scarf of the same material, might be discerned amidst the gloom. The others, as they stood together in little groups or melted away through the shadows into their stalls, might have been mistaken at first for underlings, or undertakers' men. There were no Court costumes, no Windsor uniforms, no ruddy peers' robes; the lawn of the bishop was dimly visible, but the ermine of the judge was wanting. Wigs, plumed hats, epaulettes, sword-knots—the fripperies of drawing-room and levee days— were altogether absent. Plain black, the very deepest mourning, and white cravats, were the only costume seen; but from time to time, among these unpretending-looking men, a blue ribbon, a red collar, would glance, a brilliant star would glisten, and the spectator remembered that he was gazing on an array of the proudest nobles of the proudest nation in the whole world—that yonder placid-looking gentleman with the blue ribbon was Edward Geoffrey, fourteenth Earl of Derby—that many of those present had a right to sit in their stalls not merely as guests bidden to a funeral, but as knights of the famous order of chivalry founded by Edward III—that in the adjoining chapels lay the bones of many doughty barons and paladins of immemorial descent, who fought for, and sometimes fought against, Plantagenet and Tudor and Stuart, and who were the ancestors of those who came to mourn over the Consort of Queen Victoria. Here were ambassadors, cabinet ministers, general officers, great dignitaries of state; but all were confounded in that black disguise, and less by their bearing than by their stars and ribbons could be distinguished from ordinary men. As it was, they met in a kind of equality round that black yawning gulf which swallows up alike the fourteenth earl and the fourteenth pauper, and in which we are all equal before God.

Another noticeable feature, whether the eye surveyed the crowd in the choir, the more thinly-gathered assemblage in the nave, or the small audience in the organ loft, was the plenitude of reverent white heads. Youth seemed out of place here. It was a congress of old men, of grey beards and bald heads, and quavering patriarchs, all met together to weep over one who died, alas! before his time—who died in lusty manhood and blooming prime.

The absence of two public personages most conspicuous and most illustrious was at once noticed, was much regretted, and was more commented upon. The burly form of the Duke of Cambridge, the venerable presence of Lord Palmerston, were sought in vain; and various conjectures were hazarded as to the causes which kept the Commander-in-Chief and the Prime Minister away. We believe that in both cases severe indisposition alone prevented these distinguished individuals from being present in St. George's Chapel. Another august personage whose attendance had been expected also failed to make his appearance. This was the Prince of Leiningen, who, also suffering from illness, was said to be detained at Osborne in close attendance on our afflicted Sovereign.

If anything had been wanting to mark the rigorous abstinence from mere ceremonial grandeur which characterised the proceedings, it would have been in the absence of that long train of heralds and pursuivants who in their embroidered tabards make so grand a show at the opening of Parliament. Garter King-at-Arms was indeed present, and took his customary part in the ceremony; but Sir Charles Young wore no splendid tabard, no gewgaw crown. Like every other assistant at this sad solemnity, he was in plain evening dress, wearing only his golden collar and badge, and carrying his golden sceptre, or baton of command.

All this time the bells of St. George's, and of the parochial churches of Windsor, had been ringing single and double knells at intervals; while the artillery were firing minute guns in the Long Walk. Twelve o'clock had struck, however, before the first part of the procession entered the chapel, and was marshalled by the vice-chamberlains and ushers into its proper order. The nave now became the principal point of attraction, and groups of noblemen and gentlemen, some of them richly decorated, gathered about the southern porch. The deepest and most awful silence prevailed. A sort of shivering presentiment chilled every heart that the Hearse was at the door, and that It was coming. All at once was heard the sharp, ringing word of command, as the Grenadiers presented arms outside. Then the heavy curtains of the southern door were gathered into black festoons, and the body of ALBERT THE PRINCE CONSORT was brought in to be buried in peace.

Only the extremity of the coffin could, of course, be seen, and that merely for a moment. All else was covered with the flowing pall, made of the richest black velvet, lined with white satin, and with a superb white border. The pall itself was well nigh covered with heraldic escutcheons, most elaborately and exquisitely worked in gold, silver, and colours, on white satin. The coffin, which had been at once placed on the bier, remained for a while at the porch. The auditory held their breath, knowing whom was expected, what form would soon appear to follow the corpse to its long home. Anon came Garter with his sceptre, swiftly passing through a crowd of foreign princes and officers of state; and he was soon seen to make a profound reverence as a slight young man, with fair hair, walked with a slow but firm step towards his appointed place. Then the bier, pushed by invisible hands and bearing its august burden, began slowly toiling up the southern aisle of the nave. The procession fell into rank and moved sadly onward. For the Chief Mourner was there, so close to the coffin of his father that he could touch it; that slight, fair-haired young man, with his blue Garter ribbon just peeping from beneath his closely-buttoned mourning garment, was the Hope of England, the Heir of immeasurable power, the present inheritor of unutterable woe.

The Prince of Wales bore up bravely, but he was evidently suffering profound anguish. His gait was firm, his figure erect, his features composed, his whole bearing marvellously expressive of dignified resignation; he disdained to hide his face with a handkerchief; from first to last not a sob escaped him; but his closely-drawn lips, and from time to time a convulsive twitching of the shoulders, showed how much he was enduring. His uncle, on the contrary, the Duke of Saxe-Coburg, brother to the lamented Prince Consort, gave a free and passionate expression to his grief; nor did the Duke of Nemours and Prince Louis of Hesse show a less tearful and genuine affliction. The resolute demeanour of the Prince of Wales surprised many, and may have shocked a few; but all men do not grieve in the same manner. Little Prince Arthur, in a black dress of Highland fashion, walked by his brother's side, and the poor little boy sobbed and wept as though his heart would break. It is good for children to weep thus.

We look towards the western extremity of the nave, where the procession coming from the south porch has turned and has been met by the clergy, and watch it as it approaches to the choir. First come the Prince's valets; next two of his jagers, or German huntsmen—stolid, good-humoured looking fellows, in uniforms of green and gold—who are weeping bitterly for their kind master. Then come the four physicians—whose art, alas! was impotent to save the man so prematurely cut off. Then bailiffs of the Prince's farms, his librarian, his gentleman rider, his solicitor, and his apothecaries. Next, the four chaplains to the Prince Consort, the Rev. Lord Wriothesley Russell, the Rev. Professor Stanley, the Dean of Christchurch, the Very Rev. Dr. Liddell, and the Rev. Professor Lightfoot. A knot of representatives of foreign Royal personages succeeded, comprising General Baron von Hammerstein, with an aide-de-camp, on the part of the King of Hanover; Lieut-General the Hon. Sir Edward Cust, doing duty for the King of the Belgians; Don Manoel de Camara and Lieutenant de Sampayo Pina, representing the King of Portugal; M. de Seebach, for the King of Saxony; and Colonel Boddein, for the Grand Duke of Mecklenburg-Strelitz. To every one of the potentates whom these gentlemen represented the Prince Consort was close kinsman.

Now followed a crowd of comptrollers and equerries, for whose individual enumeration we must refer our readers to the detailed programme already published. Close on them came the Master of the Household to her Majesty, Colonel Biddulph; Lord Alfred Paget, Clerk Marshal; Sir Henry Bentinck, Groom in Waiting; and the Lord in Waiting, Lord Camoys. The great officers of the household were next in order, and the Earl St. Germans, Lord Steward, and the Marquis of Ailesbury, Master of the Horse, slowly advanced. A brief space now separated the component parts of the procession, and the next section was formed by the clergy and the choir of Windsor—the little choir boys coming first, mere urchins in white surplices with broad black scarves, and the cortège gradually rising in altitude to adults and veterans. The procession of clergy was completed by the Dean of Windsor, the Hon. and Very Rev. Gerald Wellesley, D.D., who officiated throughout, albeit four prelates, the Archbishop of Canterbury, and the Bishops of London, Oxford, and Chester, were present as invited guests. Another interval took place in the procession, and then Lord George Lennox, Lord of the Bedchamber to the Prince, became an object of mournful interest, for, on black velvet cushion, richly fringed and laced with gold, he bore the insignia

277

of Prince Albert's military rank, his bâton as Field Marshal in the British army, his sword with its gilt scabbard, and his white plumed hat. Immediately after his lordship followed Earl Spencer, Groom of the Stole in the Prince's household, carrying also, on a black velvet cushion, ornamented with gold, a memorial even more interesting. This was Prince Albert's crown as Consort of the Queen, a very richly decorated coronal, more resembling that of a foreign potentate than of an English prince. The COFFIN, which next came in sight, was preceded by the Comptroller in the Chamberlain's department, the Hon. Spencer Ponsonby; the Vice-Chamberlain, Lord Castlerosse; and the Lord Chamberlain of her Majesty's Household, Viscount Sydney. It bore the following inscription:

Depositum
Illustrissimi et Celsissimi Alberti,
Principis Consortis,
Ducis Saxoniae,
de Saxe-Coburg et Gotha Principis,
Nobilissimi Ordinis Periscelidis Equitis,
Augustissimae et Potentissimae Victoriae Reginae
Conjugis percarissimi,
Obiit die decimo quarto Decembris, MDCCCLXI.,
Anno aetatis suae XLIII.

The pall-bearers were, on one side, Colonel the Hon. Sir C. B. Phipps, K.C.B., treasurer to the Prince; Lieutenant-General the Hon. C. Grey, his private secretary; Major-General Wylde, C.B., his Groom of the Bedchamber; and on the other side, Lord Waterpark, Lord of the Bedchamber; Colonel the Hon. A. N. Hood, Clerk Marshal; Lieutenant-Colonel Dudley de Ros, and Major Du Plat, Equerries. Then came Garter, and then the Chief Mourner, his Royal Highness the Prince of Wales, supported by Prince Arthur, and the Duke of Saxe-Coburg, and attended by the Crown Prince of Prussia, the Duke of Brabant, the Count of Flanders, the Duke of Nemours, Prince Louis of Hesse, Prince Edward of Saxe-Weimar, and the Maharajah Dhuleep Singh. The rear of the procession was brought up by numerous aides-de-camp and gentlemen in waiting to these Royal and noble personages.

The Bier was slowly wheeled up the choir and placed directly over the entrance to the vault, looking, as it pursued its toilsome way, the satin border of the pall swaying and flapping inertly, like some monstrous vision of an Egyptian scarabaeus bedizened in fantastic hues of gold and black. When stationary, the crown was placed at the head of the coffin, and the baton, sword, and hat at the foot. At the head of the corpse was the chief mourner and his supporters; at the foot the Lord Chamberlain, and behind him Garter.

The funeral rites comprised the full choral burial service of the Church of England. While the procession was moving up the nave, "I am the Resurrection and the Life," and "I know that my Redeemer liveth," were magnificently chanted by the choir. This was followed by "We brought nothing into this world," to Dr. Croft's music. On the arrival of the corpse within the choir, the 39th Psalm was sung to "the music of Beethoven's funeral chant." The Dean of Windsor then read the lesson for the day, in a voice which was at first clear and articulate, but which subsequently faltered, and at last grew quite choked with emotion. The clergy of Windsor were ranged behind him within the communion rails, and the effect of their white robes, mingled with the pitch blackness of the surrounding draperies, and the dusky sheen of the plate on the communion table, was most striking. It only needed the tapers on the altar to be kindled to produce a spectacle unrivalled for solemnity and grandeur, even among the most pretentious celebrations of the Roman Catholic Church. Severe, majestic, and magnificent simplicity supplied the place of fuming incense, of embroidered copes, and jewelled mitres.

After the Lesson, which was 1 Corinthians XV., a German chorale was sung, the words of which we subjoin:

> *I shall not in the grave remain,*
> *Since Thou Death's bonds hast severed*
> *By hope with Thee to rise again;*
> *From fear of death delivered,*
> *I'll come to thee where'er thou art,*
> *Live with thee, from thee never part,*
> *Therefore to die is rapture.*

After the intonation of the sentences, "Man that is born of a woman," Martin Luther's hymn, "Great God, what do I see and hear?" was sung, and after the prayer "Almighty God from whom," another German chorale.

The lowering of the coffin into the vault, which began at the termination of the Anthem (Luther's Hymn) was performed with far greater celerity than on the occasion of the funeral of the Duchess of Kent, when from fifteen to twenty minutes were occupied in its descent. In the present instance, either the machinery was in better gear, or the conductors of the ceremony were mercifully desirous to spare the feelings of the Prince's children in the agony of a protracted disappearance of the receptacle of his remains. When the pall was removed, the effect was as though a fire had suddenly burst forth in a coal pit. Some few rays of light permeated even through Benjamin West's dusky window, and lit up the gilding of the sumptuous thing, but it was chiefly through contrast of positive colour against the negation of all colour that the effect was produced; and glowing in this deluge of black appeared the gorgeous mass of crimson velvet and gold. The crown, the sword, the bâton, and the hat were now replaced at the head and foot of the coffin, which was slowly, but not tediously, lowered into the aperture. It has since, we believe, received still further garniture—an adornment furnished by kind and loving hands in the shape of three funeral wreaths, which were forwarded that morning from Osborne to be placed on the coffin after it had been removed from the spectators' gaze.

At the conclusion of the service, Garter King-at-Arms advanced to the edge of the sepulchre and proclaimed the "style" of the deceased in the following terms:

"Thus it hath pleased Almighty God to take out of this transitory life to His Divine mercy the Most High, Most Mighty, and Most Illustrious Prince Albert, the Prince Consort, Duke of Saxony, Prince of Saxe-Coburg and Gotha, Knight of the most noble Order of the Garter, and the most dear Consort of her Most Excellent Majesty Victoria, by the grace of God, of the United Kingdom of Great Britain and Ireland, Queen, Defender of the Faith, whom God bless, and preserve in long life, health, and honour."

The proclamation of this "style," ordinarily a few tame formula, was remarkable, first for the very deep emotion with which Sir Charles Young was evidently overcome, and which rendered him towards its close almost inaudible; and next, for the substitution of the word "honour" for the customary "happiness." In the dreadful grief which has overwhelmed our Sovereign, in the abandonment and despairing anguish, it may be that she thinks she will never know felicity more; but her subjects, while they re-echo the prayer of her king-at-arms, are emboldened to indulge in the hope that she may yet be spared to very many years, not only of health and honour, but of happiness.

The solemn proceedings were brought to a close by the sublime "Dead March" in *Saul*, admirably performed by Dr. Elvey, who throughout presided at the organ. The solo in the anthem was sung with exquisite feeling and purity of intonation by Mr. Tolley. While the notes of the "Dead March" were booming through the chapel, the chief mourner, his supporters and attendants, retired. The knights came down from their stalls, the nobles and prelates and soldiers from their benches, and as they passed towards Wolsey's Chapel cast a long, last glance at what lay below, so mighty and puissant nine days ago, so quenched and impassible now. And then they broke up, this gallant company— broke up, to nourish their own sorrows, or rejoice over their own delights—broke up, to go forth into the world again, to love and hate, to toil and battle, to cavil and to intrigue, to make money and to spend it, to beget children and to lose them, to live their lives in the world as worldlings—live them until the day comes when the trench shall be dug and the grave yawn for us all, and our friends, taking their long, last look at the coffin and the name-plate, may say, "But nine days since he was amongst us, and now he is gone."

In this manner was buried Albert, the Prince Consort of England. In his life he was eminently happy. In his death it must have gladdened his expiring eyes to see his children round him. To his widow and his kindred it must be a pride and a consolation to know that he was mourned by millions who had never seen his comely face or heard his eloquent voice. This was a wise and just man, and his wisdom will bear fruit, and the good that he has done will live after him. His loss was the bitterest of pangs to his wife, to his children, to us all; but Death's dart is not so cruel, so potent, nor so keen, but that an angel sent by Heaven can stretch forth his hand and tip the barbed arrow with a diamond point of Mercy. And when a good man dies in his bed, in peace and honour, and the love of friends and the reverence of children, and the respect of all mankind, the Grave has lost half its victory, and Death is robbed of half his sting.

Sources and Bibliography

Sources

CHAPTER 1

1. Lorne: *V.R.I.*, p. 120
2. Bolitho: *Reign of Queen Victoria*, p. 64
3. Emden: *Behind the Throne*, p. 52
4. Magnus: *King Edward the Seventh*, p. 20
5. Barnett Smith: *The Life of Queen Victoria*, p. 115
6. Crawford: *Victoria: Queen and Ruler*, p. 236
7. *Journal*: 11th June 1890
8. Warwick: *Afterthoughts*, p. 3
9. *The Personal Papers of Lord Rendel*, p. 50
10. *The Duke of Argyll*, Vol. II, p. 185
11. Jerrold: *Married Life of Queen Victoria*, p. VII.
12. Crawford: *Victoria: Queen and Ruler*, p. 366
13. Emden: *Behind the Throne*, p. 57
14. Benson: *Queen Victoria*, p. 104
15. *The Personal Papers of Lord Rendel*, p. 66
16. Jerrold: *Married Life of Queen Victoria*, p. 342
17. Greville: *Memories of an Old Etonian*, p. 56
18. Hibbert: *The Court at Windsor*, p. 193
19. Fulford: *Dearest Child*, p. 205
20. Albert: *Queen Victoria's Sister*, p. 191
21. Magnus: *King Edward the Seventh*, p. 27
22. *Journal*: 1st October 1842
23. In a letter to Stockmar
24. Ponsonby: *Henry Ponsonby*, p. 28
25. Bloomfield: *Reminiscences*; Colson: *Victorian Portraits*, p. 104
26. *Early Years*, p. 103
27. Kennedy: *My Dear Duchess*, p. 121
28. Bolitho: *The Reign of Queen Victoria*, p. 145
29. Princess Marie Louise: *Memories of Six Reigns*, p. 144
30. *Early Years*, p. 244
31. Arthur: *Concerning Queen Victoria and her Son*, p. 47
32. Colson: *Victorian Portraits*, p. 75
33. Kennedy: *My Dearest Duchess*, p. 127
34. Hibbert: *The Court at Windsor*, p. 200
35. Bolitho: *A Century of British Monarchy*, p. 38
36. *Early Years*, p. 295

37. Corti: *The English Empress*, p. 78
38. Bolitho: *A Century of British Monarchy*, p. 39
39. Benson: *Queen Victoria*, p. 131; Jerrold: *Married Life of Queen Victoria*, p. 223
40. *Punch*
41. Ponsonby: *Recollections of Three Reigns*, p. 19
42. Jerrold: *Married Life of Queen Victoria*, p. 224
43. *Victoria in the Highlands*
44. Benson: *Queen Victoria*, p. 132
45. Crawford: *Victoria, Queen and Ruler*, p. 267
46. Jerrold: *Married Life of Queen Victoria*, p. 263
47. Eyck: *The Prince Consort*, p. 22. (Memo by Anson, 15th August 1840, R.A.)
48. Fulford: *Dearest Mama*, p. 246
49. Fulford: *Dearest Child*, p. 308
50. *Speeches of the Prince Consort*, p. 53
51. *Early Years*
52. Creston: *The Youthful Queen Victoria*, p. 450
53. Bolitho: *The Reign of Queen Victoria*, p. 147
54. Ibid., p. 115
55. Lindsay: *Recollections of a Royal Parish*, p. 35
56. Brown: *Balmoral*, p. 99
57. McClintock: *The Queen thanks Sir Howard*, p. 47
58. Kennedy: *My Dearest Duchess*, p. 11
59. Fulford: *Dearest Child*, p. 45
60. Benson: *Queen Victoria*, p. 91
61. Ibid., p. 190
62. Corti: *The English Empress*, p. 7
63. Bolitho: *Further Letters*, p. 58
64. Emden: *Behind the Throne*, p. 42
65. Lee: *King Edward VII*, Vol. 1, p. 4
66. Emden: *Behind the Throne*, p. 280
67. *A German Prince and His Victim*; Ponsonby: *The Lost Duchess*, p. 109
68. *England als Erzieher*; Bolitho: *A Biographer's Notebook*, pp. 103–4
69. Hamilton: *Blood Royal*, pp. 29–30
70. *Early Years*, p. 92
71. Martin: *Prince Consort*, Vol. I, p. 3
72. *Early Years*, p. 389
73. Bolitho: *A Biographer's Notebook*, p. 113
74. Ponsonby: *The Lost Duchess*, p. 100
75. Ibid.
76. Bolitho: *A Biographer's Notebook*, p. 113
77. Stuart: *The Mother of Victoria*, p. 252
78. *Letters*, 2nd Series, Vol. 1, 16th January 1862

CHAPTER 2

1. Buchanan: *Queen Victoria's Relations*, p. 25
2. D'Auvergne: *The Coburgs*, p. 28
3. Ibid., p. 27
4. Green: *Queen Anne*, p. 326
5. Quennell: *Caroline of England*, p. 257
6. Archer: *Queen Victoria, Her Life and Jubilee*, Vol. 1, p. 27
7. Quennell: *Caroline of England*, p. 258
8. D'Auvergne: *The Coburgs*, p. 29
9. Huish: *Life of George III*, p. 18
10. Quennell: *Caroline of England*, p. 268
11. Huish: *Life of George III*, p. 24
12. Quennell: *Caroline of England*, p. 306
13. Huish: *Life of George III*, p. 84
14. Duff: *Edward of Kent*, p. 18
15. Morrah: *The Royal Family in Africa*, p. 49
16. Fulford: *Royal Dukes*, p. 13
17. Huish: *Memoirs of George IV*, p. 416
18. Ibid.
19. *History Today*, June 1960
20. *Reminiscences of King Leopold*
21. de Diesbach: *Secrets of the Gotha*
22. Ponsonby: *The Lost Duchess*, p. 18
23. D'Auvergne: *The Coburgs*, p. 45
24. Dennis: *Coronation Commentary*, p. 12
25. *Memoirs of Caroline Bauer*; Ponsonby: *The Lost Duchess*, pp. 26–7
26. Ibid., pp. 32–7
27. de Diesbach: *Secrets of the Gotha*
28. *Hessian Tapestry*, p. 128
29. Vibart Dixon: In *Britannia and Eve*, February 1933
30. Ibid.
31. *Reminiscences of King Leopold*; Creston: *The Regent and his Daughter*, p. 204
32. Creston: *The Regent and his Daughter*, pp. 75–83
33. Ibid.
34. Huish: *Memoirs of George IV*, p. 230
35. Stuart: *Daughter of England*, p. 267
36. Jerrold: *Married Life*, p. 2

CHAPTER 3

1. Creston: *The Regent and his Daughter*, p. 244
2. Huish: *Memoirs of Princess Charlotte*, p. 283
3. Stuart: *Daughter of England*, p. 277
4. *Wooing and Cooing*
5. Colson: *Victorian Portraits*, p. 17

6. Stuart: *Daughter of England*, p. 296; Creston: *The Regent and his Daughter*, p. 255
7. Stockmar: *Memoirs*
8. Green: *Memoirs of Her late R.H. Charlotte Augusta*
9. Stuart; Creston; *Memoirs of George IV*; *Memoirs of Princess Charlotte*
10. Fitzgerald: *The Family of George III*, Vol. II, p. 18
11. Huish: *Memoirs of Princess Charlotte*, p. 687
12. Longford: *Victoria R.I.*, p. 17
13. Fulford: *Royal Dukes*, p. 227
14. *Edward of Kent*, p. 237
15. Creston: *The Regent and his Daughter*, p. 263
16. D'Auvergne: *The Coburgs*, p. 66
17. Bolitho: *Reign of Queen Victoria*, p. 15
18. Fitzgerald: *The Family of George III*, Vol. II, p. 30
19. Hamilton: *Blood Royal*, p. 21
20. Ponsonby: *The Lost Duchess*, p. 91
21. Bolitho: *A Biographer's Notebook*, p. 113
22. Fitzgerald: *The Family of George III*, Vol. II, p. 24
23. *Reminiscences of King Leopold*

CHAPTER 4
1. *Early Years*, p. 92
2. Ibid., p. 16
3. *Queen Victoria*, p. 105
4. *Early Years*, pp. 104–5
5. Ibid., p. 99
6. Eyck: *The Prince Consort*, p. 13
7. Ponsonby: *The Lost Duchess*, p. 137
8. Hamilton: *Blood Royal*, p. 24
9. Bauer: *Memoirs*
10. Ponsonby: *The Lost Duchess*, p. 148
11. Bolitho: *A Biographer's Notebook*, p. 119
12. D'Auvergne: *The Coburgs*, p. 101
13. Bolitho: *A Biographer's Notebook*, p. 120
14. Ponsonby: *The Lost Duchess*, p. 151
15. Crawford: *Victoria, Queen and Ruler*, p. 246
16. Ponsonby: *The Lost Duchess*, p. 149
17. Eyck: *The Prince Consort*, p. 14
18. *Reminiscences*
19. Bolitho: *A Biographer's Notebook*, p. 121
20. *Early Years*, p. 8

CHAPTER 5
1. *Early Years*
2. Fulford: *The Prince Consort*, p. 22

3. Ibid., p. 21
4. *Leaves from the Journal of Our Life in the Highlands*
5. *Early Years*, p. 103
6. Ponsonby: *The Lost Duchess*, p. 157
7. Crawford: *Victoria, Queen and Ruler*, p. 246
8. Eyck: *The Prince Consort*, p. 14
9. Bolitho: *A Biographer's Notebook*, p. 121
10. Ibid., p. 122
11. Ponsonby: *The Lost Duchess*, pp. 163–7
12. Longford: *Victoria R.I.*, p. 35
13. *Memoirs of Caroline Bauer*; Creston: *The Regent and his Daughter*, pp. 291–303; Richardson: *My Dearest Uncle*, pp. 84–95
14. Aronson: *The Coburgs of Belgium*, p. 19
15. Ibid.
16. D'Auvergne: *The Coburgs*, pp. 127–8
17. Ibid., p. 164
18. *Early Years*, p. 130

CHAPTER 6
1. Tytler: *Queen Victoria*, Vol. I, p. 43
2. *Victoria, Queen and Ruler*, pp. 115–16
3. *Girlhood*, p. 82
4. Creston: *The Youthful Queen Victoria*, p. 190; D'Auvergne: *The Coburgs*
5. Maxwell: *The Creevey Papers*, p. 652
6. *Girlhood*, p. 153
7. Stuart: *The Mother of Victoria*, p. 191
8. Ibid.
9. Hopkirk: *Queen Adelaide*, p. 154
10. Creston: *The Youthful Queen Victoria*, p. 195
11. *Letters of Queen Victoria*, 13th May 1836
12. Raikes: *Journal*, 1858, Vol. I, p. 419
13. Thompson: *The Patriot King*, p. 270
14. Colson: *Victorian Portraits*, p. 22
15. Lee: *Queen Victoria*, p. 44
16. Bolitho: *Reign of Queen Victoria*, p. 40
17. Colson: *Victorian Portraits*, p. 22
18. *Early Years*, p. 136
19. *Girlhood*, pp. 157–61
20. Longford: *Victoria R.I.*, p. 117
21. Cecil: *Melbourne*, p. 272
22. Creston: *The Youthful Queen Victoria*, p. 177
23. Longford: *Victoria, R.I.*, pp. 118–19
24. Ibid., p. 57
25. Emden: *Behind the Throne*, p. 43
26. Creston: *The Youthful Queen Victoria*, p. 176

27. Fulford: *Hanover to Windsor*, p. 47
28. Crawford: *Victoria, Queen and Ruler*, p. 128
29. Fulford: *Hanover to Windsor*, p. 47; Longford: *Victoria R.I.*, p. 59
30. Greville; Creston: *The Youthful Queen Victoria*, p. 215
31. *Memoirs of Baron Stockmar*, Vol. I, p. 373
32. Creston: *The Youthful Queen Victoria*, p. 232
33. *Tales of My Father*, pp. 34–7
34. Stuart: *Mother of Queen Victoria*, p. 209
35. Longford: *Victoria R.I.*, p. 59
36. *Early Years*

CHAPTER 7
1. Richardson: *My Dearest Uncle*, p. 155
2. Crawford: *Victoria, Queen and Ruler*, p. 188
3. *Girlhood*, Vol. I, p. 391
4. Ibid., Vol. II, p. 154
5. *Dearest Child*, p. 125
6. *Tales of My Father*
7. Crawford: *Victoria, Queen and Ruler*, p. 262
8. Peel: *100 Wonderful Years*, p. 105
9. G. Greville: *Memories of an Old Etonian*, p. 85
10. Neville: *Leaves from the Note-Books of*, pp. 263–4
11. Bolitho: *A Century of British Monarchy*, p. 34
12. Jerrold: *Married Life*, p. 177
13. Battiscombe: *Queen Alexandra*, p. 4
14. Madol: *Christian IX*, p. 33
15. Ibid., pp. 34–6
16. Ibid., p. 40
17. Emden: *Behind the Throne*, pp. 85–6
18. Stuart: *The Mother of Victoria*, p. 190
19. Hopkirk: *Queen Adelaide*, p. 154
20. Creston: *The Youthful Queen Victoria*, p. 51; Crawford: *Victoria, Queen and Ruler*, p. 19
21. D'Auvergne: *The Coburgs*, p. 169
22. Crawford: *Victoria, Queen and Ruler*, p. 100
23. *Girlhood*, p. 137
24. *Victorian Portraits*, p. 70
25. *Girlhood*, Vol. II, p. 207
26. Ibid., p. 197
27. *Memoirs*, 1st June 1839
28. *Girlhood*, Vol. II, p. 158
29. Longford: *Victoria R.I.*, p. 116
30. *Girlhood*, Vol. II, pp. 188–9
31. Ibid., p. 191

CHAPTER 8

1. Warwick: *Afterthoughts*, p. 58
2. *Uncensored Recollections*, p. 209
3. Ibid., p. 206
4. Dangerfield: *Victoria's Heir*, p. 77
5. Creston: *The Youthful Queen Victoria*, p. 292
6. Fulford: *Hanover to Windsor*, p. 59
7. *Girlhood*, Vol. II, p. 294
8. Ibid., p. 67
9. Ibid., Vol. I, p. 226
10. Anglesey: *One-Leg*
11. Jerrold: *Married Life of Queen Victoria*, p. 53
12. Jerrold: *Early Court of Queen Victoria*, p. 310
13. *Girlhood*, Vol. II, p. 93
14. Crawford: *Victoria, Queen and Ruler*, p. 114
15. Gower: *Bygone Years*, p. 4
16. Fulford: *Dearest Mama*, p. 331
17. Jerrold: *The Story of Dorothy Jordan*, p. 421
18. Crawford: *Victoria, Queen and Ruler*, p. 388
19. Jerrold: *The Story of Dorothy Jordan*
20. Hopkirk: *Queen Adelaide*, p. 172
21. Le Moine: *Quebec, Past and Present*
22. Creston: *The Youthful Queen Victoria*, p. 207
23. Fulford: *Royal Dukes*, p. 315
24. *Correspondence of Sarah, Lady Lyttelton*, p. 294
25. Russell: *Collections and Recollections*, p. 210
26. Sheppard: *The Duke of Cambridge*, Vol. I
27. Greenwood: *Hanoverian Queens*, Vol. II, p. 407
28. Ibid., p. 395
29. Hopkirk: *Queen Adelaide*, p. 136
30. Sheppard: *The Duke of Cambridge*, Vol. I, p. 15
31. Creston: *The Youthful Queen Victoria*, p. 168
32. Sheppard: *The Duke of Cambridge*, Vol. I, p. 49
33. Ibid.
34. *Journal*, 10th May 1838
35. Sheppard: Ibid.
36. St. Aubyn: *The Royal George*, p. 22
37. *Memoirs*; Compton Mackenzie: *The Windsor Tapestry*, p. 341
38. Pope-Hennessy: *Queen Mary*, p. 28
39. Longford: *Victoria R.I.*, p. 91
40. *Journal*, 13th June 1838; St. Aubyn, p. 29
41. Longford, p. 91; St. Aubyn, p. 29
42. St. Aubyn, p. 29
43. Sheppard, p. 79
44. *Letters*, 18th November 1839

45. Ibid., 12th January 1840
46. Sheppard, p. 79

CHAPTER 9

1. Creston: *The Youthful Queen Victoria*, p. 346
2. Maxwell: *The Creevey Papers*, p. 669
3. Cecil: *Melbourne*, p. 267
4. Longford: *Victoria R.I.*, p. 103
5. *Greville Memoirs*, Vol. VI. p. 249
6. Cecil: *Melbourne*, p. 254
7. Ibid., p. 192
8. Ibid., p. 99
9. Creston: *The Youthful Queen Victoria*, p. 256
10. Maxwell: *The Creevey Papers*, p. 674
11. Cecil: *Melbourne*, p. 272
12. *Girlhood*, Vol. I, p. 254
13. Ibid., Vol. II, p. 179
14. *Greville Memoirs*, Vol. IV, p. 135
15. Longford: *Victoria R.I.*, pp. 79, 90
16. *Girlhood*, Vol. II, p. 96
17. Ibid., p. 144
18. Ibid., Vol. I, p. 301
19. Ibid., p. 259
20. Ibid., p. 319
21. Ibid., Vol. II, p. 14
22. Ibid., Vol. I, p. 363
23. Ibid., Vol. II, p. 244
24. *Correspondence of Sarah, Lady Lyttelton*, p. 285
25. Ibid., p. 301
26. Maxwell: *Creevey Papers*, p. 667
27. *Girlhood*, Vol. II, p. 228
28. Cecil: *Melbourne*, p. 282
29. *Girlhood*, Vol. II, p. 40
30. Ibid., Vol. I, p. 257
31. Ibid., p. 305
32. Ibid., Vol. II, p. 160
33. Ibid., p. 178
34. Ibid., p. 186
35. Longford: *Victoria R.I.*, pp. 88–9
36. Ibid.: *Girlhood*, Vol. I, p. 288
37. Pope-Hennessy: *Queen Mary*, p. 30
38. *Girlhood*, Vol. II, p. 153
39. Ibid., p. 224
40. Ibid., p. 215
41. Ibid., p. 226
42. Ibid., p. 266

CHAPTER 10

1. *Memoirs of Prince Hohenlohe*, Vol. I, p. 87
2. *Speeches of the Earl of Shaftesbury, K.G., on Social Questions*
3. *Early Years*, p. 141
4. Princess Victoria: *My Memoirs*, p. 125
5. *Early Years*, pp. 148-9
6. Ibid., pp. 153-5
7. Ibid.
8. Ibid., p. 157
9. Ibid., p. 217
10. Bolitho: *Reign of Queen Victoria*, p. 52
11. Emden: *Behind the Throne*, p. 39
12. *Letters*, 4th April 1838
13. Ibid., 13th April 1838
14. Bolitho: *Reign of Queen Victoria*, p. 52
15. *Early Years*, p. 184
16. Bullock: *Crowned to Serve*, p. 146
17. *Early Years*, p. 192
18. Martin: *Life of the Prince Consort*, Vol. I, p. 33
19. *Early Years*, p. 194
20. Ibid., p. 197
21. Ibid., p. 200
22. Ibid.
23. Bolitho: *Reign of Queen Victoria*, p. 44
24. *Letters*, 15th July 1839
25. *Early Years*, p. 207
26. Jerrold: *Married Life of Queen Victoria*, p. 240
27. Ibid., p. 239

CHAPTER 11

1. Creston: *The Youthful Queen Victoria*, p. 418
2. *Correspondence of Lady Lyttelton*, p. 291
3. *Girlhood*, Vol. II, p. 247
4. Longford: *Victoria R.I.*, p. 127
5. *Letters*, 15th July 1839
6. *Early Years*, p. 246
7. Creston: *The Youthful Queen Victoria*, p. 422
8. *Girlhood*, Vol. II, p. 255
9. *Letters*, 25th September 1839
10. Ibid., 1st October 1839
11. *Girlhood*, pp. 261-2
12. Longford: *Victoria R.I.*, p. 132
13. *Girlhood*, Vol. II, p. 262
14. Fulford: *The Prince Consort*, p. 33
15. *Girlhood*, Vol. II, p. 263
16. *Letters*, 12th October 1839

17. Ibid., 26th November 1839
18. *Our Queen*, pp. 52–3
19. Tytler: *Life of Queen Victoria*, Vol. I, p. 96
20. Bolitho: *Reign of Queen Victoria*, p. 58
21. *Girlhood*, Vol. II, pp. 268–9
22. *Letters*, 24th October 1839
23. Stuart: *The Mother of Victoria*, p. 246
24. Longford: *Victoria R.I.*, p. 134
25. *Early Years*, pp. 238–47
26. *Letters of the Prince Consort*, pp. 22–44
27. Martin: Vol. I, p. 45
28. Eyck: *The Prince Consort*, p. 19 (Coburg Archives)

CHAPTER 12

1. *Letters of the Prince Consort*, p. 34
2. *Letters*, 21st November 1839
3. Ibid., 22nd November 1839
4. Ibid., 8th December 1839
5. *Girlhood*, Vol. II, p. 281
6. Ibid., p. 284
7. Cecil: *Melbourne*, p. 337
8. Fulford: *Royal Dukes*, p. 320
9. *Early Years*, p. 263
10. Cecil: *Melbourne*, p. 337
11. Fulford: *Royal Dukes*, p. 290
12. *Hansard*
13. Longford: *Victoria R.I.*, p. 137
14. Martin: Vol. 1, pp. 61–2
15. Chancellor: *Prince Consort*, p. 64
16. *Letters*
17. *Letters of the Prince Consort*
18. *Letters*
19. Ibid.
20. *Letters of the Prince Consort*
21. Ibid.
22. Ibid.
23. Antrim: *Recollections*, p. 53
24. *Early Years*, pp. 299–300
25. Ibid., p. 301
26. *Letters*, 1st February 1840
27. Ibid., 4th February 1840
28. *Early Years*, pp. 301–3
29. *Letters of the Prince Consort*, p. 60
30. Woodham Smith: *The Reason Why*, p. 57
31. Foster: *Life of Dickens*, Vol. I, p. 195
32. Tytler: *The Life of Queen Victoria*, Vol. I, p. 130

33. Barnett Smith: *Queen Victoria*, p. 119
34. *Girlhood*, Vol. II, p. 318
35. *Letters*, 10th February
36. *Early Years*, p. 308

CHAPTER 13
1. *The Times*
2. Ibid.
3. Barnett Smith: *Queen Victoria*, p. 128
4. *The Times*
5. Longford: *Victoria R.I.*, p. 143
6. *Girlhood*, Vol. II, p. 303
7. Cecil: *Melbourne*, p. 341
8. Barnett Smith; *The Times*
9. Crawford: *Victoria, Queen and Ruler*, p. 261
10. Ibid.
11. Watson: *A Queen at Home*, p. 62
12. Lorne: *V.R.I.*, pp. 120–2
13. *The Times*
14. Barnett Smith: *Queen Victoria*, p. 136
15. *Girlhood*, Vol. II, p. 321
16. *The Times*
17. Hopkirk: *Queen Adelaide*, p. 180

CHAPTER 14
1. Kronberg Archives; Fulford: *Dearest Child*, p. 167
2. Ibid., p. 90
3. Ibid., p. 77
4. Greville: Vol. IV, p. 241
5. Bolitho: *Albert, Prince Consort*, p. 47
6. *Letters*, 11th February 1840
7. Ponsonby: *Henry Ponsonby*
8. Kronberg Archives
9. Queen Victoria Eugenia
10. Bolitho: *Albert, Prince Consort*, p. 48
11. Ibid.
12. Jerrold: *Married Life of Queen Victoria*, p. 42
13. *Correspondence of Sarah, Lady Lyttelton*, p. 282
14. *Letters*, 8th December 1839
15. *Letters of the Prince Consort*, p. 42
16. Ridley: *Lord Palmerston*, p. 275
17. Fulford: *Prince Consort*, p. 61
18. Ridley: *Lord Palmerston*, p. 314
19. Bolitho: *Reign of Queen Victoria*, p. 72
20. *Dearest Child*, p. 303
21. *Hessian Tapestry*, p. 51

22. Jerrold: *Married Life of Queen Victoria*, p. 59
23. Wintle: *Albert the Good*, p. 93; Tytler: *Queen Victoria*, Vol. I, p. 133
24. *Our Queen*, p. 75
25. *Early Years*, p. 353
26. Bolitho: *Albert, Prince Consort*, p. 47
27. *Early Years*, p. 358
28. Emden: *Behind the Throne*, p. 95
29. Memorandum by Mr. Anson, 28th May 1840
30. Barnett Smith: *Queen Victoria*, p. 149
31. Ibid.
32. Jerrold: *Married Life of Queen Victoria*, pp. 83–8
33. *Letters of the Prince Consort*, p. 71
34. Bolitho: *Albert, Prince Consort*, p. 51
35. Longford: *Victoria R.I.*, p. 153
36. Bolitho: *Albert, Prince Consort*, p. 53
37. Cecil: *Melbourne*, p. 354
38. *Early Years*, p. 363
39. *Dearest Child*, pp. 77, 115, 254, 265
40. *Early Years*, p. 366
41. *Dearest Child*, p. 151
42. Jerrold: *Married Life of Queen Victoria*, p. 78
43. *Dearest Child*, p. 152
44. Ibid., p. 165
45. Longford: *Victoria R.I.*, p. 153

CHAPTER 15
1. Jerrold: *Married Life of Queen Victoria*, p. 57
2. Bolitho: *Reign of Queen Victoria*, p. 74
3. Fulford: *Prince Consort*, p. 58
4. Ibid.
5. *Tales of My Father*, p. 84
6. Jerrold: *Married Life of Queen Victoria*, p. 80
7. In a speech in America. Reported in the *Daily Express*, 20th July 1971
8. *Dearest Child*, p. 144
9. *War Diary of Emperor Frederick III*, p. 167
10. *Dearest Child*, p. 191
11. *The Correspondence of Lady Lyttelton*, p. 319
12. *Dearest Child*, p. 167
13. *The Empress Frederick: A Memoir*, p. 8
14. Emden: *Behind the Throne*, p. 99
15. Jerrold: *Married Life of Queen Victoria*, p. 58
16. *Daisy, Princess of Pless*, p. 204
17. Albert: *Queen Victoria's Sister*, p. 109
18. Bolitho: *The Prince Consort and His Brother*

19. Ponsonby: *Henry Ponsonby*, p. 120
20. Ponsonby: *Recollections of Three Reigns*, p. 188
21. Longford: *Victoria R.I.*, p. 149
22. Emden: *Behind the Throne*, p. 106
23. Martin: Vol. I, p. 104
24. Fulford: *Prince Consort*, p. 71
25. Benson: *Queen Victoria*, p. 100
26. *Memoirs;* Colson: p. 52
27. Bolitho: *Albert Prince Consort*, p. 60
28. Martin: Vol. I, p. 103
29. Cecil: *Melbourne*, p. 353
30. Fulford: *Prince Consort*, p. 67
31. *Letters*, 15th June 1841
32. Colson: *Victorian Portraits*, p. 38
33. Bloomfield: Vol. I, p. 96
34. Cecil: *Melbourne*, pp. 358–9
35. Ibid., p. 355
36. Emden: *Behind the Throne*, p. 50
37. Ibid., p. 59
38. *Letters*, Vol. I, p. 320
39. Cecil: *Melbourne*, p. 357
40. Ibid.
41. *Letters*, Vol. I, 6th October 1841
42. Ibid., Vol. I, 25th October 1841
43. Ibid., Vol. I, 23rd November 1841
44. Ibid.
45. Ibid., Vol. I, 2nd April 1843

CHAPTER 16
1. Greville: Vol. V, p. 112
2. *Correspondence of Lady Lyttelton*, pp. 279, 282
3. Fulford; Jagow: *Königin Viktorias Mädchenjahre*
4. *Letters*, 28th June 1838
5. Fulford: *Prince Consort*, p. 71
6. Albert: *Queen Victoria's Sister*, p. 109
7. Fulford: p. 71
8. Greville: 7th September 1841
9. Fulford: p. 70
10. *Tales of My Father*, p. 84
11. Fulford: p. 71
12. Hibbert: *The Court at Windsor*, p. 196
13. *Dearest Child*, p. 151
14. *Correspondence of Lady Lyttelton*, p. 322
15. Greville: Vol. V, p. 52
16. Dangerfield: *Victoria's Heir*, p. 41
17. *Dearest Child*, p. 147

18. *Correspondence of Lady Lyttelton*, p. 321
19. In a conversation with the author
20. *Letters*, 7th December 1841 and 18th January 1842
21. *Letters*, Memorandum dated 26th December 1841
22. Lee: *Queen Victoria*, p. 139
23. Lee: *Edward VII*, Vol. I, p. 9
24. Lee: *Edward VII*, Vol. I, p. 11
25. *The Youthful Queen Victoria*, p. 456
26. *Letters*, 5th February 1842
27. Longford: *Victoria R.I.*, pp. 159–60
28. Ibid.
29. Ibid.
30. *Letters*, 18th January 1842
31. Longford: p. 161
32. *Victoria in the Highlands*, p. 25
33. *Tales of My Father*, p. 85
34. *Correspondence of Lady Lyttelton*, p. 331
35. *Your Dear Letter*, p. 301

CHAPTER 17
1. Guedalla: *The Duke*, p. 434
2. Ibid.
3. *Correspondence of Lady Lyttelton*, p. 334
4. Longford: *Victoria R.I.*, p. 170
5. *Girlhood of Queen Victoria*, Vol. II, p. 135
6. *Early Years*, p. 220
7. Prothero: *Life of Dean Stanley*, Vol. II, p. 127
8. *Journal;* Fulford, p. 74
9. Lee: *Queen Victoria*, p. 148
10. Bolitho: *Albert, Prince Consort*, p. 60
11. *Letters*, 8th February 1842
12. H.R.H. Princess Alice: *For My Grandchildren*, p. 85
13. Ibid.
14. *Correspondence of Lady Lyttelton*, p. 340
15. Colson: *Victorian Portraits*, p. 44
16. Bryant: *English Saga*, p. 71
17. Martin: Vol. I, p. 155
18. Ibid., p. 159
19. Barnett Smith: *Queen Victoria*, p. 225
20. Hibbert: *The Court at Windsor*, p. 200
21. Ponsonby: *Henry Ponsonby*, p. 359
22. Watson: *A Queen at Home*, p. 93
23. Jerrold: *Married Life of Queen Victoria*, p. 222
24. Ibid.
25. Ibid., p. 323
26. Emden: *Behind the Throne*, p. 98

27. Jerrold, p. 274
28. Watson: *A Queen at Home*, p. 91
29. Jerrold: p. 223
30. Lee: *Queen Victoria*, p. 79
31. Graeme: *The Story of Buckingham Palace*, pp. 247–50
32. Ibid.
33. *Country Life*, 29th June 1961
34. Wilkins: *Mrs. Fitzgerald*, p. 283
35. *Country Life*, 28th December 1967
36. Fulford: *The Prince Consort*, p. 78
37. *Country Life*, 19th August 1954
38. Charlton: *Osborne House*, pp. 9–10
39. *London Evening News*, 27th September 1962
40. Creston: *The Youthful Queen Victoria*, p. 450
41. *Letters of the Prince Consort*, 22nd September 1844
42. *Book of the Duffs*, Vol. II, p. 504
43. Duff: *Victoria in the Highlands*, p. 83–6
44. Gibbs-Smith: *The Great Exhibition*, p. 27
45. Ibid., p. 10
46. *London Evening News*, 8th December 1961
47. Duff: *Victoria in the Highlands*, pp. 137–44
48. *Daily Telegraph*, 27th April 1962; Aston: *Duke of Connaught*, p. 78
49. *Country Life*, 29th June 1961
50. Lee: *King Edward VII*, Vol. I, p. 143; Ashton: *Sandringham Church*, p. 24

CHAPTER 18

1. *Letters*, 3rd March 1848
2. Longford: *Victoria R.I.*, p. 195
3. Aston: *The Duke of Connaught*, p. 32
4. *Letters of the Prince Consort*, p. 273
5. Longford: *Victoria R.I.*, p. 265
6. *Letters*, 29th June 1870
7. Private information
8. *Leaves*, p. 159
9. Corti: *The English Empress*, p. 82
10. Epton: *Victoria and Her Daughters*, p. 102
11. *Dearest Child*, p. 90
12. Ibid., p. 124
13. *Correspondence of Lady Lyttelton*, p. 340
14. Longford: *Victoria R.I.*, p. 235
15. *Letters of Lady Augusta Stanley*, p. 146
16. Ibid.
17. *Letters of the Prince Consort*, p. 179
18. *Letters*, 27th July 1857

19. *Further Letters*, p. 75
20. *Correspondence of Lady Lyttelton*, p. 326
21. Emden: *Behind the Throne*, p. 98
22. Colson: *Lord Goschen and His Friends*, p. 56
23. Corti: *The English Empress*, p. 59
24. Magnus: *King Edward the Seventh*, p. 17
25. Related by Mrs. Lilly. *Sunday Express*, 14th February 1966
26. Magnus: p. 26
27. *Your Dear Letter*, p. 278
28. Magnus: p. 27
29. Benson: *Queen Victoria*, p. 194
30. Cowles: *Edward VII and his Circle*, p. 49

CHAPTER 19
1. Nevill: *My Own Times*, p. 150
2. *Queen Victoria*, p. 119
3. Colson: *Victorian Portraits*, p. 67
4. Anson Memo; Eyck: *Prince Consort*, p. 35
5. Creston: *The Youthful Queen Victoria*, p. 449
6. Martin: Vol. I, p. 165
7. Bolitho: *Reign of Queen Victoria*, p. 81
8. Arthur: *Concerning Queen Victoria and Her Son*, p. 108
9. *Uncensored Recollections*, p. 73
10. Petrie: *Monarchy in the 20th Century*, p. 41
11. Fulford: *Prince Consort*, p. 101
12. Lee: *Edward VII*, Vol. I, p. 119
13. Benson: *King Edward VII*, p. 32
14. *Daily Telegraph*, 14th December 1961
15. Lascelles: *Five Roads to Royal Exile*, p. 144
16. Fulford: *Prince Consort*, p. 92
17. Arthur: *Concerning Queen Victoria and Her Son*, p. 27
18. Benson: *Queen Victoria*, p. 141
19. *Victoria Travels*, pp. 182–6
20. Jerrold: *Married Life of Queen Victoria*, p. 234
21. Huntly: *"Auld Acquaintance"*, p. 16
22. *Dearest Child*, p. 140
23. Huntly: *"Auld Acquaintance"*, p. 18
24. Crawford: *Victoria, Queen and Ruler*, p. 301
25. Quoted in *Balmoral* by Ivor Brown, p. 14
26. Benson: *As We Were*, p. 55
27. Brown: *Balmoral*, p. 67
28. *Letters of Lady Augusta Stanley*, p. 74
29. Jerrold: *Married Life of Queen Victoria*, p. 244
30. Greville: 15th September 1849
31. Bolitho: *Albert, Prince Consort*, p. 93
32. *Correspondence of Lady Lyttelton*, p. 411

33. Mills: *Two Victorian Ladies*, p. 146
34. Lee: *Queen Victoria*, p. 320
35. Argyll: *Memoirs*, Vol. II, p. 184
36. Corti: *The English Empress*, p. 78; Fulford: *The Prince Consort*, p. 275
37. *Life and Letters of Lady Dorothy Nevill*; Peel: *A Hundred Wonderful Years*, p. 50
38. Ames: *Prince Albert and Victorian Taste*, p. 175

CHAPTER 20
1. Bolitho: *Albert, Prince Consort*, p. 221
2. Longford: *Victoria R.I.*, p. 313
3. Lee: *Queen Victoria*, p. 319
4. *Correspondence of Lady Lyttelton*, p. 422
5. Lindsay: *Recollections of a Royal Parish*, p. 35
6. Ibid., p. 52
7. *Dearest Child*, p. 365
8. Bolitho: *Albert, Prince Consort*, p. 192
9. Duke Ernest: *Memoirs*
10. Stockmar: *Memoirs*; Colson: p. 86
11. Arthur: *Concerning Queen Victoria and Her Son*, p. 73
12. Martin: Vol. II, pp. 538–62
13. Jerrold: *Married Life of Queen Victoria*, p. 356
14. Martin: Vol. II; Ibid.
15. Ibid.
16. Ibid.
17. Ponsonby: *Henry Ponsonby*, p. 27
18. Fulford: *Prince Consort*, p. 173
19. Ibid., p. 175
20. *Dearest Child*, p. 370
21. Walburga, Lady Paget
22. Benson: *Daughters of Queen Victoria*, p. 25
23. *Correspondence of Lady Lyttelton*, p. 372
24. *Memoirs* (Memorabilia, p. 43)
25. Buchanan: *Queen Victoria's Relations*, p. 34
26. Martin: Vol. I, Chap. LXVII
27. *Leaves*, p. 107
28. Martin: Vol. IV, p. 169
29. Emden: *Behind the Throne*, p. 71
30. Longford: p. 272; Bolitho: p. 197
31. Antrim: *Recollections*, p. 136
32. *Dearest Child*
33. Longford: p. 261
34. Ibid., p. 218
35. Arthur: *Concerning Queen Victoria and Her Son*, p. 107
36. Benson: *Queen Victoria*, p. 91

37. Kennedy: *My Dear Duchess*, p. 174
38. Archer: *Queen Victoria*, Vol. III, p. 207
39. *Leaves*, p. 165
40. Ibid., p. 149
41. *Letters of the Prince Consort*, p. 370
42. *Letters of Lady Augusta Stanley*, p. 263

Bibliography

Letters and Diaries

Albert, Prince Consort of Queen Victoria. *Letters of the Prince Consort, 1831–1861*. Ed. by Kurt Jagow. Trans. by E. T. S. Dugdale. London: John Murray, 1938.

————. *The Prince Consort and His Brother: Two Hundred New Letters*. Ed. by Hector Bolitho. New York: Appleton-Century, 1934.

Bloomfield, Georgiana, Baroness of. *Reminiscences of Court and Diplomatic Life*. 2 vols. New York: Putnam's, 1883.

Brookfield, Charles H., and Brookfield, Frances M. *Mrs. Brookfield and Her Circle*. 2 vols. London: Isaac Pitman, 1960.

Cambridge, George, 2d Duke of. *George, Duke of Cambridge: A Memoir of His Private Life. . . .* Ed. by Edgar Sheppard. New York: Longmans, Green, 1907.

Cavendish, Lucy C. *The Diary of Lady Frederick Cavendish*. Ed. by John Bailey. 2 vols. London: John Murray, 1927.

Creevey, Thomas. *The Creevey Papers: A Selection from the Correspondence and Diaries of the Late Thomas Creevey*. Ed. by Herbert Maxwell. New York: Dutton, 1923.

Ernest II, Duke of Saxe-Coburg-Gotha. *Memoirs of Ernest II*. 4 vols. London: Remington, 1880–90.

Gladstone, William E. *Gladstone to His Wife*. Ed. by A. Tilney Bassett. London: Methuen, 1936.

Greville, Charles C. *The Greville Memoirs*. Ed. by Roger Fulford. Rev. ed. New York: Macmillan, 1963.

Kennedy, Aubrey Leo, ed. *"My Dear Duchess:" Social and Political Letters to the Duchess of Manchester, 1858–59*. London: John Murray, 1956.

Lieven, Doroteya K., Princess. *The Private Letters of Princess Lieven to Prince Metternich, 1820–1826*. Ed. by Peter Quennell. London: John Murray, 1948.

Lyttelton, Sarah Spencer, Baroness of. *Correspondence of Sarah Spencer, Lady Lyttelton, 1787–1870*. Ed. by Mrs. Hugh Wyndham. London: John Murray, 1912.

Mills, Anthony R., ed. *Two Victorian Ladies: More Pages from the Journals of Emily and Ellen Hall*. London: Frederick Muller, 1969.

Paget, Walburga. *In My Tower*. 2 vols. London: Hutchinson, 1924.

Ponsonby, Arthur P., Baron of. *Henry Ponsonby, Queen Victoria's Private Secretary: His Life from His Letters*. London: Macmillan, 1942.

Rendel, Stuart R., Baron of. *The Personal Papers of Lord Rendell: . . . Conversations with Mr. Gladstone (1888 to 1898) and Other Famous Statesmen*. London: Ernest Benn, 1931.

Stanley, Augusta F. *Letters of Lady Augusta Stanley, a Young Lady at Court, 1849–1863*. Ed. by the Dean of Windsor and Hector Bolitho. New York: George H. Doran, 1927.

Stockmar, Ernest A., Baron of. *Memoirs of Baron Stockmar*. Ed. by F. Max

Muller. Trans. by G. A. M. 2 vols. Boston and New York: Lee and Shepard, 1873.

Victoria, Empress Consort of Frederick III. *Letters of the Empress Frederick.* Ed. by Frederick Ponsonby. London: Macmillan, 1929.

Victoria, Queen of Great Britain. *Dearest Child: Letters Between Queen Victoria and the Princess Royal, 1858–61.* Ed. by Roger Fulford. New York: Holt, Rinehart & Winston, 1964.

———. *Dearest Mama: Letters Between Queen Victoria and the Crown Princess of Prussia, 1861–1864.* Ed. by Roger Fulford. New York: Holt, Rinehart & Winston, 1969.

———. *Further Letters of Queen Victoria.* Ed. by Hector Bolitho. Trans. by Mrs. J. Pudney and Lord Sudley. New York: Kraus Reprint, 1971.

———. *The Girlhood of Queen Victoria: A Selection from Her Majesty's Diaries Between the Years 1832 and 1840.* Ed. by Viscount Esher. 2 vols. New York: Longmans, Green, 1912.

———. *Leaves from the Journal of Our Life in the Highlands, from 1848 to 1861 . . . and . . . Earlier Visits to Scotland, and Tours in England and Ireland, and Yachting Excursions.* Ed. by Arthur Helps. New York: Harper, 1868.

———. *The Letters of Queen Victoria: A Selection from Her Majesty's Correspondence Between the Years 1837 and 1861.* Ed. by Arthur C. Benson and Viscount Esher. New York: Longmans, Green, 1907.

———. *The Letters of Queen Victoria: A Selection from Her Majesty's Correspondence Between the Years 1862 and 1885.* Ed. by George E. Buckle New York: Longmans, Green, 1926–28.

———. *The Letters of Queen Victoria: A Selection from Her Majesty's Correspondence Between the Years 1886 and 1901.* Ed. by G. E. Buckle. London: John Murray, 1930–32.

Reminiscences and Memoirs

A. M. F. [Alicia M. Falls]. *Tales of My Father.* New York and London: Longmans, Green, 1902.

Airlie, Mabell Frances Ogilvy, Countess of. *Thatched with Gold: Memoirs.* Ed. by Jennifer Ellis. London: Hutchinson, 1962.

Alice, Princess of Great Britain. *For My Grandchildren: Some Reminiscences of Her Royal Highness Alice, Countess of Athlone.* Cleveland: World, 1967.

Antrim, Louisa Jane Grey, Countess of. *Recollections of Louisa, Countess of Antrim.* Shipston-on-Stour: King's Stone, 1937.

Argyll, George Douglas Campbell, Duke of. *Autobiography and Memoirs.* Ed. by the Dowager Duchess of Argyll. 2 vols. London: John Murray, 1906.

Arthur, George Compton. *Not Worth Reading.* New York and London: Longmans, Green, 1938.

Benson, Edward F. *As We Were: A Victorian Peep-Show.* London and New York: Longmans, Green, 1937.

Bolitho, Hector. *A Biographer's Notebook.* New York: Macmillan, 1950.

Derby, Mary Catherine, Countess of. *A Great Lady's Friendship: Letters to Mary, Marchioness of Salisbury, Countess of Derby.* Ed. by Winifred H. Burghclere. London: Macmillan, 1933.

Ernle, Rowland E., Baron of. *Wippingham to Westminister: The Reminiscences of Lord Ernle.* London: John Murray, 1938.

Hamilton, Gerald. *Blood Royal.* London: Gibbs and Philips, 1964.

Hohenlohe-Schillingsfürst, Chlodwig Karl Viktor, Prince. *Memoirs of Prince Hohenlohe.* Ed. by Friedrich Curtius. 2 vols. New York: Macmillan, 1906.

Leveson-Gower, Edward F. *Bygone Years.* London: John Murray, 1905.

Lindsay, Patricia. *Recollections of a Royal Parish.* London. John Murray, 1902.

McClintock, Mary Howard. *The Queen Thanks Sir Howard: The Life of Major-General Sir Howard Elphinstone.* London: John Murray, 1945.

Marie Louise, Princess. *My Memories of Six Reigns.* New York: Dutton, 1957.

Nevill, Dorothy. *Leaves from the Note-Books of Lady Dorothy Nevill.* Ed. by Ralph Nevill. London: Macmillan, 1907.

————. *My Own Times.* London: Methuen, 1912.

————. *The Reminiscences of Lady Dorothy Nevill.* Ed. by Ralph Nevill. London: Edward Arnold, 1907.

Pless, Mary Theresa Olivia, Princess of. *Daisy: Princess of Pless.* Ed. by Desmond Chapman-Huston. New York: Dutton, 1929.

Ponsonby, Frederick. *Recollections of Three Reigns.* Ed. by Colin Welch. New York: Dutton, 1952.

Radnor, Helen Matilda Bouverie, Countess of. *From a Great-Grandmother's Armchair.* London: Marshall, 1927.

Radziwill, Catherine, Princess of. *Memories of Forty Years.* New York and London: Funk and Wagnalls, 1915.

Redesdale, Algernon Bertram Freeman-Mitford, Baron of. *Further Memories.* New York: Dutton, 1917.

————. *Memories.* New York: Dutton, 1916.

Russell, George William E. *Collections and Recollections, by One Who Has Kept a Diary.* New York and London: Harper, 1898.

Uncensored Recollections. Philadelphia and London: Lippincott, 1924.

Warwick, Frances Evelyn Greville, Countess of. *Afterthoughts.* London: Cassell, 1931.

Biographies and Biographical Studies

THE HERITAGE

Cecil, David. *Lord M.: Or, The Later Life of Lord Melbourne.* London: Constable, 1954.

————. *The Young Melbourne.* Indianapolis and New York: Bobbs-Merrill, 1939.

Creston, Dormer [Dorothy J. Baynes]. *The Regent and His Daughter.* Boston: Little, Brown, 1932.

Duff, David. *Edward of Kent: The Life of Queen Victoria's Father.* London: Stanley Paul, 1938.

FitzGerald, Percy. *Royal Dukes and Princesses of the Family of George III.* 2 vols. London: Tinsley, 1882.

Fulford, Roger. *The Wicked Uncles: The Father of Queen Victoria and His Brothers.* New York: Putnam's, 1933.

Greenwood, Alice Drayton. *Lives of the Hanoverian Queens of England.* 2 vols. London: Bell, 1909–11.

Guedalla, Philip. *The Duke.* London: Hodder and Stoughton, 1931.

Hopkirk, Mary. *Queen Adelaide.* London: John Murray, 1946.

Huish, Robert, ed. *Memoirs of George IV, Descriptive of the Most Interesting Scenes of His Private and Public Life . . . .* London: printed for T. Kelly, 1830.

————. *The Public and Private Life of George III.* London: printed for T. Kelly, 1821.

————. *A Sacred Memorial of Her Late Royal Highness, Charlotte Augusta, Princess of Wales . . . .* London: printed for T. Kelly, 1818.

Jerrold, Clare. *The Story of Dorothy Jordan.* London: Nash, 1914.

Panam, Pauline A. *A German Prince and His Victim.* London: John Long, 1915.

Parry, Edward A. *Queen Caroline.* London: Ernest Benn, 1930.

Ponsonby, D. A. *The Lost Duchess: The Story of the Prince Consort's Mother.* London: Chapman and Hall, 1958.
Quennell, Peter. *Caroline of England: An Augustan Portrait.* New York: Viking, 1940.
Redman, Alvin. *The House of Hanover.* New York: Coward-McCann, 1960.
Richardson, Joanna. *My Dearest Uncle: A Life of Leopold, 1st King of the Belgians.* London: Jonathan Cape, 1961.
Stuart, Dorothy M. *Daughter of Victoria: A New Study of Princess Charlotte of Wales and Her Family.* London: Macmillan, 1952.
————. *The Mother of Victoria.* London: Macmillan, 1941.
Thompson, Grace E. *The Patriot King: The Life of William IV.* New York: Dutton, 1933.
Van Thal, Herbert. *Ernest Augustus, Duke of Cumberland and King of Hanover.* London: Arthur Barker, 1936.
Watkins, John. "The Life and Times of William IV." In *The Life and Reign of William IV.* Ed. by George N. Wright. 2 vols. London: Fisher, 1837.
Wilkins, William H. *Mrs FitzHerbert and George IV.* New York: Longmans, Green, 1905.

THE REIGN

Albert, Consort of Queen Victoria. *Principal Speeches and Addresses.* London: John Murray, 1864.
Ames, Winslow. *Prince Albert and Victorian Taste.* New York: Viking, 1968.
Archer, Thomas. *Our Sovereign Lady, Queen Victoria: Her Life and Jubilee.* 4 vols. London: Blackie, 1888.
Argyll, John George, Duke of. *V.R.I.: Her Life and Empire.* New York and London: Harper, 1901.
Aronson, Theo. *Defiant Dynasty: The Coburgs of Belgium.* Indianapolis: Bobbs-Merrill, 1968.
Benson, Edward F. *Queen Victoria.* New York: Longmans, Green, 1935.
Bolitho, Hector. *Albert, Prince Consort.* London: Max Parrish, 1964.
————. *The Reign of Queen Victoria.* New York: Macmillan, 1948.
Buchanan, Meriel. *Queen Victoria's Relations.* London: Cassell, 1954.
Chancellor, Frank B. *Prince Consort.* New York: Lincoln MacVeagh, Dial, 1931.
Colson, Percy. *Victorian Portraits.* Freeport, N. Y.: Books for Libraries, 1968.
Crawford, Emily. *Victoria, Queen and Ruler.* 2d ed. London: Simplin, Marshall, 1903.
Creston, Dormer [Dorothy J. Baynes]. *The Youthful Queen Victoria: A Discursive Narrative.* New York: Putnam's 1952.
D'Auvergne, Edmund B. *The Coburgs: The Story of the Rise of a Great Royal House.* New York: Pott, 1911.
Diesbach, Ghislain de. *Secrets of the Gotha.* Trans. by Margaret Crosland. New York: Meredith, 1968.
Emden, Paul H. *Behind the Throne.* London: Hodder and Stoughton, 1934.
Eyck, Frank. *The Prince Consort: A Political Biography.* London: Chatto and Windus, 1959.
Fulford, Roger. *The Prince Consort.* London: Macmillan, 1949.
Grey, Charles. *The Early Years of His Royal Highness The Prince Consort: Compiled for and Annotated by Queen Victoria.* New York: Kimber, 1967.
Guedalla, Philip. *The Queen and Mr. Gladstone.* New York: Kraus Reprint, 1969.
Holmes, Richard R. *Queen Victoria, 1819–1901* . . . . London and New York: Longmans, Green, 1901.
Jerrold, Clare. *The Married Life of Queen Victoria.* London, Nash, 1913.
Knight, Alfred E. *Victoria, Her Life and Reign: An Illustrated Biography* . . . . London: Partridge, 1897.

Lee, Sidney. *Queen Victoria*. New York: Macmillan, 1903.
Longford, Elizabeth. *Victoria R.I.* London: Weidenfeld and Nicolson, 1964. [Published in United States as *Queen Victoria: Born to Succeed*. New York: Harper & Row, 1964.]
Martin, Theodore. *The Life of His Royal Highness The Prince Consort*. 5 vols. London: Smith, Elder, 1875–80.
————. *Queen Victoria as I Knew Her*. London: William Blackwood, 1908.
Maxwell, Herbert E. *Sixty Years a Queen: The Story of Her Majesty's Reign*. London: Harmsworth, 1897.
Oliphant, Margaret. *Queen Victoria: A Personal Sketch*. London: Cassell, 1900.
Ponsonby, Frederick Edward Grey. *Sidelights on Queen Victoria*. New York: Sears, 1930.
The Private Life of the Queen. New York: Appleton, 1897.
Smith, George B. *Life of Her Majesty Queen Victoria*. 2d ed. New York and London: George Routledge, 1887.
Strachey, Lytton. *Queen Victoria*. New York: Harcourt, Brace, 1922.
Tytler, Sarah [Henrietta Keddie]. *The Life of Her Most Gracious Majesty The Queen*. 2 vols. London: Virtue, 1897.
Wilson, Robert. *The Life and Times of Queen Victoria*. 2 vols. London and New York: Cassell, 1887–88.

THE FAMILY

Albert, Harold A. *Queen Victoria's Sister: The Life and Letters of Princess Feodora*. London: Hale, 1967.
Anglesey, George Charles Paget, Marquis of. *One-Leg: The Life and Letters of Henry William Paget, First Marquess of Anglesey*. New York: William Morrow, 1961.
Benson, Edward F. *Queen Victoria's Daughters*. New York: Appleton-Century, 1939.
Corti, Egon C., Count of. *The English Empress: A Study in the Relations Between Queen Victoria and Her Eldest Daughter, Empress Frederick of Germany*. Trans. by E. M. Hesse. London: Cassell, 1957.
Epton, Nina C. *Victoria and Her Daughters*. New York: Norton, 1971.
Grey, George Aston. *His Royal Highness The Duke of Connaught and Strathearn: A Life and Intimate Study*. London: George G. Harrap, 1929.
Maurois, André. *Disraeli: A Picture of the Victorian Age*. Trans. by Hamish Miles. New York: Modern Library, 1955.
Morley, John, Viscount of. *The Life of William Ewart Gladstone*. New York: Macmillan, 1932.
Pope-Hennessy, James. *Queen Mary*. New York: Alfred A. Knopf, 1960.
Radziwill, Catherine, Princess of. *The Empress Frederick*. London: Cassell, 1934.
Ridley, Jasper. *Lord Palmerston*. New York: Dutton, 1971.
St. Aubyn, Files. *The Royal George, 1819–1904: The Life of His Royal Highness Prince George, Duke of Cambridge*. New York: Alfred A. Knopf, 1964.

THE SUCCESSION

Arthur, George C. *Concerning Queen Victoria and Her Son*. London: Hale, 1943.
Battiscombe, Georgina. *Queen Alexandra*. Boston: Houghton Mifflin, 1969.
Benson, Edward F. *King Edward VII*. London: Longmans, Green, 1933.
Cowles, Virginia S. *Edward VII and His Circle*. London: Hamish Hamilton, 1956.
Dangerfield, George. *Victoria's Heir: The Education of a Prince*. New York: Harcourt, Brace, 1941.
Lee, Sidney. *King Edward VII*. 2 vols. New York: Macmillan, 1925–27.

Madol, Hans R. *Christian IX*. Trans. by E. O. Lorimer. London: Collins, 1939.
――――. *The Private Life of Queen Alexandra: As Viewed by Her Friends*. London: Hutchinson, 1940.
Magnus, Philip M. *King Edward the Seventh*. New York: Dutton, 1964.
Sanderson, Edgar, and Melville, Lewis [Lewis S. Benjamin.] *King Edward VII: His Life and Reign*. 6 vols. London: Gresham, 1910.
Wortham, High E. *Edward VII: Man and King*. Boston: Little, Brown, 1931.

History, Politics, and Miscellaneous Works

Bishop, Roy. *Paintings of the Royal Collection: An Account of His Majesty's Pictures* . . . . New York: Lippincott, n.d.
Bolitho, Hector. *A Century of British Monarchy*. New York: Longmans, Green, 1953.
Brown, Ivor J. *Balmoral: The History of a Home*. London: Collins, 1955.
Bryant, Arthur. *The English Saga*. London: Collins, 1948.
Graeme, Bruce [Graham M. Jeffries.] *The Story of Buckingham Palace: An Unconventional Study of the Palace from Its Earliest Times*. London: Hutchinson, 1928.
Hibbert, Christopher. *The Court at Windsor*. New York: Harper & Row, 1964.
Mackenzie, Compton. *The Windsor Tapestry: Being a Study of the Life, Heritage, and Abdication of His Royal Highness The Duke of Windsor*. New York: Frederick A. Stokes, 1938.
Michie, Allan A. *The Crown and the People*. London: Secker and Warburg, 1952.
Petrie, Charles A. *Monarchy in the Twentieth Century*. London: Andrew Dakers, 1952.
Victoria and Albert Museum, South Kensington, Department of Museum Extension Services. *The Great Exhibition of 1851: A Commemorative Album*. Comp. by Charles H. Gibbs-Smith. London: Her Majesty's Stationery Office, 1950.
Watson, Vera. *A Queen at Home: An Intimate Account of the Social and Domestic Life of Queen Victoria's Court*. London: W. H. Allen, 1952.
Woodham-Smith, Cecil B. *The Reason Why*. New York: Dutton Paperbacks, 1957.

Index

Index

INDEX